Fisl

AUTOBIOGRAPHY

Elizabeth Butler was born in Lausanne in 1846, the elder daughter of
Thomas James Thompson. Her younger sister was the poet and essayist
Alice Meynell. Their mother, Christiana, was an accomplished amateur
pianist and water-colourist. The two girls were educated privately by
their father, who had wide cultural interests which he was able to foster
because the terms of his inheritance precluded him from having a profes-
sion. The family spent much time travelling and living abroad,
particularly in Italy.

As her talent for drawing became evident she enrolled at the South
Kensington School of Art, where she was a contemporary of Kate Green-
away; she later studied with Giuseppe Belucci in Florence. In 1872 she
witnessed some manœuvres of the British army and this quickened her
interest in military subjects. In 1874 she exhibited a large oil painting,
The Roll Call, at the Royal Academy Summer Exhibition. Its success with
the public and critics alike brought her national fame. Her reputation as
a painter of military engagements encouraged her to persist in the genre.
Ruskin described her *Quatre Bras*, which she exhibited in 1875, as "the
first fine pre-Raphaelite picture of a battle we have had." Soldiers
admired the care which she took to understand the background to the
scenes she painted, and her concern for the detail of military uniforms
and equipment.

In 1873 she followed her mother and sister into the Roman Catholic
Church, and in 1877 she married Major, later Lieutenant-General Sir
William Butler. They had three sons and three daughters. Two sons
fought in the First World War, and the third, who had become a Benedictine monk, was a military chaplain at the Front. Her youngest
daughter married Viscount Gormanston. It was at Gormanston Castle in
County Meath that she died in 1933.

Her other major pictures include: *The Remnants of an Army* (1879),
The Defence of Rorke's Drift (1880), *"Scotland for Ever!"* (1881), *An Eviction in Ireland* (1890) and *The Dawn of Waterloo* (1896). She wrote *Letters
from the Holy Land* (1903) and *From Sketch-book and Diary* (1909), as
well as her *Autobiography*.

ELIZABETH BUTLER

Battle Artist

AUTOBIOGRAPHY

With illustrations from sketches by the author

Fisher Press

Published by Fisher Press, Post Office Box 41,
Sevenoaks, Kent TN15 6YN, England

An *Autobiography* was first published in 1922
First published as a Fisher paperback 1993

British Library Cataloguing in Publication Data

A catalogue record for this book is available from
The British Library

ISBN 1 874037 08 6

Typeset by Grand Designs, London

Printed and bound in Great Britain by
Antony Rowe Ltd, Chippenham, Wiltshire

ACKNOWLEDGEMENTS

We are grateful to the Trustees of the London Irish Rifles for permission to use a detail of *The London Irish at Loos* on the cover; and to the National Portrait Gallery, London for permission to reproduce Elizabeth Butler's self-portrait in the vignette. Our thanks are also due to the library staff of the National Army Museum, The London Library, The Foreign and Commonwealth Office Library and the Central Westminster Library, for their advice on the much expanded index for this new edition.

ORIGINAL DEDICATION IN THE 1922 EDITION

To my children

Contents

MY FRIENDS: You must write your memoirs.

I: Every one writes his or her memoirs nowadays. Rather a plethora, don't you think? An exceedingly difficult thing to do without too much of the Ego.

MY FRIENDS: Oh! but yours has been such an interesting life, so varied, and you can bring in much outside yourself. Besides, you have kept a diary, you say, ever since you were twelve, and you have such an unusually long memory. A pity to waste all that. You simply *must!*

I: Very well, but remember that I am writing while the world is still knocked off its balance by the Great War, and few minds will care to attune themselves to the Victorian and Edwardian stability of my time.

MY FRIENDS: There will come a reaction.

CHAPTER ONE
FIRST IMPRESSIONS

I WAS born at the pretty "Villa Claremont," just outside Lausanne and overlooking Lake Leman. I made a good start with the parents Providence gave me. My father, cultured, good, patient, after he left Cambridge set out on the "Grand Tour," and after his unsuccessful attempt to enter Parliament devoted his leisure to my and my younger sister's education. Yes, he began with our first strokes, our "pot-hooks and hangers," our two-and-two make four; nor did his tuition really cease till, entering on matrimony, we left the paternal roof. He adopted, in giving us our lessons, the principle of "a little and often", so that we had two hours in the morning and no lessons in the afternoon, only bits of history, poetry, the collect for the Sunday and dialogues in divers languages to learn overnight by heart to be repeated to him next morning. We had no regular holidays: a day off occasionally, especially when travelling; and we travelled much. He believed that intelligent travel was a great educator. He brought us up tremendous English patriots, but our deepest contentment lay in our Italian life, because we loved the sun—all of us.

So we oscillated between our Ligurian Riviera and the home counties of Kent and Surrey, but were never long at a time in any resting place. Our father's daughter by his first wife had married, at seventeen, an Italian officer whose family we met at Nervi, and she settled in Italy, becoming one of our attractions to the beloved Land. That officer later joined Garibaldi, and was killed at the Battle of the

Volturno. She never left the country of her adoption, and that bright lure for us remained.

Although we were very strictly ruled during lessons, we ran rather wild after, and, looking back, I only wonder that no illness or accident ever befell us. Our dear Swiss nurse was often scandalised at our escapades, but our mother, bright and beautiful, loving music and landscape painting, and practising both with an amateur's enthusiasm, allowed us what she considered very salutary freedom after study. Still, I don't think she would have liked some of our wild doings and our consortings with Genoese peasant children and Surrey ploughboys, had she known of them. But, careful as she was of our physical and spiritual health, she trusted us and thought us unique.

My memory goes back to the time when I was just able to walk and we dwelt in a typically English village near Cheltenham. I see myself pretending to mind two big cart-horses during hay-making, while the fun of the rake and the pitchfork was engaging others not so interested in horses as I already was myself. Then I see the *Albergo*, with vine-covered porch, at Ruta, on the "saddle" of Porto Fino, that promontory which has been called the "Queen of the Mediterranean," where we began our lessons, and, I may say, our worship of Italy.

Then comes Villa de' Franchi for two exquisite years, a little nearer Genoa, at Sori, a *palazzo* of rose-coloured plaster and white stucco, with flights of stone steps through the vineyards right down to the sea. That sea was a joy to me in all its moods. We had our lessons on the balcony in the summer, and our mother's piano sent bright melody out of the open windows of the drawing-room when she wasn't painting the mountains, the sea, the flowers. She had the "semi-grand" piano brought out into the balcony one full-moon night and played Beethoven's "Moonlight Sonata" under those silver beams, while the sea, her audience, in its reflected glory, murmured its applause.

Often, after the babes were in bed, I cried my heart out

when, through the open windows, I could hear my mother's light soprano drowned by the strong tenor of some Italian friend in a duett, during those musical evenings so dear to the music-loving children of the South. It seemed typical of her extinction, and I felt a rage against that tenor. Our dear nurse, Amélie, would come to me with lemonade, and mamma, when apprised of the state of things, would also come to the rescue, her face, still bright from the singing, becoming sad and puckered.

A stay at Edenbridge, in Kent, found me very happy riding in big waggons during hay-making and hanging about the farm stables belonging to the house, making friends with those splendid cart-horses which contrasted with the mules of Genoa in so interesting a way. How the cuckoos sang that summer; a note never heard in Italy. I began writing verse about that time. Thus:

> The gates of Heaven open to the lovely season,
> And all the meadows sweet they lie in peace.

We children loved the Kentish beauty of our dear England. Poetry filtered into our two little hearts wherever we abode, to blossom forth in my little large-eyed, thoughtful sister in the process of time. To Nervi we went again, taking Switzerland on the way this time, into Italy by the Simplon and the Lago Maggiore.

A nice couple of children we were sometimes! At this same Nervi, one day, we little girls found the village people celebrating a *festa* at Sant' Ilario, high up on the foothills of the mountains behind our house. We mixed in the crowd outside, as the church emptied, and armed ourselves with branches. Rounding up the children, who were in swarms, we gave chase. Down, down, through the zone of chestnut trees, down through the olive woods, down through the vineyards, down to the little town the throng fled, till, landing them in the street, we went home, remarking on the evident superior power of the Anglo-Saxon race over the Latin.

As time went on my drawing-books began to show some promise, so that my father gave me great historical subjects for treatment, but warning me, in that amused way he had, that an artist must never get spoilt by celebrity, keeping in mind the fluctuations of popularity. I took all this seriously. I think that, having no boys to bring up, he tried to put all the tuition suitable to both boys and girls into us. One result was that as a child I had the ambition to be a writer as well as a painter. We children were fanatically devoted to the worship of Charlotte Brontë, since our father had read us *Jane Eyre* (with omissions). Rather strong meat for babes! We began sending poetry and prose to divers periodicals and cut our teeth on rejected MSS.

We went back to Genoa, *viâ* Jersey (as a little *détour!*). Poor old Agostino, our inevitable cook, saw us as we drove from the station, on our arrival, through the Via Carol Felice. Worse luck, for he had become too blind for his work. In days gone by he had done very well and we had not the heart to cast him off. He ran after our carriage, kissing our hands as he capered sideways alongside, at the peril of being run over. So we were in for him again, but it was the last time. On our next visit a friend told us, "Agostino is dead, thank goodness!" He and our dear nurse, Amélie, used to have the most desperate rows, principally over religion, he a devout Catholic and she a Protestant of the true Swiss fibre. They always ended by wrangling themselves at the highest pitch of their voices into papa's presence for judgment. But he never gave it, only begging them to be quiet. She declared to Agostino that if he got no wages at all he would still make a fortune out of us by his perquisites; and, indeed, considering we left all purchases in his hands, I don't think she exaggerated. The war against Austria had been won. Magenta, Solferino, Montebello—dear me, how those names resounded! One day as we were running along the road in our pinafores near the Zerbino palace, above Genoa, along came Victor Emmanuel in an open carriage looking very red and blotchy in the heat, with big, ungloved hands, one of which he raised to his hat in saluting us little imps who were shouting "Long live the King of Italy!" in English with all our might. We were only a *little* previous (!) Then the next year came the Garibaldi enthusiasm, and we, like all the children about us, became highly exalted *Garibaldians*. I saw the Liberator the day before he sailed from Quarto for his historical landing in Sicily, at the Villa Spinola, in the grounds of which we were, on a visit at the English counsul's. He was sitting in a little arbour overlooking the sea, talking to the gardener. In the following autumn, when his fame had increased a thousandfold, I made a pen and ink memory sketch of him which my father told me to keep for future times. I vividly remember, though at the time not able to understand the extraordinary meaning of the words, hearing one of Garibaldi's adoring comrades (one Colonel Vecchii) a year or two later on exclaim to my father, with hands raised to heaven, "*Garibaldi!! C'est le Christ le revolver à la main!*"

Our life at old Albaro was resumed, and I recall the pleasant English colony at Genoa in those days, headed by the very popular consul, "Monty" Brown, and the nice Church of England chaplain, the Rev. Alfred Strettell. Ah! those primitive picnics on Porto Fino, when Mr. Strettell and our father used to read aloud to the little company, including our precocious selves, Shakespeare, Wordsworth, Keats, Tennyson, under the vines and olives, between whose branches, far below the cultivated terraces which we chose for our repose, appeared the deep blue waters of the Sea of seas. My early sketch books are full of incidents in Genoese peasant life: carnival revels in the streets, so suited to the child's idea of fun; charges of Garibaldian cavalry on discomfited Neapolitan troops (the despised *Borbonici*), and waving of tricolours by bellicose patriots. I was taken to the Carlo Felice Theatre to see Ristori in *Maria Stuarda*, and became overwhelmed with adoration of that mighty creature. One night she came on the stage waving a great red, white and green tricolour, and recited to a delirious audience a fine patriotic poem to united Italy ending in the words *"E sii Regina Ancor!"* I see her now in an immense crinoline.

A charming autumn sojourn on the lakes of Orta and Maggiore filled our young minds with beauty. Early autumn is the time for the Italian lakes, while the vintage is "on" and the golden Indian corn is stored in the open loggias of the farms, hanging in rich bunches in sun and luminous shade amongst the flower pots and all the homely odds and ends of these picturesque dwellings. The following spring was clouded by our return to England and London in particularly cold and foggy weather, dark with the London smoke, and our temporary installation in a dismal abode hastily hired for us by our mother's father, where we could be close to his pretty little dwelling at Fulham. My Diary was begun there. Poor little "Mimi" (as I was called), the pages descriptive of our leaving Albaro at that time are spotted with the mementos of her tears. The journey itself was a distraction, for we returned by the long Cornice Route which then was followed by the *Malle Poste* and Diligence, the railway being only in course of construction. It was very interesting to go in that fashion, especially to me, who loved the horses and watched the changing of our teams at the end of the "stages" with the intensest zest. I made little sketches whenever halts allowed, and, as usual, my irrepressible head was out of the Diligence window most of the time. The Riviera is now known to everybody, and very delightful in its way. I have not long returned from a very pleasant visit there; everything very luxurious and up-to-date, but the local sentiment is lessened. The reason is obvious, and has been laboured enough. One can still go off the beaten paths and find the true Italy. I have found one funny little sketch showing our *Malle Poste* stopping to pick up the mail bag at a village (San Remo, perhaps), which bag is being handed out of a top window, at night, by the old postmistress. The *Malle Poste* evidently went "like the wind," for I invariably show the horses at a gallop all along the route.

My misery at the view of our approach to London through that wilderness of slums that ushers us into the Great Metropolis is all chronicled, and, what with one thing and another, the Diary sinks for a while into despondency. But not for long. I cheer up soon.

In London I took in all the amusing details of the London streets, so new to me, coming from Italy. I seem, by my entries in the Diary, to have been particularly diverted by the colour of those Dundreary whiskers that the English "swell" of the period affected. I constantly come upon "Saw no end of red whiskers." Then I read, "Mamma and I paid calls, one on Dickens (sic)—out, thank goodness." Charles Dickens, whom I dismiss in this offhand manner, had been a close friend of my father's, and it was he who introduced my father to the beautiful Miss Weller (amusing coincidence in names!) at an amateur concert where she played. The result was rapid. My vivid memory can just recall Charles Dickens's laugh. I never heard it echoed by any other man's till I heard Lord Wolseley's. The volunteer movement was in full swing, and I became even more enthusiastic over the citizen soldiers than I had been over the Garibaldini. Then there are pages and pages filled with description of the pictures at the Royal Academy; of the Zoological Gardens, describing nearly every bird, beast, reptile and fish. Laments over the fogs and the cold of that dreadful London April and May, and untiring outbursts in verse of regret for my lost Italy. But I stuffed my sketch books with British volunteers in every conceivable uniform, each corps dressed after its own taste. There was a very short-lived corps called the Six-foot Guards! I sent a design for a uniform to the Illustrated London News, which was returned with thanks. I felt hurt. Grandpapa attached himself to the St. George's Rifles, and went, later on, through storm and rain and sun in several sham fights. Well, Punch made fun of those good men and true, but I have lived to know that the "Territorials," as they came to be called, were destined in the following century to lend their strong arm in saving the nation. We next had a breezy and refreshing experience of Hastings and the joy of rides on the downs with the riding master. London fog and smoke were blown off us by the briny breezes.

CHAPTER TWO

EARLY YOUTH

IN December we migrated back to London, and shortly before Christmas our dear, faithful nurse died. That was Alice's and my first sense of sorrow, and, even now, I can't bear to go over those dreadful days. Our father told us we would never forgive ourselves if we did not take our last look at her. He said we were very young for looking on death, but "go, my children," he said, "it is right." I cannot read those heartbroken words with which I fill page after page of my Diary even now without tears. She had at first intended to remain at home at Lausanne when my parents were leaving for England, shortly after my birth, but as she was going I smiled at her from my cradle. "*Ah! Mademoiselle Mimi, ce sourire!*" brought her back irresistibly, and with us she remained to the end.

As we girls grew apace we had a Parisian mistress to try and parisianise our Swiss French and an Italian master to try and tuscanise our Genoese Italian, and every Saturday a certain Mr. Standish gave me two hours' drill in oil painting. How grand I felt! He gave me his own copies of Landseer's horses' heads and dogs as models. This wasn't very much, but it was a beginning. My lessons in the elementary class at the S. Kensington School of Art are not worth mentioning. The masters gave me hateful scrolls and patterns to copy, and I relieved my feelings by ornamenting the margins of my drawing paper with angry scribblings of horses and soldiers in every variety of fury. That did not last long. This entry in the Diary speaks for itself:—

"*Sunday, March 16th, 1862.*—We went to Mr. Lane's

house preparatory to going to see Millais in his studio. Mr. Richard Lane is an old friend of papa's. The middle Miss Lane is a favourite model of Millais' and very pretty. We entered his studio, which is hung with rich pre-Raphaelite tapestry and pre-Raphaelite everything. The smell of cigar smoke prepared me for what was to come. Millais, a tall, strapping, careless, blunt, frank, young Englishman, was smoking with two villainous friends, both with beards—red, of course. Instead of coming to be introduced they sat looking at Millais' graceful drawings calling them 'jolly' and 'stunning,' the creatures! Millais would be handsome but for his eyes, which are too small, and his hair is colourless and stands up in curls over his large head but not encroaching upon his splendid forehead. He seems to know what a universal favourite he is." I naturally did not record in this precious piece of writing a rather humiliating little detail. I wanted the company to see that I was a bit of a judge of painting, ahem! In fact, a painter myself, and, approaching very near to the wet picture of *The Ransom* (I think), I began to scrutinise. Mr. Lane took me gently, but firmly, by the shoulders and placed me in a distant chair. Had I been told by a seer that in 1875—the year I painted *Quatre Bras*—this same Millais, after entertaining me at dinner in that very house, would escort me down those very steps, and, in shaking hands, was to say, "Good night, Miss Thompson, I shall soon have the pleasure of congratulating you on your election to the Academy, an honour which you will t'oroughly deserve"—had I been told this!

Our next halt was in the Isle of Wight, at Ventnor, and then at Bonchurch, and our house was "The Dell." Bonchurch was a beautiful dwelling-place. But, alas! for what I may call the Oxford primness of the society! It took long to get ourselves attuned to it. However, we got to be fond of this society when the ice thawed. The Miss Sewells were especially charming, sisters of the then Warden of New College. Each family took a pride in the beauty of its house and gardens, the result being a rivalry in loveliness, enriching Bonchurch with flowers, woods and ornamental waters that filled us with delight. Mamma had "The Dell" further beautified to come up to the high level of the others. She made a little garden herself at the highest point of the grounds, with grass steps, bordered with tall white lilies, and called it "the Celestial Garden." The cherry trees she planted up there for the use of the blackbirds came to nothing. The water-colours she painted at "The Dell" are amongst her loveliest.

Ventnor was fond of dances, At Homes, and diversions generally, but I shall never forget my poor mother's initial trials at the musical parties where the conversation raged during her playing, rising and sinking with the *crescendos* and *diminuendos* (and this after the worship of her playing in Italy!), and once she actually stopped dead in the middle of a Mozart and silence reigned. She then tried the catching "Saltarello," with the same result exactly. "The English appreciate painting with their ears and music with their eyes," said Benjamin West (if I am not mistaken), the American painter, who became President of our Royal Academy. This hard saying had much truth in it, at least in his day. Even in ours they had to be *told* of the merits of a picture, and the *sight* of a pianist crossing his hands when performing was the signal for exchanges of knowing smiles and nods amongst the audience, who, talking, hadn't heard a note. For vocal music, however, silence was the convention. How we used inwardly to laugh when, after a song piped by some timid damsel, the music was handed round so that the words and music might be seen in black and white by the guests assembled. I thankfully record the fact that as time went on my mother's playing seemed at last to command attention, and it being whispered that silence was better suited to such music, it became quite the thing to stop talking.

Though Bonchurch was inclined to a moderate High Church tone, its rector was of a pungent Low-Churchism, and he wrote us and the other girls who sang in his choir a

very severe letter one day ordering us to discontinue turning to the east in the Creed. We all liked the much more
genial and very beautiful services at Holy Trinity Church,
midway to Ventnor, where we used to go for evensong. The
Rev. Mr. G., of Bonchurch, gave us very long sermons in
the mornings, prophesying dismal and alarming things to
come, and we took refuge finally in the Rev. A.L.B. Peile's
more heartening discourses.

The Ventnor dances were thoroughly enjoyable, and the
croquet parties and the rides with friends, and all the rest of
it. Yes, it was a nice life, but the morning lessons never
broke off. No doubt we were precocious, but we like to
dwell on the fact of the shortness of our childhood and the
consequent length of our youth. I now and then come upon
funny juvenile sketch books where I find my Ventnor partners at these dances clashing with charges of Garibaldian
cavalry. There they are, the desirable ones and the undesir-
able; the drawling "heavy swell" and the raw stripling; the
handsome and the ugly. The girls, too, are there; the flirt
and the wallflower. They all went in.

These festive Ventnor doings were all very well, but it
became more and more borne in upon me that, if I intended to be a "great artist" (oh! seductive words), my young
'teens were the right time for study. "Very well, then—
attention!—miss!" No sooner did my father perceive that I
meant business than he got me books on anatomy, architecture, costume, arms and armour, Ruskin's inspiring writings,
and everything he thought the most appropriate for my
training. But I longed for regular training in some academy.
I chafed, as my Diaries show. For some time yet I was to
learn in this irregular way, petitioning for real severe study
till my dear parents satisfied me at last. "You will be entering into a tremendous ruck of painters, though, my child,"
my father said one day, with a shake of his head. I answered,
"I will single myself out of it."

So, then, the lovely "Dell" was given up, and soon there
began the happiest period of my girlhood—my life as an art

student at South Kensington; *not* in the elementary class of unpleasant memory, but in the "antique" and the "life."

But our father wanted first to show us Bruges and the Rhine, so we were off again on our travels in the summer. Two new countries for us girls, hurrah! and a little glimpse of a part of our own by the way. I find an entry made at Henley.

"*Henley, May 31st.*—Before to-day I could not boast with justice of knowing more than a fraction of England! This afternoon I saw her in one of her loveliest phases on a row to Medmenham Abbey. Skies of the most telling effect, ever changing as we rowed on, every reach we came to revealing fresh beauties of a kind so new to me. The banks of long grass full of flowers, the farmsteads gliding by, the willows allowed to grow according to Nature's intention into exquisitely graceful trees, the garden lawns sloping to the water's edge as a delicious contrast to the predominating rural loveliness, and then that unruffled river! I have seen the Thames! At Medmenham Abbey we had tea, and one of the most beautiful parts of the river and meadowland, flowery to overflowing, was seen before us through the arcades, the sky just there being of the most delicious dappled warm greys, and further on the storm clouds towered, red in the low sun. What pictures wherever you turn; and turn and turn and turn we did, until my eyes ached, on our smooth row back. The evening effects put the afternoon ones out of my head. I imagined a score of pictures, peopling the rich, sweet banks with men and women of the olden time. The skies received double glory and poetry from the perfectly motionless water, which reflected all things as in a mirror—as if it wasn't enough to see that overwhelming beauty without seeing it doubled! At last I could look no more at the effects nor hear the blackbirds and thrushes that sang all the way, and to Mamma's sympathetic amusement, I covered my eyes and ears with a shawl. Alas! for the artist, there is no peace for him. He cannot gaze and peacefully admire; he frets because he cannot 'get the thing down' in paint. Having finished my row in that Paradise, let me also descend from the poetic heights, and record the victory of the Frenchman. Yes, 'Gladiateur' has carried off the blue ribbon of the turf. "Upon my word, these Frenchmen!" It was the first time a French horse had won the Derby.

Bruges was after my own heart. Medieval without being mouldy, kept bright and clean by loving restorations done with care and knowledge. No beautiful old building allowed to crumble away or be demolished to make room for some dreary hideosity, but kept whole and wholesome for modern use in all its own beauty. Would that the Italians possessed that same spirit. My Diary records our daily walks through the beautiful, bright streets with their curious signs named in Flemish and French, and the charm of a certain *place* planted with trees and surrounded by gabled houses. Above every building or tree, go where you would, you always saw rising up either the wondrous tower of the Halle (the *Beffroi*), dark against the bright sky, or the beautiful red spire on the top of the enormous grey brick tower of Notre Dame, a spire, I should say, unequalled in the world not only for its lovely shape and proportions, but for its exquisite style and colour: a delicious red for its upper part, most refined and delicate, with white lines across, and as delicate a yellow lower down. Or else you had the grey tower of the cathedral, plain and imposing, made of small bricks like that of Notre Dame, having a massive effect one would not expect from the material. Over the little river, which runs nearly round the town, are oft-recurring drawbridges with ponderous grey gates, flanked by two strong, round, tower-like wings. Most effective. On this river glided barges pulled painfully by men, who trudged along like animals. I record with horror that one barge was pulled by a woman! "It was quite painful to see her bent forward doing an English horse's work, with the band across her chest, casting sullen upward glances at us as we passed, and the perspiration running down her face. From the river diverge canals into the town, and nothing can describe the beauty of those water

streets reflecting the picturesque houses whose bases those
waters wash, as at Venice. When it comes to seeing two
towers of the Halle, two spires of Notre Dame, two towers
of the cathedral, etc., etc., the duplicate slightly quivering
downwards in the calm water! Here and there, as we
crossed some canal or other, one special bit would come
upon us and startle us with its beauty. Such combinations of
gables and corner turrets and figures of saints and little
water-side gardens with trees, and always two or more of the
towers and spires rising up, hazy in the golden flood of the
evening sun!"

In our month at Bruges I made the most of every hour. It
is one of the few towns one loves with a personal love. I
don't know what it looks like to-day, after the blight of war
that passed over Belgium, but I trust not much harm was
done there. How one trembled for the old *beffroi*, which one
heard was mined by the Huns when they were in possession.

"*August 24th.*—Dear, exquisite, lovely, sunny, smiling
Bruges, good-bye! Good-bye, fair city of happy, ever happy,
recollections. Bright, gabled Bruges, we shall not look upon
thy like again."

I will make extracts from my German Diary, as Germany
in those days was still a land of kindly people whom we
liked much before they became spoilt by the Prussianism
only then beginning to assert itself over the civil population. The Rhine, too, was still unspoilt. That part of
Germany was agricultural; not yet industrialised out of its
charm. I also think these extracts, though so crude and
"green," may show young readers how we can enjoy travel
by being interested in all we see. I may become tiresome to
older ones who have passed the Golden Gates, and for
some of whom Rhine or Nile or Seine or Loire has run dry.

"Adieu! Camarade."
at Nice

At a Café. Genoa

At Fort San Giugliano
Genoa — Il dolce far niente

Garibaldine

Enjoyment
Nice

How English Soldiers take their stroll

How French do the same

A LEAF FROM A VERY EARLY SKETCH-BOOK.

Market Cart Bruges

Royal Prussian Postillions

FLYING SHOTS IN BELGIUM AND RHINELAND IN /65.

CHAPTER THREE
MORE TRAVEL

"ALAS! for railway travellers one approach to a place is like another. Fancy arriving at Cologne through ragged factory outskirts and being deposited under a glazed shed from which nothing but the railway objects can be seen! We made a dash to the cathedral, I on the way remarking the badly-dressed Düppel heroes (!) with their cook's caps and tight trousers; and oh dear! the officers are of a very different mould here from what they are in Belgium. Big-whiskered fellows with waists enough to make the Belgians faint. But I am trifling. We went into the cathedral by a most glorious old portal covered with rich Gothic mouldings. Happy am I to be able to say I have seen Cologne Cathedral. Now, hurrah for the Rhine! that river I have so longed, for years, to see."

We don't seem to have cared much for Bonn, though I intensely enjoyed watching the swift river from the hotel garden and the Seven Mountains beyond. The people too, amused and interested me very much, and the long porcelain pipe dangling from every male mouth gave me much matter for sketching.

My Diary on board the *Germania*: "Koenigswinter at the foot of the Dragenfels began that series of exquisite towns at the foot of ruined castles of which we have had more than a sufficient feast—that is, to be able to do them all the justice which their excessive beauty calls loudly for. We rounded the Dragenfels and saw it 'frowning' more Byronically than on the Bonn side, and altogether more impressive. And soon began the vines in all their sweet abundance on the smiling hill slopes. Romantic Rolandsec expanded on our right as we neared it, and there stood the fragment of the ruined castle peering down, as its builder is said to have done, upon the Convent amidst the trees on its island below. And then how fine looked the Seven Mountains as we looked back upon them, closing in the river as though it were a lake, and away we sped from them and left them growing mistier, and passed russet roofs and white-walled houses with black beams across, and passed lovely Unkel, picturesque to the core, bordering the water, and containing a most delicious old church. Opposite rose curious hills, wild and round, half vine-clad, half bare, and so on to Apollinarisberg on our right, with its new four-pinnacled church on the hill, above Remagen and its old church below. The last sight of the Dragenfels was a very happy one, in misty sunlight, as it finally disappeared behind the near hills. On, on we went, and passed the dark Erpeler Lei and the round, blasted and dismal ruin of Okenfels; and Ling, with a cloud-capped mountain frowning over it. As we glided by the fine restored *château* of Argenfels and the village of Hönningen the sky was red with the reflection of the sunset which we could not see, and was reflected in the swirling river. We did our Rhine pretty conscientiously by going first aft, then forward, and then to starboard, and then to port, and glories were always before us, look which way we would. So the Rhine has *not* been much cried up, say what you will, Messrs. Blasé and Bore. The views were constantly interrupted by the heads of the lack-lustre people on board, who, just like the visitors at the R.A., hide the beauties they can't appreciate from those who long to see them. But it soon began to grow dark.

"As we glided by Neuwied and stopped to take and discharge passengers a band was playing the 'Düppel March,' so called because the Prussians played it before Düppel. They are so blatantly proud of having beaten the Danes and getting Schleswig-Holstein. Fireworks were spluttering, and, altogether, a great deal of festivity was going on. It was quite black on the afterdeck by this time, *minus* lanterns. To go below to the stuffy, lighted cabin was not to be thought of, so we walked up and down, sometimes coming in contact with our fellow-man, or, rather, woman, for the men carried lights at the fore (*i.e.* at the ends of their cigars). At last, by the number of lights ahead, we knew we were approaching Coblenz. We went to the "Giant" Hotel, close to the landing. It was most tantalising to know that Ehrenbreitstein was towering opposite, invisible, and that such masses of picturesqueness must be all around. Papa and I had supper in the *Speise-saal*, and then I gladly sought my couch, in my sweet room which looked on the front, after a very enjoyable day.

"Most glorious of glorious days! The theory held so drearily by Messrs. Blasé and Bore about the mist and rain of the Rhine is knocked on the head. We were off to Bingen, to my regret, for it was hard to leave such a place as Coblenz, although greater beauties awaited us further up, perhaps, than we had yet seen. But I must begin with the morning and record the glorious sight before us as we looked out of our windows. Strong Ehrenbreitstein against the pearly, hot, morning sky, the furrowed rock laid bare in many places, and precipitous, sun-tinted and shadow-stained; the bright little town just opposite, the hill behind thickly clothed in rich vines athwart which the sun shone deliciously. The green of the river, too, was beautifully soft. After breakfast we took that charming invention, an open carriage, and went up to the Chartreuse, the proper thing to do, as this hill overlooks one of *the* views of the world. We went first through part of the town, by the large and rather ugly King's Palace, passing much picturesqueness. The women have very pleasing headdresses about here of various patterns. Of course, the place is full of soldiers and everything seems fortified. On our ascent we passed great forts of immense strength, hard nuts for the French to crack, if they ever have the wickedness (*sic*) to put their pet notion of the Rhine being France's boundary into execution. What a view we had all the way up; to our left, the winding Rhine disappearing in the distance into the gorge, its beautiful valley smiling below, and the vine-clad hills rising on either side, with their exquisite surfaces. Purple shadows, and golden vines, and walnut trees, that contrast which so often has enchanted my eyes on the Genoese

Riviera, the Italian lakes, and my own dear Lake Leman, gladdened them once more. And then the really clear sky (no factory chimneys here) and those intense white clouds casting shadows on the hills of lovely purple. We went across the wide plateau on the top, a magnificent exercise ground for the soldiers, health itself, and then we beheld, winding below us in its sweet valley and by two picturesque villages, the little Moselle, by no means 'blue,' as the song says, but of a pinky brown and apparently very shallow. We were at a great height, and having got out of the carriage we stood on the very verge of a sheer precipice, at the far-down base of which wound the high road. Sweet little Moselle! I was so loth to leave that view behind. It really does seem such a shame to say so little of it. The air up there was full of the scent of wild thyme, and mountain flowers grew thick in that hot sun, and the short mountain grass was brown.

"We descended by another road and were taken right through the town to the old Moselle bridge which crosses that river near its confluence with the green Rhine. What turreted corners, what gable ends, what exquisite David Roberts 'bits' at every turn! The bridge and its old gate were a picture in themselves, and the view from the middle of the bridge of the walls, the old buildings, church towers and spires, and boats and rafts moored below, was the essence of the picturesque. Market women and *pelotons* of soldiers with glittering helmets and bayonets make excellent fore-ground groups. How unlike nearly-deserted Bruges is this busy, thronged city! Oxen are as much used about here as horses, and add much to the artist's joy. But I must hurry on; there is all the glorious Rhine to Bingen to ascend. What a feast of beauty we have been partaking of since leaving Failure Bonn!

"Lots of people at 1 o'clock *table d'hôte:* staring Prooshan officers in 'wings' and whiskers, more or less tightly clad, talking loud and clattering their swords unnecessarily; swarms of English and a great many honeymoon couples of all nations. It was very hot when we left to dive into that glorious region we had seen from the Chartreuse. Those were golden hours on board the *Lorelei*. But more 'spoons'; more English; more Ya-ing natives and small boys always in the way, and so we paddled away from beautiful Coblenz, and very fine did the 'Broadstone of Honour'[1] look as we left it gradually behind. And now we began again the castles and the villages, the former more numerous than below stream. Happy Mr. Moriarty to possess such a castle as Lahneck; and then the beautiful town below, and the gorgeous wooded steep hills and the beautiful tints on the water. Golden walnut trees on the banks and old church towers— such rich loveliness gliding by perpetually. The towns are certainly half the battle; they add immensely to the scene. Rhense was the oldest town we had yet seen, and the old dark walls are crumbling down. Such bits of archways, such corner bits, such old age-tinted roofs! I *must* not pass over Marksburg, the most perfect old castle on the Rhine, quite unaltered and not quite ruinous, as it is garrisoned by a corps of Invalides. It therefore looks stronger and grander than the others. Below the cone which it crowns nestled the inevitable picturesque town (Braubach) upon the shore.

"Soon after passing this beautiful part we rounded another old village and church on our right, for the river takes a great bend here. Of course, new beauties appeared ahead as we swept round, soft purple mountains, one behind the other, and hillsides golden with vines and walnut trees. And then we came to Boppart, in the midst of the gorge, one of the most enchanting old walled towns we had yet seen, with a large water-cure establishment above it upon the orchard slopes of the hill. Then the old castle called 'The Mouse' drew our attention to the left again, and then to the right appeared, after we had passed the twin castles of Sternberg and Liebenstein, or the 'Brothers,' the magnificent ruin of Rheinfels above the town of St. Goar in the shadow of the steep hill. How splendidly those blasted arches come out against the sunny sky! Then 'The Cat' appeared on our left, supposed to be watching 'The Mouse' round the corner; then, with the last gleam of the sun upon it, appeared the castle of 'Schönberg' after we had passed the Lorelei rock, tunnelled through by the railway, and hills glowing autumn tints. Sunset colour began to add new charm to mountains, hills, and river. Two guns were fired in this part of the gorge for the echo. It rolled away like thunder very satisfactorily. Gutenfels on its rock was splendid in the sunset, with the town of Caub at its feet, and the curious old tower called the Pfalz in mid-stream, where poor Louis le Débonnaire came to die. I can hardly individualise the towns and their over-looking castles that followed. There was Bacharach, with its curious three-sided towers and church of St. Werner; then more castles, getting dimmer and dimmer in the deepening twilight. The last was swallowed up in the night."

I need not dwell on Bingen. I see us, happy wanderers, dropping down to Boppart, to halt there for very fondly-remembered days at the water-cure of "Marienberg," which we made our habitation for want of an hotel. Being there I did the "cure" for nothing in particular, but was none the worse for it. At any rate it passed me as "sound" after the ordeal by water. The ordeal was severe, and so was the Spartan food. To any one who wasn't going through the water ordeal the Spartan food ordeal seemed impossible. But soon one got to like the whole thing and delight in the freshness of that life in the warm sunny weather. We both accepted the "Grape Cure" with unmixed feelings—2 lbs. each of grapes a day; and even the cold, deep plate of sour milk (*dicke milch*), sprinkled with brown breadcrumbs, and that *kraut* preserve which so dashed us at our first breakfast, became rather fascinating. We took our pre-breakfast walk on four glasses of cold water, though, to *wet* our appetites. I see now, in memory, the swimming baths, with the blue water rushing through them from the hills, and feel the exhilaration of the six-in-the-morning plunge. Oh! *La jeunesse! La joie de vivre!*

They had dancing every Thursday evening in what was the great vaulted refectory of the monks before that monastery was secularised. One gala evening many people came in from outside. The young ladies were in muslin frocks, which they, no doubt, had washed themselves, and the ballroom was redolent of soap. The gentlemen went into the drawing-room after each dance and combed their blond hair and beards at the looking-glass over the mantel-piece, having brought brush and comb with them. The next morning I was very elaborately saluted by a man in a blouse, driving oxen, and I recognised in him one of my partners of the evening before who had worn the correct *frac* and white tie. What a strange amalgamation of democracy and aris-tocracy we found in Germany! The Diary tells of the music we had every evening till 10 o'clock and "lights out." My mother and one or two typical German musical geniuses—women patients—kept the piano in constant request, and the evenings were really very bright and the tone so homely and kind. Kindness was the prevailing spirit which we noticed amongst the Germans in those far-away days. How they complimented us all on our halting German; how the women admired our frocks, especially the buttons! I hope they didn't expect us to go into equal ecstasies over their own costumes. We sang and were in great voice, perhaps on account of the "plunge baths," or was it the "sour milk"?

A big Saxon cavalry officer who was doing the cure for a kick from a horse and, being in mufti, had put off his "jack-boot" manners, was full of enthusiasm about our voices. He expressed himself in graceful pantomime after each of my songs by pointing to his ear and running his finger down to his heart, for he spoke neither English nor French, and wor-shipfully paid homage to Mamma's pianoforte playing. She played indeed superbly. He was a big man. We called him "the Athlete." We had nicknames for all the patients. There was "the *Sauer-kraut*," there was the "Flighty," the funniest little shrivelled creature, a truly wonderful musical genius, who, having heard me practising one morning, flew to Mamma, telling her she had heard me go up to *Si* and that I must make my name as a *prima donna*—no less. That Mendelssohn had proposed to her was a treasured memory. Her mother, with true German pride of birth, forbade the union. There was a very great dame doing the cure, the "*Incog*," who confided her card to Mamma with an Imperial embrace before leaving, which revealed her as Marie, Prinzessin zu Hohenzollern Hechingen. Then there was a most interesting and ugly duellist, who a short time previously had killed a prince. His wife wore blue spectacles, having cried herself blind over the regrettable incident. And so on, and so on.

The vintage began, and we visited many a vineyard on both banks of the rapid, eddying river, watching the peasants at their wholesome work in the mellowing sunlight. Whenever we bought grapes of these pleasant people, they insisted on giving us extra bunches *gratis* in that old-fashioned way so prevalent in Italy. I record in the Diary one classic-looking youth, with the sunset gold behind his serious, handsome face, bent slightly over the vine he was picking, on the hillside where we sat. He seemed the personification of the sanctity of labour. All this sounds very sentimental to us war-weary ones of the twentieth century, but we need refreshment in the pleasures of memory; memory of more secure times. The Diary says:—

"When we left Boppart, Mamma and we two girls were half hidden in bouquets, and our Marienberg friends clustered at the railway carriage door and on the step—the '*Sauer-kraut*,' the 'Flighty,' the 'Athlete' and all, and, as we started, the salutations were repeated for the twentieth time, the 'Athlete' taking a long sniff of my bouquet, then quickly blocking his nose hard to keep the scent in, after going through the pantomime of the ear, the finger, and the heart. As Papa said, 'One gets quite reconciled to the two-legged creature when meeting such people as these.' Good-bye, lovely Boppart, of ever sweet recollections!"

We tarried at Cologne on our way to England. I see,

together with admiring and elaborate descriptions of the cathedral, a note on the kindly manners of the Germans, so curiously at variance with the impression left on the present generation by the episodes of the late war. At the *table d'hôte* one evening the two guests who happened to sit opposite our parents, on opening their champagne at dessert, first insisted on filling the two glasses of their English *vis-à-vis* before proceeding to fill their own. German manners then! The military class kept, however, very much aloof, and were very irritating to us with their wilfully offensive attitude. That unfortunate spirit had already taken a further step forward after the conquest of Schleswig-Holstein, and was to go further still after the knock-down blow to Austria; then in 1870 comes more arrogance, and so on to its own undoing in our time.

"*Aix la Chapelle.*—Good-bye, Cologne, ever to remain bright by the remembrance of its cathedral and that museum containing pictures which have so inspired my mind. And so good-bye, dear, familiar Rhine; not the Rhine of the hurried tourist and his John Murray Red Book, but the glorious river about whose banks we have so often wandered at our leisure.

"And now 'Vorwärts, marsch!' Northwards, to the Land of Roast Beef plus Rinderpest.[2] But first, Aachen. Ineffable poetry surrounds this evening of our arrival, for from the three churches which stand out sharp against the bright moonlight sky in front of the hotel there peal forth many mellow bells, filling my mind with that sort of sadness so familiar to me. This is All Hallows' Eve.

"*November 1st.*—We saw the magnificent frescoes in the long, low, arched hall of the Rathhaus, which is being magnificently restored, as is the case with all the fine things of the Prussia we have seen. We only just skimmed these great works of art, for the horses were waiting in the pelting rain...The first four frescoes we saw were by Rethel, the first representing the finding of the body of Charlemagne sitting in his tomb on his throne, crowned and robed, holding the ball and sceptre; a very impressive subject, treated with all its requisite poetry and feeling. The next fresco represents in a forcible manner Charlemagne ordering a Saxon idol to be broken; the third is a superb episode from the Battle of Cordova, where Charlemagne is wresting the standard from the Infidel. The horses are all blindfolded, not to be frightened by the masks which the enemy had prepared to frighten them with. The great white bulls which draw the chariot are magnificently conceived. The fourth fresco represents the entry of the great emperor—whose face, by the by, lends itself well to the grand style of art—into Pavia; a superb composition, as, indeed they all are. After painting this the artist lost his senses. No doubt such efforts as these may have caused his mind to fail at last. He had supplied the compositions for the other four frescoes which Kehren has painted, without the genius of the originator. We were shown the narrow little old stone staircase up which all those many German emperors came to the hall. I could almost fancy I saw an emperor's head coming bobbing up round the bend, and a figure in Imperial purple appear. Strange that such a steep little winding staircase should be the only approach to such a splendid hall. The new staircase, up which a different sort of monarch from the old German emperors came a few days ago, in tight blue and silver uniform, is indeed in keeping with the hall, and should have been trodden by the emperors, whereas this old cad of a king[3] (sic) would get his due were he to descend the little old worn stair head foremost."

At Brussels my entry runs: "*November 3rd.*—My birthday. I feel too much buoyed up with the promise of doing something this year to feel as wretched as I might have felt at the thought of my precious 'teens dribbling away. Never say die; never, never, never! This birthday is ever to be marked by our visit to Waterloo, which has impressed me so deeply. The day was most enjoyable, but what an inexpressibly sad feeling was mixed with my pleasure; what thoughts came crowding into my mind on that awful field, smiling in

the sunshine, and how, even now, my whole mind is over-
shadowed with sadness as I think of those slaughtered
legions, dead half a century ago, lying in heaps of mouldering bones under that undulating plain. We had not driven
far out of Brussels when a fine old man with a long white
beard, and having a stout stick for scarcely-needed support,
and from whose waistcoat dangled a blue and red ribbon
with a silver medal attached bearing the words 'Wellington'
and 'Waterloo,' stopped the carriage and asked whether we
were not going to the Field and offering his services as
guide, which we readily accepted, and he mounted the box.
This was Sergeant-Major Mundy of the 7th Hussars, who
was twenty-seven when he fought on that memorable 18th
June, 1815. In time we got into the old road, that road
which the British trod on their way to Quatre Bras, ten
miles beyond Waterloo, on the 16th. We passed the forest
of Soignies, which is fast being cleared, and at no very distant period, I suppose, merely the name will remain. What
a road was this, bearing a history of thousands of sad incidents! We visited the church at Waterloo where are the
many tablets on the walls to the memory of British officers
and men who died in the great fight. Touching inscriptions
are on them. An old woman of eighty-eight told us that she
had tended the wounded after the battle. Is it possible!
There she was, she who at thirty-eight had beheld those
men just half a century ago! It was overpowering to my
young mind. The old lady seems steadier than the serjeant-
major, eleven years her junior, and wears a brown wig.
Thanks to the old sergeant, we had no bothering vendors of
'relics.' He says they have sold enough bullets to supply a
dozen battles.

    "We then resumed our way, now upon more historic
ground than ever, the field of the battle proper. The Lion
Mound soon appeared, that much abused monument. Certainly, as a monument to mark where the Prince of Orange
was wounded in the left shoulder it is much to be censured,
particularly with that Belgian lion on the top with its paw

on Belgium, looking defiance towards France, whose soldiers, as the truthful old sergeant expressed himself, 'could any day, before breakfast, come and make short work of the Belgians' (sic). But I look upon this pyramid as marking the field of the fifteenth decisive battle of the world. In a hundred years the original field may have been changed or built upon, and then the mound will be more useful than ever as marking the centre of the battlefield that was. To make it much ground has been cut away and the surface of one part of the field materially lowered. On being shown the plan for this 'Lion Mound,' Wellington exclaimed, 'Well, if they make it, I shall never come here again,' or something to that effect, and, as old Mundy said, 'the Duke was not one to break his word, and he never did come again.' Do you know that, Sir Edwin Landseer, who have it in the background of your picture of Wellington revisiting the field? We drove up to the little Hotel du Musée, kept by the sergeant's daughter, a dejected sort of person with a glib tongue and herself rather grey. We just looked over Sergeant Cotton's museum, a collection of the most pathetic old shakos and casques and blundering muskets, with pans and flints, belonging to friend and foe; rusty bullets and cannon balls, mouldering bits of accoutrements of men and horses, evil-smelling bits of uniforms and even hair, under glass cases; skulls perforated with balls, leg and arm bones in a heap in a wooden box; extracts from newspapers of that sensational time, most interesting; rusty swords and breastplates; medals and crosses, etc., etc., a dismal collection of relics of the dead and gone. Those mouldy relics! Let us get out into the sunshine. Not until, however, the positive old soldier had marshalled us around him and explained to us, map in hand, the ground and the leading features of the battle he was going to show us.

"We then went, first, a short way up the mound, and the old warrior in our midst began his most interesting talk, full of stirring and touching anecdotes. What a story was that he was telling us, with the scenes of that story before our eyes! I, all eagerness to learn from the lips of one who took part in the fight, the story of that great victory of my country, was always throughout that long day by the side of the old hussar, and drank in the stirring narrative with avidity. There lay before us the farm of La Haie Sainte—'lerhigh saint' as he called it—restored to what it was before the battle, where the gallant Germans held out so bravely, fighting only with the bayonet, for when they came to load their firearms, oh, horror! the ammunition was found to be too large for the muskets, and was, therefore, useless. There the great Life Guard charge took place, there is the grave of the mighty Shaw, and on the skyline the several hedges and knolls that mark this and that, and where Napoleon took up his first position. And there lies La Belle Alliance where Wellington and Blücher did *not* meet—oh, Mr. Maclise!— and a hundred other landmarks, all pointed out by the notched stick of old Mundy. The stories attached to them were all clearly related to us. After standing a long time on the mound until the man of discipline had done quite his regulation story, with its stirring and amusing touches and its minute details, we descended and set off on our way to Hougoumont. What a walk was that! On that space raged most of the battle; it was a walk through ghosts with agonised faces and distorted bodies, crying noiselessly.

"Our guide stopped us very often as we reached certain spots of leading interest, one of them—the most important of all—being the place where the last fearful tussle was made and the Old Guard broke and ran. There was the field, planted with turnips, where our Guards lay down, and I could not believe that the seemingly insignificant little bank of the road, which sloped down to it, could have served to hide all those men until I went down and stooped, and then I understood, for only just the blades of the grass near me could I see against the sky. Our Guards must indeed have seemed to start out of the ground to the bewildered French, who were, by the by, just then deploying. That dreadful V formed by our soldiers, with its two sides

and point pouring in volley after volley into the deploying
Imperial Guard, must have indeed been a 'staggerer,' and so
Napoleon's best soldiers turned tail, yelling 'Sauve qui peut!'
and ran down that now peaceful undulation on the other
side of the road.

"Many another spot with its grim story attached did I
gaze at, and my thoughts became more and more overpowering. And there stood a survivor before us, relating this
tale of a battle which, to me, seems to belong to the olden
time. But what made the deepest impression on my mind
was the sergeant's pointing out to us the place where he lay
all night after the battle, wounded, 'just a few yards from
that hedge, there.' I repeat this to myself often, and always
wonder. We then left that historic rutted road and, following a little path, soon came, after many more stoppages, to
the outer orchard of Hougoumont. Victor Hugo's thoughts
upon this awful place came crowding into my mind also.
Yet the place did look so sweet and happy: the sun shining
on the rich, velvety grass, chequered with the shade of the
bare apple trees, and the contented cows grazing on the
grass which, on the fearful day fifty years ago, was not green
between the heaps of dead and dying wretches.

"Ah! the wall with the loopholes. I knew all about it and
hastened to look at it. Again all the wonderful stratagems
and deeds of valour, etc., etc., were related, and I have
learnt the importance, not only of a little hedge, but of the
slightest depression on a battlefield. Riddled with shot is
this old brick wall and the walls of the farm, too. Oh! this
place of slaughter, of burning, of burying alive, this place of
concentrated horror! It was there that I most felt the sickening terror of war, and that I looked upon it from the dark
side, a thing I have seldom had so strong an impulse to do
before. The farm is peaceful again and the pigs and poultry
grunt and cluck amongst the straw, but there are ruins
inside. There's the door so bravely defended by that British
officer and sergeant, hanging on its hinges; there's the well
which served as a grave for living as well as dead, where

Sergeant Mundy was the last to fill his canteen; and there's the little chapel which served as an oven to roast a lot of poor fellows who were pent up there by the fire raging outside. We went into the terror-fraught inner orchard, heard more interesting and saddening talk from the old soldier who says there is nothing so nice as fighting one's battles over again, and then we went out and returned to the inn and dined. After that we streamed after our mentor to the Charleroi road, just to glance at the left part of the field which the sergeant said he always liked going over the best. 'Oh!' he said, looking lovingly at his pet, 'this was the strongest position, except Hougoumont.' It was in this region that Wellington was moved to tears at the loss of so many of his friends as he rode off the field. Papa told me his memorable words on that occasion: 'A defeat is the only thing sadder than a victory.' What a scene of carnage it was! We looked at poor Gordon's monument and then got into our carriage and left that great, immortal place, with the sun shedding its last gleams upon it. I feel virtuous in having written this much, seeing what I have done since. We drove back, in the clear night, I a wiser and a sadder girl."

About this same Battle of Waterloo. Before the Great War it always loomed large to me, as it were from the very summit of military history, indeed of all history. During the terrible years of the late War I thought my Waterloo would diminish in grandeur by comparison, and that the awful glamour so peculiar to it would be obliterated in the fumes of a later terror. But no, there it remains, that lurid glamour glows around it as before, and for the writer and for the painter its colour, its great form, its deep tones, remain. We see through its blood-red veil of smoke Napoleon fall. There never will be a fall like that again: it is he who makes Waterloo colossal.

CHAPTER FOUR

IN THE ART SCHOOLS

AFTER tarrying in Brussels, doing the galleries thoroughly, we went to Dover. I had been anything but in love with the exuberant Rubenses gathered together in one surfeited room, but imbibed enthusiastic stimulus from some of the moderns. I write: "Oh! that I had time to tell of my admiration of Ambroise Thomas' *Judas Iscariot*, of Charles Verlat's wonderful *Siege of Jerusalem by Godfrey of Bouillon*, with its strikingly terrible incidents, given with wonderful vividness, so free from coarseness; of Tschaggeny's *Malle Poste*, with its capital horses. There was not much study to be done in the time, but enthusiasm to be caught, and I caught it."

At Dover I find myself saying: "Still at my drawing of the soldiers working at the new fort on the cliff, just outside the castle, which forms the background of the scene. I am sending it to the *Illustrated London News*. Then, a few days later: "Woe is me! my drawing is returned with the usual apologies. Well, never mind, the world will hear of me yet." And there, above my "diminished head," right over No. 2, Sydney Villas, our temporary resting-place, stood that very castle, biding its time when it should receive me as its official *châtelaine*, and all through that art which I was so bent on.

At Brompton I said "good-bye" to a year to me very bright and full of adventure; a year rich in changes, full of varied scenes and emotions. I say: "Enter, 1866, bearing for me happy promise for my future, for to-day I had the interview with Mr. Burchett, the Headmaster of the South Kensington School of Art, and everything proved satisfactory and sunny. First, Papa and I trotted off to Mr. Burchett's office and saw him, a bearded, velvet-skull-capped and cold-searching-eyed man. After a little talk, we galloped off home, packed the drawings and the oil, then, Mamma with us, we returned, and came into The Presence once more. The office being at the end of the passage of the male schools, I could see, and envy, the students going about. So the drawings were scrutinised by *that Eye*, and I must say I never expected things to go so well. Of course, this austere, rigid master is not one to say much, but, on the contrary, to dwell upon the shortcomings and weaknesses; to have no pity. He looked longer at my soldiers at work at Dover Castle and some hands that I had done yesterday, saying they showed much feeling. He said he did not know whether I only wished to make my studies superficial, but strongly advised me to become an artist. I scarcely needed such advice, I think, but it was very gratifying. I told him I wished for severe study, and that I did *not* wish to begin at the wrong end. We were a long time talking, and he was very kind, and told me off to the Life School after preliminary work in the Antique. I join to-morrow. I now really feel as though fairly launched. Ah! they shall hear of me some day. But, believe me, my ambition is of the right sort.

"*January 2nd.*—A very pleasant day for me. At ten marched off, with board, paper, chalk, etc., etc., to the schools, and signed my name and went through all the rest of the formalities, and was put to do a huge eye in chalk. I felt very raw indeed, never having drawn from a cast before. Everything was strange to me. I worked away until twenty minutes to two, when I sped home to have my lunch. Five hours' work would be too long were I not to break the time by this charming spin home and back in the open air, which makes me set to work again with redoubled energy and spirits sky-high. A man comes round at a certain time to the rooms to see by the thermometer whether the temperature is according to rule, which is a very excellent precaution; 65° seems to be the fixed degree. Of course, I did not make any friends to-day; besides, we sit far apart, on our own hooks, and not on forms. Much twining about of arms and *darling-ing*, etc., went on, however, but we all seem to work here so much more in earnest than over those dreary scrolls in the Elementary. One girl in our room was a capital hit, short hair brushed back from a clever forehead and a double eyeglass on an out-thrust nose. Then there is a dear little pale girl, with a pretty head and large eyes, who is struggling with that tremendous *Fighting Gladiator*. She and he make a charming *motif* for a sketch. But I am too intent on my work to notice much. The skeleton behind me seems, with outstretched arm, to encourage me in my work, and smiles (we won't say *grins*) upon me, whilst behind him—it?—the *écorché* man seems to be digging his grave, for he is in the attitude of using a spade. But enough for to-day. I was very much excited all day afterwards. And no wonder, seeing that my prayer for a beginning of my real study has now been granted and that I am at length on the high road. Oh, joy, joy!

"*January 15th.*—Did very well at the schools. Upon my word, I am getting on very smoothly. I peeped into the Life room for the first time whilst work was going on, and beheld a splendid halberdier standing above the girls' heads and looking very uncomfortable. He had a steel headpiece and his hands were crossed upon the hilt of his sword in front, and his face, excessively picturesque with its grizzly moustache, was a tantalising sight for me!

"*January 16th.*—Oh, how I am getting on! I can't bear to look at my old things. Was much encouraged by Mr. Burchett, who talked to me a good deal, the mistress standing deferentially and smilingly by. He said, 'Ah! you seem to get over your difficulties very well,' and said with what immense satisfaction I shall look back upon this work I'm doing. Altogether it was very encouraging, and he said this last thing of mine was excellent. He remarked that my early education in those matters had been neglected, but I console myself with the thought that I have not wasted my time so utterly, for all the travel I have had all my life has put crowds of ideas into my head, and now I am learning how to bring those ideas to good account.

"*January 24th.*—I shall soon have done the big head and shall soon reach a full-length statue, and I shall go in for anatomy rather than give so much time to this shading which the students waste so much time over. I don't believe in carrying it so far. The little pale girl I like, on the completion of her gladiator, has been promoted to the Life class. A girl made friends with me, a big grenadier of a girl, who says she wants to know 'all about the joints and muscles' and seems a 'thoroughgoer' like myself."

This is how I write of dear Miss Vyvyan, a fine, rosy specimen of a well-bred English girl, who became one of my dearest fellow students—and drew well. In writing of me after I had come out in the art world, she records this meeting in words all the more deserving of remembrance for being those of a voice that is still. Of my other fellow-students the Diary will have more to say, left to its own diction.

"*February 13th.*—It is very pleasant at the schools—oh, charming! In coming home at the end of my work I fell in with Mr. Lane, my friend in the truest sense of the word. He was coming over to us. His first inquiry was about me and my work. He was very much disappointed that I was not in the Life class, fully expecting that I should be there, seeing how highly Mr. Burchett twice spoke of my drawings to Mr. Lane, and that I was quite ready for the Life. But, of course, Mr. B. is desirous of putting me as much through the regular course as possible. Mr. Lane shares Millais' opinion that 'the antique is all very well, but that there is nothing like the living model, and that they are too fond of black and white at the Museum.' I was enrolled as a member of the Sketching Club this morning, and have only a week to do 'On the Watch' in, the title they have given us to illustrate. *Only* a week, Mimi? That's an age to do a sketch in! Ah! yes, my dear, but I shall have five hours in the schools every day except Saturdays. I have chosen for a subject a freebooter in a morion and cloak upon a bony horse, watching the plain below him as night comes on, with his blunderbus ready cocked. Wind is blowing, and makes the horse's mane and tail to stream out."

There follow pages and pages describing the daily doings at the schools: the commotion amongst girls at the drawings I used to bring to show them of battle scenes; the Sketching Club competitions, and all the work and the play of an art school. At last I was promoted to the Life class.

"*March 19th.*—Oh, joyous day! oh, white! oh, snowy Monday! or should I say *golden* Monday? I entered the Life this joyous morn, and, what's more, acquitted myself there not only to my satisfaction (for how could I be satisfied if the masters weren't?), but to Mr. Denby's and the oil master's *par excellence*, Mr. Collinson's. I own I was rather diffident, feeling such a greenhorn in that room, but I may joyfully say 'So far, so good,' and do my very best of bests, and I can't fail to progress. How willingly I would write down all the pleasant incidents that occur every day, and those, above all, of to-day, which make this delightful student life I am leading so bright and happy and amusing. However, I shall write down all that my spare moments will allow me. Little 'Pale Face' took me in hand and got me a nice position quite near the sitter, as I am only to do his head. There was a good deal of struggling as the number of girls increased, and late comers tried amicably to badger me out of my good position. We waited more than half an hour for the sitter, and beguiled the time as we are wont. Three semi-circles surround the sitter and his platform. The inner and smaller circle is for us who do his head only, and is formed by desks and low chairs; the next is formed by small fixed easels, and the outer one by the loose-easel brigade, so there are lots of us at work. At length the martyr issued from the curtained closet where Messrs. Burchett, Denby and Collinson had been helping the unhappy victim to make a lobster of his upper self with heavy plates of armour. He became sadly modern below the waist, for his nether part was not wanted. To see Mr. Denby pinning on the man's refractory Puritan starched collar was rich. The model is a small man, perfectly clean shaven with a most picturesque face; quite a study. Very finely-chiselled mouth, with thin lips and well-marked chin and jaw. The poor fellow was dreadfully nervous. He was posed standing, morion on head, with a book in one hand, the other raised as though he were discoursing to some fellow soldiers—maybe Covenanters—in a camp. I never saw a man in such agony as he evinced, his nervousness seeming at times to overpower him, and the weight of the armour and of the huge morion (too big for him) told upon him in a painfully evident manner. He was, consequently, allowed frequent rests, when down his trembling arm would clatter and the instrument of torture on his heated forehead come down with a great thump on the table. Mr. Denby was much pleased with my drawing in, and Mr. Collinson commended my carefulness. This pleases me more than anything else, for I know that carefulness is the most essential quality in a student.

"*March 27th.*—Mr. Burchett showed me how to proceed with the finishing of the face. He liked the way I had done the morion, which astonished me, as I had done it all unaided. I am now a friend of more girls than I can individualise, and they seem all to like me. 'Little Pale Face' is very charming with me indeed. One girl told me a dream she had had of me, and Mrs. C., wife of the *Athenaeum* art critic, clapped me on the back very cordially."

I give these extracts just to launch the Memoirs into that student life which was of such importance to me. Till the Easter vacation I did all I could to retrieve what I considered a good deal of leeway in my art training. There were Sketching Club competitions of intense effort on my part, and how joyful I felt at such events as my illustrations to Thackeray's *Newcomes* coming through marked "Best" by the judges.

"*May 9th.*—*Veni, vidi, vici!* My re-entry into the schools after the vacation has been a triumphal one, for my *Newcomes* have been returned 'The Best.' The girls were so glad to see me back. I have chosen, as there is not to be a model till next Monday week, a beautiful headpiece of elaborate design on whose surface the red drapery near it is reflected. Some time after lunch Mrs. C. came running to me from the Antique triumphantly waving a bunch of lilac above her head and crying out that my *Newcomes* had won! I jumped up, overjoyed, and went to see the sketches, around which a crowd of students was buzzing. Mr. Denby, who couldn't help knowing whose the 'Best' were, gave me a nod of approbation. I was very happy. Returning to Fulham, I told the glad tidings to Papa, Mamma, Grandpapa and Grandmamma as they each came in. So this has been a charming day indeed."

Page after page, closely written, describes the student life, than which there cannot be a happier one for a boy or girl; thorough searchings through the Royal Academy rooms for everything I could find for instruction, admiration and criticism. I joined a class in Bolsover Street for the study of the "undraped" female model, and worked very hard there on alternate days. This necessitated long omnibus rides to that dismal locality, but I always managed to post myself near the omnibus door, so as to study the horses in motion in the crowded streets from that coign of vantage. I also joined a painting class in Conduit Street, but that venture was not a success. I went in about the same time for very thorough artistic anatomy at the schools. I gave sketches to nearly all my fellow students—fights round standards, cavalry charges, thundering guns. I wonder where they are all now! I had always had a great liking for the representation of movement, but at the same time a deep well of melancholy existed in my nature, and caused me to draw from its depths some very sad subjects for my sketches and plans for future pictures. How strange it seems that I should have been so impregnated, if I may use the word, with the warrior spirit in art, seeing that we had had no soldiers in either my father's or mother's family! My father had a deep admiration for the great captains of war, but my mother detested war, though respecting deeply the heroism of the soldier. Though she and I had much in common, yet, as regards the military idea, we were somewhat far asunder; my dear and devoted mother wished to see me lean towards other phases of art as well, especially the religious phase, and my Italian studies in days to come very much inclined me to sacred subjects. But as time went on circumstances conducted me to the *genre militaire*, and there I have remained, as regards my principal oil paintings, with few exceptions. My own reading of war—that mysteriously inevitable recurrence throughout the sorrowful history of our world—is that it calls forth the noblest and the basest impulses of human nature. The painter should be careful to keep himself at a distance, lest the ignoble and vile details under his eyes should blind him irretrievably to the noble things that rise beyond. To see the mountain tops we must not approach the base, where the foot-hills mask the summits. Wellington's answer to enthusiastic artists and writers seeking information concerning the details of his crowning victory was full of meaning: "The best thing you can do for the Battle of Waterloo is to leave it alone." He had passed along the dreadful foot-hills which blocked his vision of the Alps.

I worked hard at the schools and in the country throughout 1867, and, with many ups and downs, progressed in the Life class. My fellow students were a great delight to me, so enthusiastically did they watch my progress and foretell great things for me. We formed a little club of four or five students—kindred spirits—for mutual help and all sorts of good deeds, the badge being a red cross and the motto "Thorough." I remember a money-box into which we were, by the rules, to drop what coins we could spare for the Poor. We were to read a chapter of the New Testament every day, and a chapter of Thomas à Kempis, and all our works were to be signed with the red cross and the club monogram. Seeing this little sign in the corner of *The Roll Call* over my name set one of those absurd stories circulating in the Press with which the public was amused in 1874, namely that I had been a Red Cross nurse in the Crimea. As a counterpoise to this more "Copy" was obtained for the papers by paragraphs representing me as an infant prodigy, which I thank my stars I was *not!*

One day in this year 1867 I had, with great trepidation, asked Mr. Burchett to accept two pen and ink illustrations I had made to Morris's poem, 'Riding together.' Great commotion amongst the students. Some preferred the drawing for the gay and happy first verse:

> Our spears stood bright and thick together,
> Straight out the banners streamed behind,
> As we galloped on in the sunny weather,
> With our faces turned toward the wind.

and others the tragic sequel:

> They bound my blood-stained hands together,
> They bound his corpse to nod by my side,
> Then on we rode in the bright March weather,
> With clash of cymbal did we ride.

The Diary says: "Mr. Burchett, surrounded by my dear fellow red crosses, Va., B., and Vy., talked about the drawings in a way which pleased me very much. When he was gone, Va. and B. disappeared and soon reappeared, Va. with a crown of leaves to crown me with and B. with a comb and some paper on which to play 'See the Conquering Hero comes' whilst Va. and Vy. should carry me along the great corridor in a dandy chair. They had great trouble to crown me, and then to get me to mount. It was a most uncomfortable triumphal progress, Vy. being nearly six foot and Va. rather short. They just put me down in time, for, had we gone an inch further on, we should have confronted Miss Truelock,[4] who swooped round the corner. I cannot describe the homage these three pay me, Va.'s in particular—Vy.'s is measured, and not humble like Va.'s or radiantly enthusiastic like B.'s. I am glad that I stand proof against all this, but it is hard to do so, as I know it is so thoroughly sincere, and that they say even more out of my hearing than to my face."

The Sultan Abdul Aziz and the Khedive Ismail paid a visit to London that year. We were in the midst of the festivities; and such church-bell ringing, fireworks, musical uproar, especially at the Crystal Palace, where the "Hallelujah," "Moses in Egypt," and other Biblical choruses vied with the cheering of the crowds in expressions of exultation, seldom had London known. This fills pages and pages of the Diary. As we looked on from Willis and Sotheran's shop window, out of which all the books had been cleared for us, in Trafalgar Square, at the arrival of the "Father of the Faithful," it seemed a strange thing for the bells of our churches to be pealing forth their joyous welcome. But how vain all these political doings appear as time goes by! What sort of reception would we give the present Sultan I wonder? We have even *abolished* Khedives. Much more reasonable and sane was the mob's welcome to the Belgian volunteers, who were also England's guests that year. We English were very courteous to the Belgians. Papa took us to the great Belgian ball, where we appeared wearing red, black, and yellow sashes. He offered to hold a Belgian officer's sword for him while he (the Belgian) waltzed me round the hall. A silver medal was struck to commemorate this visit, and every Belgian was presented with this decoration. On it were engraved the words "*Vive La Belge.*" No one could tell who the lady was.

This year saw my meek beginning in the showing of an oil picture (*Horses in Sunshine*) at the Women Artists' Exhibition, and then followed a water colour, *Bavarian Artillery going into Action*, at the Dudley Gallery—that delightful gallery which is now no more and which *The Times* designated the "nursery of young reputations." I continued exhibiting water colours and black-and-whites for some years there. I had the rare sensation of walking on air when my father, meeting me on parting with Tom Taylor, the critic of *The Times*, told me the latter had just come from the Dudley's press view and seen my *Bavarian Artillery* on its walls. I had begun!

In the latter part of this year's work at South Kensington Mr. Burchett stirred us up by giving us "time" and "memory" drawing to do from the antique, and many things which required quickness, imagination and concentration, all of which suited me well. Charcoal studies on tinted paper delighted me. I was always at home in such things. We often had "time" drawings to do on very rough paper, using charcoal with the hog's hair paint brush. What a good change from the dawdling chalk work formerly in vogue when I joined. I had by this time painted my way in oils through many models, male and female, with all the ups and downs recorded elaborately, the encouragements and depressions, and the happy, though slow, progress in the management of the brush. I had won a medal for two life-size female heads in oils, and through all the ups and downs the devotion of my dear "Red Cross" fellow students never fluctuated.

The year 1868 saw me steadily working away at the Schools and doing a great many drawings for sketching clubs and various competitions during this period, till we were off once more to Italy in October. On March 19th of that year I wrote in the Diary: "Ruskin has invited himself to tea here on Monday!!!" Then: "Memorable Monday. On thee I was introduced to Ruskin! Punctually at six came the great man. If I had been disposed to be nervous with him, his cold formal bow and closing of the eyes, his somewhat supercilious under-lip and sensitive nostrils would not have put me at my ease. But, fortunately, I felt quite normal—unlike Mamma and Alice, the latter of whom had reason for quaking, seeing that one of her young poems, sent him by a friend, had been scanned by that eye and pondered by that greatest of living minds.

"He sat talking a little, not commonplaces at all; on the contrary, he immediately began on great topics, Mamma and he coinciding all through, particularly on the subject of modern ugliness, railways, factory chimneys, backs of English houses, sash windows, etc., etc. Then he directed his talk to me, and we sat talking together about art, of course, and I showed him two life studies, which he expressed himself as exceedingly pleased with in a very emphatic manner. But here we went down to tea. After tea I showed him my imaginative drawings, which he criticised a good deal. He said there was no reason why I should not become a great artist (!), that I was 'destined to do great things.' But he remarked, after this too kindly beginning, that it was evident I had not studied enough from nature in those drawings, the light and shade being incorrect and the relations of tones, etc., etc. He told me to beware of sensational subjects, as yet, à propos of the Lancelot and Guinevere drawing; that such were dangerous, leading me to think I had quite succeeded by virtue of the strength of my subject and to overlook the consideration of minor points. He said, 'Do fewer of these things, but what you do do right and never mind the subject.' I did not like that; my great idea is that an artist should choose a worthy subject and concentrate his attention on the chief point. But Ruskin is a lover of landscape art and loves to see every blade of grass in a foreground lovingly dwelt upon. I cannot write down all he said as he and I leant over the piano where my drawings were. But it was with my artillery water colour, The Crest of the Hill, that he was most pleased. He knelt down before where it hung low down and held a candle before it the better to see it, and exclaimed 'Wonderful!' two or three times, and said it had 'immense power.' Thank you, Dudley Gallery, for not hanging it where Ruskin would never have seen it!

"He listened to Mamma's playing and Alice's singing of Mamma's 'Ave Maria' with perfectly absorbed attention, and seemed to enjoy the lovely sounds. He had many kind things to say to Alice about her poem, saying that he knew she was forced to write it; but was she always obliged to write so sadly? Then he spied out Mamma's pictures, and insisted on seeing lots of her water colours, which I know he must have enjoyed more than my imaginative things, seeing with what humble lovingness Mamma paints her landscapes. In fact, we showed him our paces all the evening. Papa says he (P.) was like the circus man, standing in the middle with the long whip, touching us up as we were trotted out before the great man. He seems, by the by, to have a great contempt for the modern French school, as I expected."

Daily records follow of steady work, much more to the purpose than in the humdrum old days. Mr. Burchett continued the new system with increasing energy. He seemed to have taken it up in our Life class with real pleasure latterly. In July the session ended, and I was not to re-enter the schools till after my Italian art training had brought me a long way forward.

CHAPTER FIVE

STUDY IN FLORENCE

ITALY once more! Again the old palazzo at Albaro and the old friends surrounding us! My work never relaxed, for I set up a little studio and went in for life-size heads, and got more and more facility with the brush. The kindly peasants let me paint them, and I victimised my obliging friends and had professional models out from Genoa. That was a very greatly enjoyed autumn, winter and spring, and the gaieties of the English Colony, the private theatricals, the concerts at Villa Novello—all those things did me good. The childish carnival revels had still power over me—yea, more—though I was grown up, and to tell the truth, I got all the fun out of them that was possible within bounds. "The Red Cross Sketch Book," which I filled with illustrations of our journey out and of life at Genoa, I dedicated to the club and sent to them when we left for Florence.

We found Genoa just as we had left it, still the brilliantly picturesque city of the sea, its populace brightly clad in their Ligurian national dress, the women still wearing the pezzotto, and the men the red cap I loved; the port all delightful with oriental character, its shouting muleteers and *facchini*, its fruit and flower sellers in the narrow streets and entrances to the palaces—all the old local colour. Alas! I was there only the other day, and found all the local charm had gone—modernised away!

When we left Genoa in April my father tried to get a *vetturino* to take us as far as Pisa by road on our way to Florence, for auld lang syne, but Antonio—he who used to drive us into Genoa in the old days—said that was now impossible on account of the railway—"*Non ci conviene, signore!*"—but he would take us as far as Spezzia. So, to our delight, we were able once more to experience the pleasures of the road and avoid that truly horrible series of suffocating tunnels that tries us so much on that portion of the coastline. At Sestri Levante I wrote: "I sit down at this pleasant hotel, with the silent sea glimmering in the early night before me outside the open window, to note down our journey thus far. The day has been truly glorious, the sea without even the thinnest rim of white along the coast, and such exquisite combinations of clouds. We left Villa Quartara at ten, with Madame Vittorina and the servants in tears. Majolina comes with us; she is such a good little maid. We had three good horses, but for the Bracco Pass we shall have an extra one. There is no way of travelling like this, in an open carriage; it is so placid; there is no hurrying to catch trains and struggling in crowds, no waiting in dismal *salles d'attente*. And then compare the entry into the towns by the high road and through the principal streets, perhaps through a city gate, the horse's hoofs clattering and the whip cracking so merrily and the people standing about in groups watching us pass, to sneaking into a station, one of which is just like the other, which hasn't the slightest *couleur locale* about it, and is sure to have unsightly surroundings.

"Away we went merrily, I feeling very jolly. The colour all along was ravishing, as may be imagined, seeing what a

perfect day it was and that this is the loveliest season of the
year. We dined at dear old Ruta, where also the horses had
a good rest and where I was able to sketch something down.
From Ruta to Sestri I rode by Majolina on the box, by far
the best position of all, and didn't I enjoy it! The horses'
bells jingled so cheerily and those three sturdy horses took
us along so well. Rapallo and Chiavari! Dear old friends,
what delicious picturesqueness they had, what lovely
approaches to them by roads bordered with trees! The
views were simply distracting. Sestri is a gem. Why don't
water-colour painters come here in shoals? What colouring
the mountains had at sunset, and I had only a pencil and
wretched little sketch book.

"*Spezzia, April 28th, 1869.*—A repetition of yesterday in
point of weather. I feel as though I had been steeped all day
in some balmy liquid of gold, purple, and blue. I have a
Titianesque feeling hovering about me produced by the
style of landscape we have passed through and the faces of
the people who are working in the patches of cultivation
under the mulberries and vines, and that intense, deep blue
sky with massive white clouds floating over it. We
exclaimed as much at the beauty of the women as at the
purple of the mountains and the green of the budding mulberries and poplars. And the men and boys; what perfect
types; such fine figures and handsome faces, such healthy
colour! We left the hotel at Sestri, with its avenue of
orange trees in flower, at ten o'clock, and, of course, crossed
the Bracco to-day. We dined at a little place called Boglias-
co, in whose street, under our windows, handsome youths
with bare legs and arms were playing at a game of ball
which called forth fine action. I did not know at first
whether to look well at them all or sketch them down one
by one, but did both, and I hope to make a regular drawing
of the group from the sketch I took and from memory. We
stopped at the top of the hill, from which is seen La Spezzia
lying below, with its beautiful bay and the Carara Mountains beyond. Here ends our drive, for to-morrow we take

the train for Florence.

"*Florence, April 29th.*—Magnificent, cloudless weather. But, oh! what a wearisome journey we had, the train crawling from one station to another and stopping at each such a time, whilst we baked in the cushioned carriage and couldn't even have lovely things to look at, surrounded by the usual railway eyesores. We passed close by the Pisan Campo Santo, and had a very good view of the Leaning Tower and the Duomo. Such hurrying and struggling at the Pisa station to get into the train for Florence, having, of course, to carry all our small baggage ourselves. Railway travelling in Italy is odious. It was very lovely to see Florence in the distance, with those domes and towers I know so well by heart from pictures, but we were very limp indeed, the wearisome train having taken all our enthusiasm away. Everything as we arrived struck us as small, and I am still so dazzled by the splendour of Genoa that my eyes cannot, as it were, comprehend the brown, grey and white tones of this quiet-coloured little city. I must *Florentine* myself as fast as I can. This hotel is on the Lung' Arno, and charming was it to look out of the windows in the lovely evening and see the river below and the dome of the Carmine and tower of Santo Spirito against the clear sky with, further off, the hills with their convents (alas! empty now) and clusters of cypresses. No greater contrast to Genoa could be than Florence in every way. Oh! may this city of the arts see me begin (and finish) my first regular picture. *April 30th.*—I and Papa strolled about the streets to get a general impression of 'Firenze la gentile,' and looked into the Duomo, which is indeed bare and sad-coloured inside except in its delicious painted windows over the altars, the harmonious richness of which I should think could not be exceeded by any earthly means. The outside is very gay and cheerful, but some of the marble has browned itself into an appearance of wood. Oh! dear Giotto's Tower, could elegance go beyond this? Is not this an example of the complete *savoir faire* of those true-born artists of old?

And the 'Gates of Paradise'! The delight of seeing these from the street is great, instead of in a museum. But Michael Angelo's enthusiastic exclamation in their praise rather makes one smile, for we know that it must have been in admiration of their purely technical beauties, as the gates are by no means large and grand *as* gates, and the bronze is rather dark for an entrance into Paradise! I reverently saluted the Palazzo Vecchio, and am quite ready to get very much attached to the brown stone of Florence in time.

"*Villa Lamporecchi, May 1st.*—We two and Papa had a good spell at the Uffizi in the morning, and in the afternoon we took possession of this pleasing house, which is so cool and has far-spreading views, one of Florence from a terrace leading out of what I shall make my studio. A garden and vineyards sloping down to the valley where Brunelleschi's brown dome shows above the olives."

Our mother did many lovely water colours, one especially exquisite one of Fiesole seen in a shimmering blue midsummer light. That, and one done on the Lung' Arno, to which Shelley's line

"The purple noon's transparent might"

could justly be applied, are treasured by me. She understood sunshine and how to paint it.

"*May 3rd.*—I already feel Florence growing upon me. I begin to understand the love English people of culture and taste get for this most interesting and gentle city. The ground one treads on is all historic, but it is in the artistic side of its history that I naturally feel the greatest interest, and it is a delightful thing to go about those streets and be reminded at every turn of the great Painters, Architects, Sculptors I have read so much of. Here a palace designed by Raphael, there a glorious row of windows carved by Michael Angelo, there some exquisite ironwork wrought by some other born genius. I think the style of architecture of the Strozzi Palace, the Ricardi, and others, is perfection in its way, though at first, with the brilliant whites, yellows

and pinks of Genoa still in my eye, I felt rather depressed by
the uniform brown of the huge stones of which they are
built. No wonder I haunt the well-known gallery which
runs over the Ponte Vecchio, lined with the sketches, studies, and first thoughts of most of the great masters. One
delights almost more in these than in many of the finished
pictures. They bring one much more in contact, as it were,
with the great dead, and make one familiar with their
methods of work. One sees what little slips they made, how
they modified their first thoughts, over and over again,
before finally fixing their choice. Very encouraging to the
struggling beginner to see these evidences of their troubles!

"I have never, before I came here where so many of them
have lived, realised the old masters as our comrades; I have
never been so near them and felt them to be mortals exactly like ourselves. This city and its environs are so little
changed, the greater part of them not at all, since those
grand old Michael Angelesque days that one feels brought
quite close to the old painters, seeing what they saw and
walking on the very same old pavement as they walked on,
passing the houses where they lived, and so forth."

I was at that time bent on achieving my first "great picture," to be taken from Keats's poem "The Pot of Basil":
Lorenzo riding to his death between the two brothers:

> So the two brothers and their murdered man
> Rode past fair Florence,

but, fortunately, I resolved instead to put in further training
before attacking such a canvas, and I became the pupil of a
very fine academic draughtsman, though no great colourist,
Giuseppe Belluci. On alternate days to those spent in his
studio I copied in careful pencil some of the exquisite
figures in Andrea del Sarto's frescoes in the cloisters of the
SS. Annunziata.

The heat was so great that, as it became more intense, I
had to be at Bellucci's, in the Via Santa Reparata, at eight
o'clock instead of 8.30, getting there in the comparative

cool of the morning, after a salutary walk into Florence, accompanied by little Majolina, no *signorina* being at liberty to walk alone. What heat! The sound of the ceaseless hiss of the *cicale* gave one the impression of the country's undergoing the ordeal of being *frizzled* by the sun. I record the appearance of my first fire-fly on the night of May 6th. What more pleasing rest could one have, after the heat and work of the day, than by a stroll through the vineyards in the early night escorted by these little creatures with their golden lamps?

The cloisters were always cool, and I enjoyed my lonely hours there, but the Bellucci studio became at last too much of a furnace. My master had already several times suggested a rest, mopping his brow, when I also began to doze over my work at last, and the model wouldn't keep his eyes open. I record mine as "rolling in my head."

I see in memory the blinding street outside, and hear the fretful stamping of some tethered mule teased with the flies. The very Members of Parliament in the Palazzo Vecchio had departed out of the impossible Chamber, and, all things considered, I allowed Bellucci to persuade me to take a little month of rest—"*un mesetto di riposo*"—at home during part of July and August. That little month of rest was very nice. I did a water colour of the white oxen ploughing in our *podere*; I helped (?) the *contadini* to cut the wheat with my sickle, and sketched them while they went through the elaborate process of threshing, enlivened with that rough innocent romping peculiar to young peasants, which gave me delightful groups in movement. I love and respect the Italian peasant. He has high ideas of religion, simplicity of living, honour. I can't say I feel the same towards his *betters*(?) in the Italian social scale.

The grapes ripened. The scorched *cicale* became silent, having, as the country people declared, returned to the earth whence they sprang. The heat had passed even *cicala* pitch. I went back to the studio when the "little month" had run out and the heat had sensibly cooled, and worked very well there. I find this record of a birthday expedition:

"I suggested a visit to the convent of San Salvi out at the Porta alla Croce, where is to be seen Andrea del Sarto's *Cenacolo*. This we did in the forenoon, and in the afternoon visited Careggi. Enough isn't said about Andrea. What volumes of praise have been written, what endless talk goes on, about Raphael, and how little do people seem to appreciate the quiet truth and soberness and subtlety of Andrea. This great fresco is very striking as one enters the vaulted whitewashed rectory and sees it facing the entrance at the further end. The great point in this composition is the wonderful way in which this master has disposed the hands of all those figures as they sit at the long table. In the row of heads Andrea has revelled in his love of variety, and each is stamped, as usual, with strong individuality. This beautifully coloured fresco has impressed me with another great fact, viz., the wonderful value of *bright yellow* as well as white in a composition to light it up. The second Apostle on our Saviour's left, who is slightly leaning forward on his elbow and loosely clasping one hand in the other, has his shoulders wrapped round with yellow drapery, the horizontally disposed folds of which are the *ne plus ultra* of artistic arrangement. There is something very realistic in these figures and their attitudes. Some people are down on me when they hear me going on about the rendering of individual character being the most admirable of artistic qualities.

"At 3.30 we went for such a drive to Careggi, once Lorenzo de' Medici's villa—where, indeed, he died—and now belonging to Mr. Sloane, a 'bloated capitalist' of distant England. The 'keepsake' beauty of the views thence was perfect. A combination of garden kept in English order and lovely Italian landscape is indeed a rich feast for the eye. I was in ecstasies all along. We made a great *détour* on our return and reached home in the after-glow, which cast a light on the houses as of a second sun.

"*October 18th.*—Went with Papa and Alice to see

Raphael's *Last Supper* at the Egyptian Museum, long ago a convent. It is not perfectly sure that Raphael painted it, but, be that as it may, its excellence is there, evident to all true artists. It seems to me, considering that it is an early work, that none but one of the first-class men could have painted it. It offers a very instructive contrast with del Sarto's at San Salvi. The latter immediately strikes the spectator with its effect, and makes him exclaim with admiration at the very first moment—at least, I am speaking for myself. The former (Raphael's) grew upon me in an extraordinary way after I had come close up to it and dwelt long on the heads, separately; but on entering the room the rigidity and formality of the figures, whose aureoles of solid metal are all on one level, the want of connection of these figures one with the other, and the uniform light over them all had an unprepossessing effect. Artistically considered this fresco is not to be mentioned with Andrea's, but then del Sarto was a ripe and experienced artist when he painted the San Salvi fresco, whereas they conjecture Raphael to have been only twenty-two when he painted this. There is more spiritual feeling in Raphael's, more dignity and ideality altogether; no doubt a higher conception, and some feel more satisfied with it than with Andrea's. The refinement and melancholy look of St. Matthew is a thing to be thought of through life. St. Andrew's face, with the long, double-peaked white beard, is glorious, and is a contrast to the other old man's head next to it, St. Peter's, which is of a harder kind, but not less wonderful. St. Bartholomew, with his dark complexion and black beard, is strongly marked from the others, who are either fair or grey-headed. The profile of St. Philip, with a pointed white beard, gave me great delight, and I wish I could have been been left an hour there to solitary contemplation. St. James Major, a beardless youth, is a true Perugino type, a very familiar face. Judas is a miserable little figure, smaller than the others, though on the spectator's side of the table in the foreground. He seems not to have been taken from life at all.

"On one of the walls of the room are hung some little chalk studies of hands, etc., for the fresco, most exquisitely drawn, and seeming, some of them, better modelled than in the finished work; notably St. Peter's hand which holds the knife. Is there no Modern who can give us a *Last Supper* to rank with this, Andrea's and Leonardo's?"

This entry in my Diary of student days leads my thoughts to poor Leonardo da Vinci. A painter must sympathise with him through his recorded struggles to accomplish, in his *Cenacolo*, what may be called the almost superhuman, achievement of worthily representing the Saviour's face. Had he but been content to use the study which we see in the Brera gallery! But, no! he must try to do better at Santa Maria delle Grazie—and fails. How many sleepless nights and nerve-racking days he must have suffered during this supreme attempt, ending in complete discouragement. I think the Brera study one of the very few satisfactory representations of the divine Countenance left us in art. To me it is supreme in its infinite pathos. But it is always the way with the truly great geniuses; they never feel that they have reached the heights they hoped to win.

Ruskin tells us that Albert Dürer, on finishing one of his own works, felt absolutely satisfied. "It could not be done better," was the complacent German's verdict. Ruskin praises him for this, because the verdict was true. So it was, as regarding a piece of mere handicraft. But to return to the Diary.

"We went then to pay a call on Michael Angelo at his apartment in the Via Ghibellina. I do not put it in those words as a silly joke, but because it expresses the feeling I had at the moment. To go to his house, up his staircase to his flat, and ring at his door produced in my mind a vivid impression that he was alive, and living there, would receive us in his drawing-room. Everything is well nigh as it was in his time, but restored and made to look like new, the place being far more as he saw it than if it were half ruinous and going to decay. Even the furniture is the same, but new

velveted and varnished. It is a pretty apartment, such as
one can see any day in nice modern houses. I touched his
little slippers, which are preserved, together with his two
walking sticks, in a tiny cabinet where he used to write, and
where I wondered how he found space to stretch his legs.
The slippers are very small and of a peculiar, rather Eastern,
shape, and very little worn. Altogether, I could not realise
the lapse of time between his date and ours. The little
sketches round the walls of the room, which is furnished
with yellow satin chairs and sofa, are very admirable and
free. The Titian hung here is a very splendid bit of colour.
This was a very impressive visit. The bronze bust of M. A.
by Giovanni da Bologna is magnificent; it gives immense
character, and must be the image of the man."

On October 21st I bade good-bye to Bellucci. His system
forbade praise for the pupil, which was rather depressing,
but he relaxed sufficiently to tell my father at parting that I
would do things (*Farà delle cose*) and that I was untiring
(*istancabile*), taking study seriously, not like the others (*le
altre*). With this I had to be content. He had drilled me in
drawing more severely than I could have been drilled in
England. For that purpose he had kept me a good deal to
painting in monochrome, so as to have my attention
absorbed by the drawing and modelling and *chiaroscuro* of
an object without the distraction of colour. He also said to
me I could now walk alone (*può camminare da sè*), and with
this valedictory good-bye we parted. Being free, I spent the
remaining time at Florence in visits to the churches and
galleries with my father and sister, seeing works I had not
had time to study up till then.

"*October 22nd.*—We first went to see the Ghirlandajos at
Santa Trinità, which I had not yet seen. They are fading, as,
indeed, most of the grand old frescoes are doing, but the
heads are full of character, and the grand old costumes are
still plainly visible. From thence we went to the small cloister called *dello Scalzo*, where are the exquisite
monochromes of Andrea del Sarto. Would that this cloister

had been roofed in long ago, for the weather has made sad havoc of these precious things. Being in monochrome and much washed out, they have a faded look indeed; but how the drawing tells! What a master of anatomy was he, and yet how unexaggerated, how true: he was content to limit himself to Nature; *knew where to draw the line*, had, in fact, the reticence which Michael Angelo couldn't recognise; could stop at the limit of truth and good taste through which the great sculptor burst with coarse violence. There are some backs of legs in those frescoes which are simply perfect. These works illustrate the events in the life of John the Baptist. Here, again, how marvellous and admirable are all the hands, not only in drawing, but in action, how touching the heads, how grand and thoroughly artistic the draperies and the poses of the figures. A splendid lesson in the management of drapery is, especially, the fresco to the right of the entrance, the *Vision of Zacharias*. There are four figures, two immediately in the foreground and at either extremity of the composition; the two others, seen between them, further off. The nearest ones are in draperies of the grandest and largest folds, with such masses of light and dark, of the most satisfying breadth; and the two more distant ones have folds of a slightly more complex nature, if such a word can be used with regard to such a thoroughly broadly treated work. This gives such contrast and relief between the near and distant figures, and the absence of the aid of colour makes the science of art all the more simply perceived. Most beautiful is the fresco representing the birth of St. John, though the lower part is quite lost. What consummate drapery arrangements! The nude figure *vue de dos* in the fresco of St. John baptising his disciples is a masterly bit of drawing. Though the paint has fallen off many parts of these frescoes, one can trace the drawing by the incision which was made on the wet plaster to mark all the outlines preparatory to beginning the painting."

These are but a few of my art student's impressions of this fondly-remembered Florentine epoch, which are recorded

My Studio. Florence 1869

The Vintage Florence

Pounding the Grapes

IN FLORENCE DURING MY STUDIES IN /69.

ROMAN IMPRESSIONS IN 1870.

THE LAST OF THE RIDERLESS HORSE-RACES, AND A WET TRUDGE
TO THE VATICAN COUNCIL.

at great length in the Diary for my own study. And now
away to Rome!

CHAPTER SIX

ROME

THAT was a memorable journey to Rome by Perugia. I
have travelled more than once by that line, and the
more direct one as well, since then, and I feel as though I
could never have enough of either, though to be on the
road again, as we now can be by motor, would be still
greater bliss. But the original journey took place so long ago
that it has positively an old-world glamour about it, and a
certain roughness in the flavour, so difficult to enjoy in
these times of Pulman cars and Palace Hotels, which make
all places taste so much alike. The old towns on the
foothills of the Apennines drew me to the left and the great
sunlit plains to the right of the carriage in an *embarras de
choix* as we sped along. Cortona, Arezzo, Castiglione—
Fiorentin—each little old city putting out its predecessor, as
it seemed to me, as more perfect in its picturesque effect
than the last one seen. It was the story of the Rhine castles
and villages over again. The Lake of Trasimene appeared on
our right towards sundown, a sheet of still water so tender
in its tints and so lonely; no town on its malaria-stricken
banks; a boat or two, water-fowl among the rushes and, as
we proceeded, the great, magnified globe of the sun sinking
behind the rim of the lake. We were going deep into the
Umbrian Hills, deep into old Italy; the deeper the better.
We neared Perugia, where we passed the night, before dark,
and saw the old brown city tinged faintly with the after-
glow, afar off on its hill. A massive castle stood there in
those days which I have not regretted since, as it symbol-
ised the old time of foreign tyranny. It is gone now, but how
mediæval it looked, frowning on the world that darkening
evening. Hills stood behind the city in deep blue masses

against a sky singularly red, where a great planet was shining. There was a Perugino picture come to life for us! Even
the little spindly trees tracing their slender branches on the
red sky were in the true naïf Perugino spirit! How pleased
we were! We rumbled in the four-horse station 'bus under
two echoing gateways piercing the massive outer and inner
city walls and along the silent streets, lit with rare oil
lamps. Not a gas jet, aha! But we were to feel still more
deeply mediæval, whether we liked it or not, for on reaching the Hotel de la Poste we found it was full, and had to
wander off to seek what hostel could take us in through
very dark, ancient streets. I will let the Diary speak:

"The *facchino* of the hotel conducted us to a place little
better than a *cabaret*, belonging, no doubt, to a chum. I
wouldn't have minded putting up there, but Mamma knew
better, and, rewarding the woman of the *cabaret* with two
francs, much against her protestations, we went off up the
steep street again and made for the 'Corona,' a shade better,
close to the market place. My bedroom was as though it had
once been a dungeon, so massive were the walls and deep
the vaulting of the low ceiling. We went to bed almost
immediately after our dinner, which was enlivened by the
conversation of men who were eating at a neighbouring
table, all, except a priest, with their hats on. One was very
loquacious, shouting politics. He held forth about 'Il
Mastai,' as he called His Holiness Pope Pius the Ninth, and
flourished renegade *Padre Giacinto* in the priest's face, the
courteous and laconic priest's eyebrows remaining at high-
water mark all the time. The shouter went on to say that
English was '*una lingua povera e meschina*' ('Poor and
mean'!)"

The next morning before leaving we saw all that time
allowed us of Perugia, the bronze statue of Pope Julius III
impressing me deeply. Indeed, there is no statue more eloquent than this one. Alas! the Italians have removed it
from its right place, and when I revisited the city in 1900 I
found the tram terminus in place of the Pope.

"*October 27th.*—After the morning's doings in sunshine the day became sad, and from Foligno, where we had a long wait, the story is but of rain and dusk and night. We became more and more apathetic and bored, though we were roused up at the frontier station, where I saw the Papal *gendarmes* and gave the alarm. Mamma went on her knees in the carriage and cried, '*Viva Il Papa Rè!*' We all joined in, drinking his health in some very flat 'red *grignolino*' we had with us. I became more and more excited as we neared the centre of the earth, the capital of Christendom, the highest city in the world. In the rainy darkness we ran into the Roman station, which might have been that of Brighton for aught we could see. I strained my eyes right and left for Papal uniforms, and was rewarded by Zouaves and others, and lots of French (of the Legion) into the bargain.

Then a long wait, in the 'bus of the Anglo-American Hotel, for our luggage; and at last we rattled over the pavement, which, with its cobble stones, was a great contrast to the large flat flags of Florence, along very dark and gloomy streets. An apartment all crimson damask was ready prepared for us, which looked cheery and revived us.

"*October 28th, 56, Via del Babuino.*—The day began rather dismally—looking for apartments in the rain! The coming of the Œcumenical Council has greatly inflated the prices; Rome is crammed. At last we took this attractive one for six months, '*esposto a mezzogiorno.*' Facing due south, fortunately.

"The sun came out then, and all things were bright and joyous as we rattled off in a little victoria to feast our eyes (we two for the first time) on St. Peter's. Papa, knowing Rome already, knew what to do and how best to give us our first impressions. An epoch in my life, never to be forgotten, a moment in my existence too solemn and beyond my power of writing to allow of my describing it! I have seen St. Peter's. No, indeed, no descriptions have ever given me an adequate idea of what I have just seen. The sensation of seeing the real thing one has gazed at in pictures and photographs with longing is one of peculiar delight.

"To find myself really on the Ponte Sant' Angelo! No
dream this. There is the huge castle and the angel with outstretched wings, and there is St. Peter's in very truth. The
sight of it made the tears rise and my throat tighten, so
greatly was I overcome by that soul-moving sight. The
dome is perfect; the whole, with its great piazza and colon-
nade, is perfect; I am utterly overpowered and, as to writing,
it is too inadequate, and I do so merely because I must do
my duty by this journal.

"What a state I was in, though exteriorly so quiet. And
all around us other beauties—the yellow Tiber, the old
houses, the great fortress-tomb—oh, Mimi, the artist, is not
all the enthusiasm in you at full power? We got out of the
carriage at the bottom of the piazza and walked up to the
basilica on foot. The two familiar fountains—so familiar,
yet seen for the first time in reality—were sending up their
spray in such magnificent abundance, which the wind took
and sent in cascade-like forms far out over the reflecting
pavement. The interior of St. Peter's, which impresses different people in such various ways, was a radiant revelation
to me. We had but a preliminary taste to-day. We drove
thence to the Piazza del Popolo, and then had an entrancing walk on Monte Pincio. We came down by the French
Academy, with its row of clipped ilexes, under which you
see one of the most exquisite views of silvery Rome, St.
Peter's in the middle. We dipped down by the steps of the
Trinità, where the models congregate, flecking the wide
grey steps with all the colours of the rainbow.

"*October 29th.*—Papa would not let us linger in the
Colosseum too long, for to-day he wanted us to have only a
general idea of things. Those bits of distance seen through
triumphal arches, between old pillars, through gaps in
ancient walls, how they please! As we were climbing the
Palatine hill a Black Franciscan came up to us for alms, and
in return offered us his snuff-box, out of which Alice and I
took a pinch, and we went sneezing over the ruins. On to

the Capitol, and down thence homeward through streets
full of priests, monks and soldiers. All the afternoon given
to being tossed about, with poor Papa, by the Dogana from
the railway station to the custom-house in the Baths of
Diocletian, and from there to the artist commissioned by
the Government to examine incoming works of art. They
would not let me have my box of studies, calling them
'modern pictures' on which we must pay duty."

Rome under the Temporal Power was so unlike Rome,
capital of Italy, as we see it to-day, that I think it just as well
to draw largely from the Diary, which is crammed with
descriptions of men and things belonging to the old order
which can never be seen again. I love to recall it all. We
were in Rome just in time. We left it in May and the Italians entered it in September. Though I was not a Catholic
then, and found delight in Rome almost entirely as an
artist, the power and vitality of the Church could not but
impress me there.

"*October 30th.*—This has been one of the most perfectly
enjoyable days of my life. Papa and I drove to the Vatican
through that bright light air which gives one such energy.
The Vatican! What a place wherein to revel. We climbed
one of the mighty staircases guarded by the interesting
Papal Guards, halberd on shoulder, until we got to the top
loggia and went into the picture gallery, I to enchant my
eyes with the grandest pictures that men have conceived.
But I will not touch on them till I go there to study. And so
on from one glory to another. We turned into St. Peter's
and there strolled a long time. Before we went in, and as we
were standing at the bottom of the Scala Regia enjoying
the clearness of the sunshine on the city, we saw the *gendarmes*, the Zouaves and others standing at attention, and,
looking back, we saw the red, black, and yellow Swiss running with operatic effect to seize their halberds, and
Cardinal Antonelli came down to get into his carriage,
almost stumbling over me, who didn't know he was so near.
Before he got into his great old-fashioned coach, harnessed

to those heavy black horses with the trailing scarlet traces, a picturesque incident occurred. A girl-faced young priest tremulously accosted the Cardinal, hat in hand, no doubt begging some favour of the great man. The Cardinal spoke a little time to him with grand kindness, and then the priest fell on one knee, kissed the Cardinal's ring, and got up blushing pink all over his beautiful young face, and passed on, gracefully and modestly, as he had done the rest. Then off rattled the carriage, the Zouaves presented arms, salutes were made, hats lifted, and Antonelli was gone.

"In St. Peter's were crowds of priests in different colours, forming masses of black, purple, and scarlet of great beauty. Two Oriental bishops were making the round, one, a Dominican, having with him a sort of Malay for a chaplain in turban and robe. Two others had Chinamen with pigtails in attendance, these two emaciated prelates bearing signs of recent torture endured in China, living martyrs out of Florentine frescoes. Yonder comes a bearded Oriental with mild, beautiful face, and following him a scarlet-clad German with yellow hair, projecting ears, coarse mouth, and spectacles over his little eyes; and then a sharp-visaged Jesuit, or a spiritual, wan Franciscan and a burly Roman secular. No end of types. One very young Italian monk had the face of a saint, all ready made for a fresco. I looked at him in unspeakable admiration as he stood looking up at some inscription, probably translating it in his own mind. On our way home, to crown all, we met the Pope. His outrider in cocked hat and feathers came clattering along the narrow street in advance, then a red-and-gold coach, black prancing horses—all shadowy to me, as I was intent only on catching a view of the Holy Father. We got out of the carriage, as in duty bound, and bent the knee like the rest as he passed by. I saw his profile well, with that well-known smile on his kind face. As we looked after the carriages and horsemen the effect was touching of the people kneeling in masses along the way. The sight of Italian men kneeling is novel to me in the extreme.

"*October 31st.*—I went first, with Mamma and Alice, to St. Peter's, where I studied types, attitudes and costumes. The sight of a Zouave officer kneeling, booted and spurred, his sword by his side, and his face shaded with his hand, is indeed striking, and one knows all those have enrolled themselves for a sacred cause they have at heart—higher even than for love of any particular country. The difference of types among these Zouaves is most interesting. The Belgian and Dutch decidedly predominate. Papa and I went thence for a fascinating stroll of many hours, finding it hard to turn back. We went up to Sant' Onofrio and then round by the great Farnese Palace. The view from Sant' Onofrio over Rome is—well, my language is utterly annihilated here. How invigorated I felt, and not a bit tired."

I have never been able to call up enthusiasm over the Pantheon, low-lying, black and pagan in every line. Why does Byron lash himself into calling it "Pride of Rome"? For the same reason, I suppose, that he laments and sighs over the disappearance of Dodona's "aged grove and oracle divine." As if any one cares! The view of Rome from Monte Mario, being *the* view, should have a place here as we saw it one of those richly-coloured days.

"*November 3rd.*—My birthday, marked by the customary birthday expedition, this time to Monte Mario. Nothing could be more splendid than looked the Capital of the World as it lay below us when we reached the top of that commanding height. The Campagna lay beyond it, ending in that direction with the Sabine and Alban Mountains, the furthest all white with snow. Buildings, cypresses, pines, formed foreground groups to the silver city as they only can do to such perfection in these parts. In another direction we could see the Campagna with its straight horizon like a calm rosy-brown sea meeting the limpid sky. We drove a long way on the high road across the Campagna Florence-wards. No high walls as in the Florentine drives were here to shut out the views, which unfolded themselves on all sides as we trotted on. We got out of the carriage on the

Campagna and strolled about on the brown grass, enjoying the sweet free breeze and the great sweep of country stretching away to the luminous horizon towards the sun, and to the lilac mountains in the other direction. These mountains became tender pink as we went Romewards, and when the city again appeared it was in a richly-coloured light, the Campagna beyond in warm shadow from large chocolate-coloured clouds which were rising heaped up into the sky. A superb effect."

Here follow many days chiefly given up to studio hunting and "property" seeking for my work, soon to be set up. Models there were in plenty, of course, as Rome was then still the artists' headquarters. How things have changed!

I began with a *ciociara* spinning with a distaff in the well-known and very much used-up costume, just for practice, and another peasant girl. Then I painted, at my dear mother's earnest desire, 'The Magnificat'—Mary's visit to Elizabeth—and on off days my father and I "did" all the pictures contained in various palaces, the Vatican, and the Villa Borghese, filling pages and pages of notes in the old Diary. I felt the value of every day in Rome. Many people might think I ought not to have worked so much in a studio, but I think I divided the time well. I felt I must keep my hand in, and practice with the brush, though how often I was tempted to join the others on some fascinating ramble may be imagined. Soon, however, the rains of a Roman December set in, and Rome became very wet indeed. Our father read us Roman history every evening when there were no visitors. We had a good many, our mother and her music and brightness soon attracting all that was nice in the English and American colonies. Dear old Mr. Severn, he in whose arms Keats died, often took tea with us (we kept our way of having dinner early and tea in the evening), and there was an antiquarian who took interest in nothing whatever except the old Roman walls, and he used to come and hold forth about the "Agger of Servius Tullius" till my head went round. He kept his own on, it

seemed to me, by pressing his hand on the bald top of it as
he explained to us about that bit of "agger" which he had
discovered, and the herring-bone brick of which it was
built. Often as I have revisited Rome, I cannot become
enthusiastic over the discovery of some old Roman sewer,
or bit of hot-water pipe, or horrible stone basin with a hole
in the bottom for draining off the blood of sacrificial oxen. I
always long to get back into the sunshine and fresh air from
the mouldy depths of Pagan Rome when I get caught in a
party to whom the antiquarian enthusiasts like to hold
forth below the surface of the earth. Alice listens, deferential and controlled, while I fidget, supporting myself on my
umbrella, with such a face! Here is a little bit of Papal
Rome impossible to-day:

"*November 29th.*—In the course of our long ramble after
my work Papa and I, in the soft evening, came upon a scene
which I shall not forget, made by a young priest preaching
to a little crowd in the street before the side door of Santa
Maria Sopra Minerva, a Rembrandtesque effect being produced by the two lamps held by a priest at either side of the
platform on which the preacher stood. One of these held
the large crucifix to which the preacher turned at times,
with gestures of rapture such as only an Italian could use in
so natural a way. To see him, lighted from below, in his
black habit and hear his impassioned voice! All the men
were bareheaded, and such as passed by took their hats off.
Penetrating as the priest's voice was, it was now and then
quite drowned by the street noises, especially the rattling of
wheels on the rough stones."

The days that follow are filled with my work on *The Visi-
tation*, with few intervals of sight-seeing. Then comes the
great ecclesiastical event to be marked in history, which
brought all the world to Rome.

"*Opening of the Œcumenical Council, December 8th.*—A
memorable day, this! We got up by candle-light, as at a
quarter past seven we were to drive to St. Peter's. The dreary raining dawn was announced, just as it broke, by the

heavy cannon of Castel Sant' Angelo, the flash of which
was reflected in the blue-grey sky long before the sound
reached us, and the cannon on the Aventine echoed those
of the Castel. How dreary it felt, yet how imposing for any
one who has got into the right feeling about this solemn
event. On our way we overtook scores of priests on foot,
trying to walk clear of the puddles in those thin, buckled
shoes of theirs. It must have been trying for the old ones.
There were bishops amongst them, too poor to afford a cab.
We have seen them day after day thus going to the Vatican
meetings. One great blessing the rain brought: it kept hundreds of people from coming to the church, and thus saved
many crushings to death, for it is terrible to contemplate,
seeing what a crowd there actually was, what it might have
been had the building been crammed. Entrance and egress
were both at one end of the church. That thought must
console me for the terrible toning down and darkening of
what, otherwise, would have been a great pageant. So many
thousands of wet feet brought something like a lake half
way up the floor; so slippery was it that, had the crowd
swayed in a panic, it wouldn't have been very nice.

"Papa and I insinuated ourselves into the hedge of people
kept back by Zouaves and Palatine Guards, as we came
opposite the statue of St. Peter, and I eventually got fixed
three rows back from the soldiers, and was lucky to get in so
far. I was jammed between a monk and a short youth of the
'horsey' kind. The atmosphere in that warm, wet crowd was
trying. I could see into the Council Hall opposite.

"The passage kept clear for the great procession was very
wide. On the other side I could see rows of English and
American girls and elderly females in the best places, as
usual, right to the front, as bold as brass, and didn't they eye
the bishops over through their *pince-nez!* We must have
been waiting two hours before the procession entered the
church. I ought to have mentioned that the sacred dark
bronze statue of St. Peter was robed in gorgeous golden
vestments with a splendid triple crown on its head, making

it look like a black Pope, and very life-like from where I saw it. It seemed very strange.

"At last there was a buzz as people perceived the slowly-moving *silhouette* of the procession as it passed along in a far-off gallery, veiled from us by pink curtains against the light and very high up, over the entrance. We could see the prelates had all vested by the outlines of the mitres and the high-shouldered look of the figures in stiff copes. As the procession entered the church the 'Veni Creator' swelled up majestically and floated through the immense space. The effect of the procession to me was *nil;* all I could do was to catch a glimpse of each bishop as he passed between the bobbing heads of the men in front of me. All the European and United States Bishops were in white and silver, but now and then there passed Oriental Patriarchs in rich vestments, their picturesque dark faces (two were quite brown) telling so strikingly amongst the pale or rosy Europeans. Each had his solemn secretary, with imperturbable Eastern face, bearing his jewelled crown, something in shape like the dome of a mosque. One Oriental wore a jewel on his dusky forehead, another a black cowl over his head, shading his keen, dark face, the coarse cowl contrasting in a startling way with the delicate splendour of the gold and pink and amber vestments worn over the rough monk's habit. Still, all this could not be imposing to me, having to squint and crane as I did, seldom being able to see with both eyes at once. I could at intervals see the silvery prelates, most of them with snowy heads, and the dark Easterns mount into their seats in the Council Chamber, our Archbishop Manning amongst them. I had a quite good glimpse of Cardinal Bonaparte, very like the great Napoleon. Of the Pope I saw nothing. He was closely surrounded, as he walked past, by the high-helmeted Noble Guard, and, of course, at that supreme moment every one in front of me strove to get a better sight of him. Then Papa and I gladly struggled our way out of the great crowd and went to seek Mamma, who, very wisely, had not attempted to get a place, but was meekly sitting on the steps of a confessional in a quiet chapel. Mamma then went home, and we went into the crowd again to try and see the Council from a point opposite. We saw it pretty well, the two white banks of mitred bishops on each side and, far back, the little red Pope in the middle. Mass was being sung, all Gregorian, but it was faintly heard from our great distance.

"No council business was being done to-day; it was only the Mass to open the meeting. The crowd was most interesting. Surely every nation was represented in it. An officer of the 42nd Highlanders had an excellent effect. What shall I do in London, with its dead level of monotony? Oh! dear, oh! dear. I was quite loth to go home. And so the council is opened. God speed!"

The Ghetto was in existence in those days, so I have even experienced the sight of *that*. Very horrible, packed with "red-haired, blear-eyed creatures, with loose lips and long, baggy noses." Thus I describe them in this warren, during our drive one day. What a "*sventramento*" that must have been when the Italians cleared away and cleaned up all that congested horror. Wide, wind-swept spaces and a shining, though hideous, syngagoue met my astonished gaze when next I went there and couldn't find the Ghetto.

At the end of the year La Signorina Elizabetta Thompson had to apply to his Eminenza Riverendissima Cardinal Berardi, Minister of Public Works, to announce her intention of sending the *Magnificat* to the Pope's international exhibition. At that picture I worked hard, my mother being my model for Our Lady, and an old *ciociara* from the Trinità steps for St. Elizabeth. How it rained that December! But we had radiant sunshine in between the days when the streets were all running with red-brown rivulets, through which the horses splashed as if fording a stream.

January 25th, 1870.—I finished my *Magnificat* to-day. Yet ought I to say I ceased to paint at it, for 'finish' suggests something far beyond what this picture is. Well, I shall enjoy being on the loose now. To stroll about Rome after having passed through a picture is perfect enjoyment. I should feel very uncomfortable at the present time if I had, up till now, done nothing but lionise. I have no hope of my picture being accepted now, but still it is pleasant to think that I have worked hard.

February 3rd.—I took my picture to the Calcografia place, as warned to do. There, in dusty horror, it awaits the selecting committee's review, which takes place to-morrow. Mamma and I held it manfully in the little open carriage to keep it from tumbling out, our arms stretched to their utmost. Lots of men were shuffling about in that dusty place with pictures of all sizes. But, oh! what a scene of horror was that collection of daubs. Oh! mercy on us.

"*February 5th.*—My *Magnificat* is accepted. First, off goes Mamma with Celestina to the Calcografia to learn the fate of the picture, and bring it back triumphant, she and the maid holding it steady in the little open carriage. Soon after, off we go to the Palazzo Poli to see nice Mr. Severn, who says he is so proud of me, and will do all he can to help me in art matters, to see whether he could make the exhibition people hang my picture well, as we were told the artists had to see to that themselves if they wanted it well done. I, for my part, would leave it to them and rather shirk a place on the line, for my picture is depressingly unsatisfactory to me, but Mamma, for whom I have painted it, loves it, and wants it well placed 'so that the Pope may see it'! From thence off we go to the abode of the Minister of Commerce, Cardinal B., for my pass. We were there told, to our dismay, that we could not take the picture ourselves to the exhibition, as it was held in the cloisters of Sta. Maria degli Angeli, and no permission had yet been given to admit women before the opening. But I knew that between Papa and Mr. Severn the picture would be seen to inside the cloistered walls. After lunch, off goes Papa with my pass, we following in the little open carriage as before, holding the old picture before us with straining arms and knitted brows, very much jolted and bumped. We are stopped at the cloisters, and told to drive out again, and there we pull up, our faces turned in the opposite direction. The hood of the carriage suddenly collapses, and we are revealed, unable to let go the picture, with the soldiers collected about the place grinning. Papa arrives, and he and two *facchini* come to the rescue, and then disappear with the picture amongst the forbidden regions enclosed in the gloomy ruins of Diocletian's Baths. Papa, on returning home, told me how charmed old Severn, who was there, was with the picture, and even Podesti, the judge, after some criticisms, and in no way ready to give it a good place, said to Severn he had expected the signorina's picture to be rubbish (*porcheria*). I suppose because it was a woman's work. He retracted, and said he would like to see me.

"*February 14th.*—I began another picture to-day, after all my resolutions to the contrary, the subject, two Roman shepherds playing at 'Morra,' sitting on a fallen pilar, a third *contadino*, in a cloak, looking on. I posed my first model, putting a light background to him, the effect being capital, he coming rich and dusky against it. He soon understood I wanted energy thrown into the action. I shall delight in this subject, because the hands figure so conspicuously in the game.

"*February 15th.*—I went up alone to the Trinità to choose the other young man for my *Morra*, and, after a little inspection of the group of lolling Romagnoli, gave the apple to one with a finely-cut profile and black hair, the other models, male and female, clustering round to hear, and many bystanders and the Zouave sentry, hard by, looking on."

On one evening in this eventful Roman period I had the opportunity of seeing the famous race of the riderless horses (the *barberi*), which closed the Carnival doings. The impression remains with me quite vividly to this day. The colour, the movement; the fast-deepening twilight; the historic associations of that vast Piazza del Popolo, where I see the great obelisk retaining, on its upper part, the last flush from the west; the impetuous waters of the fountains at its base in cool shadow; St. Peter's dome away to the left—this is the setting. Then I hear the clatter of the dragoon's horses as the detachment forms up for clearing the course. The stands, at the foot of the obelisk, are full, some of the crowd in carnival costume and with masks. A sharp word of command rings out in the chilly air. Away go the dragoons, down the narrow Corso and back, at full gallop, splitting the surging crowd with theatrical effect. The line is clear. Now comes the moment of expectancy! At that unique starting post, the obelisk upon which Moses in Egypt may have looked as upon an interesting monument of antiquity in pre-Exodus days, there appear eleven highly-nervous barbs, tricked out with plumes and painted with white spots and stripes. The convicts who lead them in (each man, one may say, carrying his life in his hand) are trying, with iron grip, to keep their horses quiet, for the spiked balls and other irritants are now unfastened and dangling loose from the horses' backs. But one terrified beast comes on "kicking against the pricks" already. The whole pack become wild. The more they plunge, the more the balls bang and prick. One furious creature, wrenching itself free, whirls round in the wrong direction. But there is no time to lose; the restraining rope must be cut. A gun booms; there is a shout and clapping of hands. Ten of the horses, with heads down, get off in a bunch, shooting straight as arrows for the Corso; the eleventh slips on the cobbles, rolls over and, recovering itself, tears after its pals, straining every nerve. I hear a voice shout "*E capace di vincere!*" ("He is fit to win!") and in an instant the lot are engulfed in that dark, narrow street, the squibs on their backs going off like pistol shots, and the crackling bits of metallic tinsel, getting detached, fly back in a shower of light. The sparks from the iron heels splash out in red fire through the dusk. The course is just one mile—the whole length of the straight street. At the winning post a great sheet is stretched across the way, through which some of the horses burst, to be captured some days

afterwards while roaming about the open spaces of the
Campagna. It is the dense crowd, forming two walls along
the course, that forces the horses to keep the centre. This
was the last of the *barberi*. They were more frightened than
hurt, yet I am not sorry that these races have been abolished.

Here follow records of expeditions in weather of spring
freshness—to catacombs, along the Via Appia, to the wild
Campagna, and all the delights of that Roman time when
the lark inspires the poet. I got on well with my *Morra* picture, which wasn't bad, and which has a niche in my art
career, because it turned out to be the first picture I sold,
which joyful event happened in London.

"*March 25th.*—A brilliant day, full of colour. This is a
great feast, the Annunciation, and I gave up work to see
the Pope come in grand procession to the Church of the
Minerva with his Cross Bearer on a white mule, and all the
cardinals, bishops, ambassadors and officials in carriages of
antique magnificence, a spectacle of great pomp, and
nowhere else to be seen. We did it in this wise. At nine we
drove to the Minerva, the sun very brilliant and the air very
cold, and soon posted ourselves on the steps of the church
in the midst of a tight crowd, I quite helpless in a knot of
French soldiers of the Legion, who chaffed each other good-
humouredly over my head. The piazza, in the midst of
which rises the funny little obelisk on the elephant's back,
swarmed with people, black being quite the exception in
that motley crowd. Zouaves and the Legion formed a square
to keep the piazza open, and dragoons pranced officiously
about, as is their wont. Every balcony was thronged with
gay ladies and full-dressed officers (some most gallant and
smart Austrians were at a window near us), and crimson
cloth and brocade flapped from every window, here in powerful sunshine, there in effective shadow. Some dark,
Florentine-coloured houses opposite, mostly in shade, as
they were between us and the sun, had a strong effect
against the bright sky, their crimson cloths and gaily dressed

ladies relieving their dark masses, and their beautiful roofs and chimneys making a lovely sky line.

"Presently the gilt and painted coaches of the cardinals began to arrive, huge, high-swung vehicles drawn by very fat black horses dressed out with gold and crimson trappings, but the servants and coachmen, in spite of their extra full get-up, having that inimitable shabby-genteel appearance which belongs exclusively to them. The Prior of the Dominicans, to which order this church belongs, stood outside the archway through which the Pope and all went into the church after alighting from their coaches. He was there to welcome them, and, oh! the number of bows he must have made, and his mouth must have ached again with all those wide smiles. Near him also stood the Noble Guards and all the general officers, plastered over with orders; and all these, too, saluted and salaamed as each ecclesiastical bigwig grandly and courteously swept by under the archway, glowing in his scarlet and shining in his purple. The carriages pulled up at the spot of all others best suited to us. Everything was filled with light, the cardinals glowing like rubies inside their coaches, even their faces all aglow with the red reflections thrown up from their ardent robes. But there presently came a sight which I could hardly stand; it was eloquent of the olden time and filled the mind with a strange feeling of awe and solemnity, as though long ages had rolled back and by a miracle the dead time had been revived and shown to us for a brief and precious moment. On a sleek white mule came a prelate, all in pure lilac, his grey head bare to the sunshine and carrying in his right hand the gold and jewelled Cross. The trappings of the mule were black and gold, a large black, square cloth thrown over its back in the mediæval fashion. The Cross, which was large and must have weighed considerably, was very conspicuous. The beauty of the colour of mule and rider, the black and gold housings of that white beast, the lilac of the rider's robes, and the tender glory of the embossed Cross—how these things enchant me! An attendant took the Cross as the priest dismounted. Then a flourish of modern Zouave bugles and a sharp roll of the drum intruded the forgotten present day on our notice, and soon on came the gallant *gendarmerie* and dragoons, and then the coach of His Holiness, seeming to bubble over with molten gold in the sunshine. Its six black horses ambled fatly along, all but the wheelers trailing their long, red traces almost on the ground, as seems to be the ecclesiastical fashion in harness (only the wheelers really pull), and guided by bedizened postillions in wigs decidedly like those worn by English Q.C.'s. Flowers were showered down on this coach from the windows, and much cheering rang in the fresh, clear air. I see now in my mind's eye the outthrust chins and long, bare necks of a clump of enthusiastic Zouaves shouting with all their hearts under the Pope's carriage windows in divers tongues. But the English 'Long live the Pope King,' though given with a will, did not travel as far as the open '*Viva il Papa Rè*, or '*Vive le Pape Roi.*' I put in my British 'Hurrah!' as did Papa, splendidly, just as three old and very fat cardinals had painfully got down from His Holiness's high coach and he himself had begun to emerge. We could see him quite well in the coach, because the sides were more glass than gilding, and very assiduously did the kind-looking old man bless the people right and left as he drove up. He had on his head, not the skull cap I have hitherto seen him in, which allows his silver locks to be seen, but the old-lady-like headgear so familiar to me from pictures, notably several portraits of Leo X. at Florence, which covers the ears and is bound with ermine. It makes the lower part of the face look very large, and is not becoming. After getting down he stood a long time receiving homage from many grandees, and smiled and beamed with kindness on everybody. Then we all bundled into the church, but as every one there was standing on, instead of sitting on, the chairs, we could see nothing of the ceremonies. We struggled out, after listening a little to the singing, and Papa and I strolled delightedly to St. Peter's, on whose great piazza we awaited the return of the procession. It was very beautiful, winding along towards us, with my white mule and all, over that vast space."

Remember, Reader, that these things can never more be seen, and that is why I give these extracts in *extenso*. Merely as history they are precious. How we would like to have some word pictures of Rome in the seventeenth, sixteenth and fifteenth centuries, but we don't get them. The chronicles tell us of magnificence, numbers, illustrious people, dress, and so forth; but, somehow, we would like something more intimate and descriptive of local colour—effects of weather, etc.—to help us to realise life as it was in the olden time. I think in this age of ugliness we prize the picturesque and the artistic all the more for their rarer charm.

"After *Morra* I did a life-size oil study of the head of the celebrated model, Francesco, which was a great advance in freedom of brush work. But the walks were not abandoned, and many a delightful round we made with our father, who was very happy in Rome. The Colosseum was rich in flowers and trees, which clothed with colour its hideous stages of seats. The same abundant foliage beautified the brickwork of Caracalla's Baths, but those beautiful veils were, unfortunately, slowly helping further to demolish the ruins, and had to be all cleared away later on. I have several times managed to wander over those eerie ruins in later years by full moon, but I have never again enjoyed the awe-inspiring sensation produced by the first visit, when those trees waved and sighed, and the owls hooted, as in Byron's time. And then the loneliness of the Colosseum was more impressive, and helped one to detach oneself in thought from the present day more easily. Now the town is creeping out that way.

"*April 3rd.*—Our goal was Santa Croce to-day, beyond the Lateran, for there the Pope was to come to bless the 'Agnus Dei.' This ceremony takes place only once in seven years. Everything was *en petite tenue*, the quietest carriages, the seediest servants, but oh! how glorious it all was in that fervent sunlight. We stood outside the church, I greatly enjoying the amusing crowd, full of such varied types. The effect of the Pope's two carriages and the horsemen coming trotting along the straight, long road from St. John's to this church, the luminous dust rising in clouds in the wind, was very pretty. The shouting and cheering and waving of handkerchiefs were quite frantic, more hearty even than at the Minerva. People seemed to feel more easy and jolly here, with no grandeur to awe them. His Holiness looked much more spry than when I last saw him. We lost poor little Mamma and, in despair, returned without her, and she didn't turn up till 7 o'clock!"

The Roman Diary of 1870 must end with the last Easter Benediction given under the temporal power, *Urbi et Orbi*.

"*Easter Sunday, April 17th.*—What a day, brimming over with rich eye-feasts, with pomp and splendour! What can the eye see nowadays to come anywhere near what I saw today, except on this anniversary here in unique Rome? Of course, all the world knows that the splendour of this great ceremony outshines that of any other here or in the whole world. Mamma and I reserved ourselves for the benediction alone, so did not start for St. Peter's till ten o'clock, and got there long before the troops. On getting out of the carriage we strolled leisurely to the steps leading up to the church, where we took up our stand, enjoying the delicious sunshine and fresh, clear air, and also the interesting people that were gradually filling the piazza, amongst whom were pilgrims with long staves, many being Neapolitans, the women in new costumes of the brightest dyes and with snowy *tovaglie* artistically folded. Some of these women carried the family luggage on their heads, this luggage being great bundles wrapped in rugs of red, black and yellow stripes, some with the big coloured umbrella passed through and cleverly balanced. All these people had trudged on foot all the way. Their shoes hung at their waists, and also their water flasks. As the troops came pouring in we were requested by the sappers to range ourselves and not to encroach beyond the bottom step. Here was a position to see from! We watched the different corps forming to the stirring bugle and trumpet sounds, the officers mounting their horses, all splendid in velvet housings, the officers in the fullest of full dress. There was no pushing in the crowd, and we were as comfortable as possible. But there was a scene to our left, up on the terrace that runs along the upper part of the piazza and is part of the Vatican, which was worth to me all the rest; it was, pictorially, the most beautiful sight of all. Along this terrace, the balustrade of which was hung with mellow old faded tapestry, and bears those dark-toned, effective statues standing out so well against the blue sky, were collected in a long line, I should say, nearly all the bishops who are gathered here in Rome for the Council, in their white and silver vestments, and wearing their snowy mitres, a few dark-dressed ladies in veils and an officer in bright colour here and there supporting most artistically those long masses of white. Above the heads of this assembly stretched the long white awning, through which the strong sun sent a glowing shade, and above that the clear sky, with the Papal white and yellow flags and standards in great quantities fluttering in the breeze! My delighted eyes kept wandering up to that terrace away from the coarser military picturesqueness in front. Up there was a real bit of the olden time. There was a feeling as of lilies about those white-robed pontiffs. At last a sign from a little balcony high up on the façade was given, and all the troops sprang to attention, and then the gentle-faced old Pope glided into view there, borne on his chair and wearing the triple crown. Clang go the rifles and sabres in a general salute, and a few '*evvivas*' burst from the crowd, which are immediately suppressed by a general 'sh-sh-sh,' and amidst a most imposing silence, the silence of a great multitude, the Pope begins to read from a crimson book held before him with the voice of a strong young man. Curiously enough, in this stillness all the horses began to neigh, but their voices could not drown the single one of

Pio Nono. After the reading the Pope rose, and down went, on their knees, the mass of people and soldiers, 'like one man,' and the old Pope pressed his hands together a moment and then flung open his arms upwards with an action full of electrifying fervour as he pronounced the grand words of the blessing which rang out, it seemed, to the ends of the Earth.

"In the evening we saw the famous illumination of the dome of St. Peter's from the Pincian. The wind rather spoiled the first or silver one, but the next, the golden, was a grand sight, beginning with the cross at the top and running down in streams over the dome. As I looked, I heard a funny bit of Latin from an English tourist, who asked a priest '*Quis est illuminatio, olio o gas?*' '*Olio, olio,*' answered the priest good-naturedly."

And so our Papal Rome on May 2nd, 1870, retreated into my very appreciative memory, and we returned for a few days to Florence, and thence to Padua and Venice and Verona on our way to England through the Tyrol and Bavaria. What a downward slope in art it is from Italy into Germany! We girls felt a great irritation at the change, and were too recalcitrant to attend to the German sights properly.

But I filled the Diary with very searching notes of the wonderful things I saw in Venice, thanks to Veronese, Titian, Tintoretto, Palma Vecchio and others, who filled me with all that an artist can desire in the way of colour. I was anxious to improve my weak point, and here was a lesson!

It is curious, however, to watch through the succeeding years how I was gradually inducted by circumstances into that line of painting which is so far removed from what inspired me just then. It was the Franco-German War and a return to the Isle of Wight that sent me back on the military road with ever diminishing digressions. Well, perhaps my father's fear, which I have already mentioned in my early 'teens, that I was joining in a "tremendous ruck" in taking the field would have been justified had I not taken up a line of painting almost non-exploited by English artists. The statement of a French art critic when writing of one of my war pictures, "*L'Angleterre n'a guère qu'un peintre militaire, c'est une femme,*" shows the position. I wish I could have another life here below to share the joys of those who paint what I studied in Italy, if only for the love of such work, though I am very certain I should be quite indistinguishable in *that* "ruck."

CHAPTER SEVEN

WAR. BATTLE PAINTINGS

PADUA I greatly enjoyed—its academic quiet, its Shakespearean atmosphere; and still more did Shakespearean Verona enchant me. I had a good study of the modern French school at the Paris Salon, and on getting back to London rejoined the South Kensington schools till the end of the summer session. Then a studio and practice from the living model. In July we were all absorbed in the great Franco-German War, declared in the middle of that month. It seems so absurd to us to-day that we should have been pro-German in England. This little entry in the Diary shows how Bismarck's dishonest manœuvres had hoodwinked the world. "France *will* fight, so Prussia *must*, and all for nothing but jealousy—a pretty spectacle!" We all believed it was France that was the guilty party. I call to mind how some one came running upstairs to find me and, subsiding on the top step with *The Times* in her hand, announced the surrender of MacMahon's army and the Emperor. I wrote "the Germans are pro-di-gious!" and I have lived to see them prostrate. Such is history.

I was asked, as the war developed, if I had been inspired by it, and this caused me to turn my attention pictorially that way. Once I began on that line I went at a gallop, in water-colour at first, and many a subject did I send to the "Dudley Gallery" and to Manchester, all the drawings selling quickly, but I never relaxed that serious practice in oil painting which was my solid foundation. I sent the poor *Magnificat* to the Royal Academy in the spring of 1871. It was rejected, and returned to me with a large hole in it.

That summer, which we spent at well-loved Henley-on-Thames, was marred by the awful doings of the Commune in Paris. *The Times* had a stereotyped heading for a long time: "The Destruction of Paris." What horrible suspense there was while we feared the destruction of the Louvre and Notre Dame. I see in the Diary: "*May 28th, 1871.*—Oh! that tomorrow's papers may bring a decided contradiction of the oft-repeated report that the great Louvre pictures are lost and that Notre Dame no longer stands intact. As yet all is confusion and dismay, and one clings, therefore, to the hope that little by little we may hear that some fragments, at least, may be spared to bereaved humanity and that all that beauty is not annihilated."

In August, 1871, we were off again. From London back to Ventnor! There I kept my hand in by painting in oils life-sized portraits of friends and relations and some Italian ecclesiastical subjects, such as young Franciscan monks, disciples of him who loved the birds, feeding their doves in a cloister; an old friar teaching schoolboys, *al fresco*, outside a church, as I had seen one doing in Rome. For this friar I commandeered our landlord as a model, for he had just the white beard and portly figure I required. Yet he was one of the most *furibond* dissenters I ever met—a Congregationalist—but very obliging. Also a candlelight effect in the Church of San Pietro in Vincoli, in Rome; a large altarpiece for our little Church of St. Wilfred, and so on, a mixture of the ecclesiastical and the military. The dances, theatricals, croquet parties, rides—all the old ways were linked up again at Ventnor, and I have a very bright memory of our second dwelling there and reunion with our old friends. In the spring of 1872 I sent one of the many Roman subjects I was painting to the Academy, a water-colour of a Papal Zouave saluting two bishops in a Roman street. It was rejected, but this time without a hole. This year was full of promise, and I very nearly reached the top of my long hill climb, for in it I began what proved to be my first Academy picture.

What proved of great importance to me, this year of 1872, was my introduction, if I may put it so, to the British Army! I then saw the British soldier as I never had the opportunity of seeing him before. My father took me to see something of the autumn manœuvres near Southampton. Subjects for water-colour drawings appeared in abundance to my delighted observation. One of the generals who was to be an umpire at these manœuvres, Sir F.C., had become greatly interested in me, as a mutual friend had described my battle scenes to him, and said he would speak about me to Sir Charles Staveley, one of the commanders in the impending "war," so that I might have facilities for seeing the interesting movements. He hoped that, if I saw the manœuvres, I would "give the British soldiers a turn," which I did with alacrity. I sent some of the sketches to Manchester and to my old friend the "Dudley." One of them, *Soldiers Watering Horses*, found a purchaser in a Mr. Galloway, of Manchester, who asked through an agent if I would paint him an oil picture. I said "Yes," and in time painted him *The Roll Call*. Meanwhile, in the spring of 1873, I sent my first really large war picture in oils to the Academy. It was accepted, but "skyed," well noticed in the Press and, to my great delight, sold. The subject was, of course, from the war which was still uppermost in our thoughts: a wounded French colonel (for whom my father sat), riding a spent horse, and a young subaltern of Cuirassiers, walking alongside (studied from a young Irish officer friend), "missing" after one of the French defeats, making their way over a forlorn landscape. The Cameron Highlanders were quartered at Parkhurst, near Ventnor, about this time, and I was able to make a good many sketches of these splendid troops, so essentially pictorial. I have ever since then liked to make Highlanders subjects for my brush.

In this same year of 1873 my sister and I, now both belonging to the old faith, whither our mother had preceded us, joined the first pilgrimage to leave the shores of England since the Reformation. I had arranged with the *Graphic* to make pen-and-ink sketches of the pilgrimage, which was arousing an extraordinary amount of public interest. Our goal was the primitive little town of Paray-le-Monial, deep in the heart of France, where Margaret Mary Alacoque received our Lord's message. I cannot convey to my readers who are not "of us" the fresh and exultant impressions we received on that visit. There was a mixture of religious and national patriotism in our minds which produced feelings of the purest happiness. The steamer that took us English pilgrims from Newhaven to Dieppe on September 2nd flew the standard of the Sacred Heart at the main and the Union Jack at the peak, seeming thus to symbolise the whole character of the enterprise. Those *Graphic* sketches proved a very great burden to me. Nowadays one of the pilgrims would have done all by "snapshots." I tried to sketch as I walked in the processions at Paray and to sing the hymn at the same time. There was hardly a moment's rest for us, except for a few intervals of sleep. The long ceremonies and prescribed devotions, the processions, the stirring hymns and the journey there and back, all crowded into a week from start to finish, called for all one's strength. But how joyfully given!

I can never forget the hearty, well-mannered welcome the French gave us, lay and clerical. The place itself was lovely and the weather kind. It is good to have had such an experience as this in our weary world. The Bishop of Salford, the future Cardinal Vaughan, led us, and our clergy mustered in great force. The dear French people never showed so well as during their welcome of us. It suited their courteous and hospitable natures. Most of our hosts were peasants and owners of little picturesque shops in this jewel of a little town. We two were billeted at a shoemaker's. The urbanity of the French clergy in receiving our own may be imagined. I love to think back on the truly beautiful sights and sounds of Paray, with the dominant note of the church bells vibrating over all. They gave us a graceful send-off, pleased to have the assurance of our approval of our reception. Many compliments on our *solide piété*, with regrets as to their own *"légèreté,"* and so forth. *"Vive l'Angleterre!"* *"Vive la France!"* *"Adieu!"*

CHAPTER EIGHT
"THE ROLL CALL"

I HAD quite a large number of commissions for military water-colours to get through on my return home, and an oil of French artillery on the march to paint, in my little glass studio under St. Boniface Down. But after my not inconsiderable success with *Missing* at the Academy, I became more and more convinced that a London studio *must* be my destiny for the coming winter. Of course, my father demurred. He couldn't bear to part with me. Still, it must be done, and to London I went, with his sad consent. I had long been turning *The Roll Call* in my mind. My father shook his head; the Crimea was "forgotten." My mother rather shivered at the idea of the snow. It was no use; they saw I was bent on that subject. My dear mother and our devoted family doctor in London (Dr. Pollard[5]), who would do anything in his power to help me, between them got me the studio, No. 76, Fulham Road, where I painted the picture which brought me such utterly unexpected celebrity.

Mr. Burchett, still headmaster at South Kensington, was delighted to see me with all the necessary facilities for carrying out my work, and he sent me the best models in London, nearly all ex-soldiers. One in particular, who had been in the Crimea, was invaluable. He stood for the sergeant who calls the roll. I engaged my models for five hours each day, but often asked them to give me an extra half-hour. Towards the end, as always happens, I had to put on pressure, and had them for six hours. My preliminary expeditions for the old uniforms of the Crimean epoch were directed by my kind Dr. Pollard, who rooted about Chelsea back streets to find what I required among the Jews. One, Mr. Abrahams, found me a good customer. I say in my Diary:

"Dr. Pollard and I had a delightful time at Mr. Abrahams' dingy little pawnshop in a hideous Chelsea slum, and, indeed, I enjoyed it *far* more than I should have enjoyed the same length of time at a West End milliner's. I got nearly all the old accoutrements I had so much longed for, and in the evening my Jew turned up at Dr. Pollard's after a long tramp in the city for more accoutrements, helmets, coatees, haversacks, etc., and I sallied forth with the 'Ole Clo!' in the rain to my boarding house under our mutual umbrella, and he under his great bag as well. We chatted about the trade 'chemin faisant.'"

I called Saturday, December 13th, 1873, a "red-letter day," for I then began my picture at the London studio. Having made a little water-colour sketch previously, very carefully, of every attitude to the figures, I had none of those alterations to make in the course of my work which waste so much time. Each figure was drawn in first without the great coat, my models posing in a tight "shell jacket," so as to get the figure well drawn first. How easily then could the thick, less shapely great coat be painted on the well-secured foundation. No matter how its heavy folds, the cross-belts, haversacks, water-bottles, and everything else broke the lines, they were there, safe and sound, underneath. An artist remarked, "What an absurdly easy picture!" Yes, no doubt it was, but it was all the more so owing to the care taken at the beginning. This may be useful to young painters, though, really, it seems to me just now that sound drawing is at a discount. It will come by its own again. Some people might say I was too anxious to be correct in minor military details, but I feared making the least mistake in these technical matters, and gave myself some unnecessary trouble. For instance, on one of my last days at the picture I became anxious as to the correct letters that should appear stamped on the Guards' haversacks. I sought professional advice. Dr. Pollard sent me the beery old Crimean pensioner who used to stand at the Museum gate wearing a gold-laced hat, to answer my urgent inquiry as to this matter. Up comes the puffing old gentleman, redolent of rum. I, full of expectation, ask him the question: "What should the letters be?" "B.O.!" he roars out—"Board of Ordnance!" Then, after a congested stare, he calls out, correcting himself, "W.D.—War Deportment!" "Oh!" I say, faintly, "War Department; thank you." Then he mixes up the two together and roars, "W.O.!" And that was all I got. He mopped his rubicund face and, to my relief, stumped away down my stairs. Another Crimean hero came to tell me whether I was right in having put a grenade on the pouches. "Well, miss, the natural *hinference* would be that it *was* a grenade, but it was something like my 'and." Desperation! I got the thing "like his hand" just in time to put it in before *The Roll Call* left—a brass badge lent me by the War Office—and obliterated the much more effective grenade.

On March 29th and 30th, 1874 came my first "Studio Sunday" and Monday, and on the Tuesday the poor old *Roll Call* was sent in. I watched the men take it down my narrow stairs and said "Au revoir," for I was disappointed with it, and apprehensive of its rejection and speedy return. So it always is with artists. We never feel we have fulfilled our hopes.

The two show days were very tiring. Somehow the studio, after church time on the Sunday, was crowded. Good Dr. Pollard hired a "Buttons" for me, to open the door, and busied himself with the people, and enjoyed it. So did I, though so tired. It was "the thing" in those days to make the round of the studios on the eve of "sending-in day."

Mr. Galloway's agent came, and, to my intense relief, told me the picture went far beyond his expectations. He had been nervous about it, as it was through him the owner had bought it, without ever seeing it. On receiving the agent's report, Mr. Galloway sent me a cheque at once—£126—being more than the hundred agreed to. The copyright was mine.

The days that followed felt quite strange. Not a dab with a brush, and my time my own. It was the end of Lent, and then Easter brought such church ceremonial as our poor little Ventnor St. Wilfrid's could not aspire to. A little more Diary:

"*Saturday, April 11th.*—A charming morning, for Dr. Pollard had a fine piece of news to tell me. First, Elmore, R.A., had burst out to him yesterday about my picture at the Academy, saying that all the Academicians are in quite a commotion about it, and Elmore wants to make my acquaintance very much. He told Dr. P. I might get £500 for *The Roll Call*! I little expected to have such early and gratifying news of the picture which I sent in with such forebodings. After Dr. P. had delivered this broadside of Elmore's compliments he brought the following battery of heavy guns to bear upon me which compelled me to sink into a chair. It is a note from Herbert, R.A., in answer to a few lines which kind Father Bagshawe had volunteered to write to him, as a friend, to ask him, as one of the Selecting Committee, just simply to let me know, as soon as convenient, whether my picture was accepted or rejected. The note is as follows:

'DEAR MISS THOMPSON,—I have just received a note from Father Bagshawe of the Oratory in which he wished me to address a few lines to you on the subject of your picture in the R.A. To tell the truth I desired to do so a day or two since but did not for two reasons: the first being that as a custom the doings of the R.A. are for a time kept secret; the second that I felt I was a stranger to you and you would hear what I wished to say from some friend—but Father Bagshawe's note, and the decision being over, I may tell you with what pleasure I greeted the picture and the painter of it when it came before us for judgment. It was simply this: I was so struck by the excellent work in it that I proposed we should lift our hats and give it and you, though, as I thought, unknown to me, a round of huzzahs, which was generally done. You now know my feeling with regard to your work, and may be sure that I shall do everything as one of the hangers that it shall be *perfectly seen* on our walls.

I am tired and hurried, and ask you to excuse this very hasty note, but *accept my hearty congratulations*, and

Believe me to be, dear Miss Thompson,
Most faithfully yours,

J.R. HERBERT.'

I trotted off at once to show Father Bagshawe the note, and then left for home with my brilliant news."

While at home at Ventnor I received from many sources most extraordinary rumours of the stir the picture was making in London amongst those who were behind the scenes. How it was "the talk of the clubs" and spoken of as the "coming picture of the year," "the hit of the season," and all that kind of thing. Friends wrote to me to give me this pleasant news from different quarters. Ventnor society rejoiced most kindly. I went to London to what I call in the Diary "the scene of my possible triumphs," having taken rooms at a boarding house. I had better let the Diary speak:

"'*Varnishing Day*,' *Tuesday, April 28th.*—My real feelings as, laden like last year, with palette brushes and paint box, I ascended the great staircase all alone, though meeting and being overtaken by hurrying men similarly equipped to myself, were not happy ones. Before reaching the top stairs I sighed to myself, 'After all your working extra hours through the winter, what has it been for? That you may have a cause of mortification in having an unsatisfactory picture on the Academy walls for people to stare at.' I tried to feel indifferent, but had not to make the effort for long, for I soon espied my dark battalion in Room II. *on the line,* with a knot of artists before it. Then began my ovation (!)

(which, meaning a second-class triumph, is *not* quite the word). I never expected anything so perfectly satisfactory and so like the realisation of a castle in the air as the events of this day. It would be impossible to say all that was said to me by the swells. Millais, R.A., talked and talked, so did Calderon, R.A., and Val Prinsep, asking me questions as to where I studied, and praising this figure and that. Herbert, R.A., hung about me all day, and introduced me to his two sons. Du Maurier told me how highly Tom Taylor had spoken to him of the picture. Mr. S., our Roman friend, cleaned the picture for me beautifully, insisting on doing so lest I should spoil my new velveteen frock. At lunch-time I returned to the boarding house to fetch a sketch of a better Russian helmet I had done at Ventnor, to replace the bad one I had been obliged to put in the foreground from a Prussian one for want of a better. I sent a gleeful telegram home to say the picture was on the line. I could hardly do the little helmet alterations necessary, so crowded was I by congratulating and questioning artists and starers. I by no means disliked it all. Delightful is it to be an object of interest to so many people. I am sure I cannot have looked very glum that day. In the most distant rooms people steered towards me to felicitate me most cordially. 'Only send as *good* a picture next year' was Millais' answer to my expressed hope that next year I should do better. This was after overhearing Mr. C. tell me I might be elected A.R.A. if I kept up to the mark next year. O'Neil, R.A., seemed rather to deprecate all the applause I had to-day and, shaking his head, warned me of the dangers of sudden popularity. I know all about *that*, I think.

"*Thursday, April 30th.*—The Royalties' private view. The Prince of Wales wants 'The Roll Call.' It is not mine to let him have, and Galloway won't give it up.

"*Friday, May 1st.*—The to-me-glorious private view of 1874. I insert here my letter to Papa about it:

'DEAREST—, I feel as though I were undertaking a really difficult work in attempting to describe to you the events of this most memorable day. I don't suppose I ever can have another such day, because, however great my future successes may be, they can never partake of the character of this one. It is my first great success. As Tom Taylor told me to-day, I have suddenly burst into fame, and this *first time* can never come again. It has a character peculiar to all *first things* and to them alone. You know that "the *élite* of London society" goes to the Private View. Well, the greater part of the *élite* have been presented to me this day, all with the same hearty words of congratulation on their lips and the same warm shake of the hand ready to follow the introductory bow. I was not at all disconcerted by these bigwigs. The Duke of Westminster invited me to come and see the pictures at Grosvenor House, and the old Duchess of Beaufort was so delighted with *The Roll Call* that she asked me to tell her the history of each soldier, which I did, the knot of people which, by the bye, is always before the picture swelling into a little crowd to see me and, if possible, catch what I was saying. Galloway's tall figure was almost a fixture near the painting. That poor man, he was sadly distracted about this Prince of Wales affair, but the last I heard from him was that he *couldn't* part with it.

Some one at the Academy offered him £1,000 for it, and T. Agnew told him he would give him anything he asked, but he refused those offers without a moment's hesitation. He has telegraphed to his wife at Manchester, as he says women can decide so much better than men on the spur of the moment. The Prince gives him till the dinner to-morrow to make up his mind. The Duchess of Beaufort introduced Lord Raglan's daughters who were pleased with the interest I took in their father. Old Kinglake was also introduced, and we had a comparatively long talk in that huge assembly where you are perpetually interrupted in your conversation by fresh arrivals of friends or new introductions. Do you remember joking with me, when I was a child, about the exaggerations of popularity? How strange it felt to-day to be realizing, in actual experience, what you warned me of, in fun, when looking at my drawings. You need not be afraid that I shall forget. What I *do* feel is great pleasure at having "arrived," at last. The great banker Bunbury has invited me and a friend to the ball at the Goldsmiths' Hall on Wednesday night. He is one of the wardens. Oh! if you could only come up in time to take me. Col. Lloyd Lindsay, of Alma fame, and his wife were wild to have *The Roll Call*. She shyly told me she had cried before the picture. But, for enthusiasm, William Agnew beat them all. He came up to be introduced, and spoke in such expressions of admiration that his voice positively shook, and he said that, having missed purchasing this work, he would feel "proud and happy" if I would paint him one, the time, subject and price, whatever it might be, being left entirely to me. Sir Richard Airey, the man who wrote the fatally misconstrued order on his holster and handed it to Nolan on the 25th October, 1854, was very cordial, and showed that he took a keen pleasure in the picture. I told him I valued a Crimean man's praise more than anybody else's, and I repeated the observation later to old Sir William Codrington under similar circumstances, and to other Crimean officers. One of them, whose father was killed at the assault on the Redan, pressed me very hard to consent to paint him two Crimean subjects, but I cannot promise anything more till I have worked out my already too numerous commissions, old ones, at the horrible old prices.

Sir Henry Thompson, a great surgeon, I understand, was very polite, and introduced his little daughter who paints. Lady Salisbury had a long chat with me and showed a great intelligence on art matters. Many others were introduced, or I to them, but most of them exist as ghosts in my memory. I have forgotten some of their names and, as some only wrote their addresses on my catalogue, I don't know who is who. The others gave me their cards, so that is all right. Horsely, R.A., is such a genial, hearty sort of man. He says he shouldn't wonder if my name was mentioned in the Royal speeches at the dinner. Lady Somebody introduced me to Miss Florence Nightingale's sister, who wanted to know if there was any possibility of my "most kindly" letting the picture be taken, at the close of the exhibition, to her poor sister to see. Miss Nightingale, you know, is now bedridden. Now I must stop. More to-morrow...'

I remember how on the following Sunday my good friend Dr. Pollard, who lived close to my boarding house, waylaid me on my way to mass at the Oratory, and from his front garden called me in stentorian tones, waving the *Observer* over his head. On crossing over I learnt of the speeches of the Prince of Wales and the Duke of Cambridge at the Academy banquet the evening before, in which most surprising words were uttered about me and the picture.

"*Monday, May 4th.*—The opening day of the Royal Academy. A dense crowd before my grenadiers. I fear that fully half of that crowd have been sent there by the royal speeches on Saturday. I may say that I awoke this morning and found myself famous. Great fun at the Academy, where were some of my dear fellow students rejoicing in the fulfilment of their prophecies in the old days. Overwhelmed with congratulations on all sides; and as to the papers, it is impossible to copy their magnificent critiques, from *The Times* downwards.

"*Wednesday, May 6th.*—The Queen had my picture abstracted from the R.A. last night to gaze at, at Buckingham Palace! It is now, of course, in its place again. Went with Papa to the brilliant Goldsmiths' Ball, where I danced. I was a bit of a lion there, or shall I say lioness? Sir William Ferguson was introduced to me; and he, in his turn, introduced his daughter and drank to my further success at the supper. Sir. F. Chapman also was presented, and expressed his astonishment at the accuracy of the military details in my picture. He is a Crimean man. The King of the Goldsmiths was brought up to me to express his thanks at my 'honouring' their ball with my presence. The engravers are already at me to buy the copyright, but my dear counsellor and friend, Seymour Haden, says I am to accept nothing short of £1,000, and get still more if I can!

"*May 10th.*—The Dowager Lady Westmoreland, who is about 80, and who has lost pleasure in seeing new faces, when she heard of my Crimean picture, expressed a great wish to see me, and to-day I went to dine at her house, meeting there the present earl and countess, an old Waterloo lord, and Her.ry Weigall and his wife, Lady Rose. The dear old lady was so sweet. She was the Duke of Wellington's favourite niece, and his Grace's portraits deck the walls of more than one room. Her pleasure was in talking of the Florence of the old pre-Austrian days, where she lived sixteen years, but my great pleasure was talking with the earl and the Waterloo lord, who were most loquacious. Lord Westmoreland was on Lord Raglan's staff in the Crimea.

"*May 11th.*—Received cheque for the *San Pietro in Vincoli* and *Children of St. Francis.* My popularity has *levered* those two poor little pictures off. Messrs. Dickinson & Co. have bought my copyright for £1,200!!!"

There follows a good deal in the Diary concerning the trouble with Mr. Galloway, who made hard conditions regarding his ceding *The Roll Call* to the Queen, who wished to have it. He felt he was bound to let it go to his Sovereign, but only on condition that I should paint him my next Academy picture for the same price as he had given for the one he was ceding, and that the Queen should sign with her own hand six of the artist's proofs when the engraving of her picture came out. I had set my heart on painting the 28th Regiment in square receiving the last charge of the French Cuirassiers at Quatre Bras, but as that picture would necessitate far more work than *The Roll Call,* I could not paint it for that little £126—so very puny now! So I most reluctantly suggested a subject I had long had *in petto, The Dawn of Sedan,* French Cuirassiers watching by their horses in the historic fog of that fateful morning—a very simple composition. To cut a very long story short, he finally consented to have *Quatre Bras* at my own price, £1,126, the copyright remaining his. All this talk went on for a long time, and meanwhile, all through the London society doings, I made oil studies of all the grey horses for *Sedan.* The General Omnibus Company sent me all shades of grey *percherons* for this purpose. I also made life-size oil studies of hands for *Quatre Bras,* where hands were to be

very strong points, gripping "Brown Besses." So I took time
by the forelock for either subject. I was very fortunate in
having the help of wise business heads to grapple with the
business part of my work, for I have not been favoured that
way myself.

There is no mention in the Diary of the policeman who,
a few days after the opening of the Academy, had to be
posted, poor hot man, in my corner to keep the crowd from
too closely approaching the picture and to ask the people to
"move on." That policeman was there instead of the brass
bar which, as a child, I had pleased myself by imagining in
front of one of my works, à la Frith's *Derby Day*. The R.A.'s
told me the bar created so much jealously, when used, that
it had been decided never to use it again. But I think a live
policeman quite as much calculated to produce the undesir-
able result. I learnt later that his services were quite as
necessary for the protection of two lovely little pictures of
Leighton's, past which the people *scraped* to get at mine,
they being, unfortunately, hung at right angles to mine in
its corner. What an unfortunate arrangement of the hangers! Horsley told me that they went every evening after the
closing, with a lantern, to see if the two gems had been
scratched. They were never seen. I wonder if Leighton had
any feelings of dislike towards "that girl." She who in her
'teens records her prostrations of worship before his earlier
works, ere he became so coldly classical.

It is a curious condition of the mind between gratitude
for the appreciation of one's work by those who know, and
the uncomfortable sense of an exaggerated popularity with
the crowd. The exaggeration is unavoidable, and, no doubt,
passes, but the fact that counts is the power of touching the
people's heart, an "organ" which remains the same through
all the changing fashions in art. I remember an argument I
once had with Alma Tadema on this matter of touching the
heart. He laughed at me, and didn't believe in it at all.

"*Tuesday, May 12th.*—Mr. Charles Manning and his wife
have been so very nice to me, and this morning Mrs M.

bore me off to be presented to His Grace of Westminster, with whom I had a long interview. What a face! all spirit and no flesh. After that, to the School of Art Needlework to meet Lady Marion Alford and other Catholic ladies. I ordered there a pretty screen for my studio on the strength of my £1,200! Thence I proceeded on a round of calls, going first to the Desanges, where I lunched. There they told me the Prince of Wales was coming at four o'clock to see the Ashanti picture Desanges is just finishing. They begged me to come back a little before then, so as to be ready to be presented when the moment should arrive. I returned accordingly, and found the place crowded with people who had come to see the picture. As soon as H.R.H. was announced, all the people were sent below to the drawing-room and kept under hatches until Royalty should take its departure; but I alone was to remain in the back studio, to be handy. All this was much against my will, as I hate being thrust forward. But, as it turned out, there was no thrusting forward on this occasion, and all was very nice and natural. The Prince soon came in to where I was, Mr. Desanges saying 'Here she is' in answer to a question. His first remark to me was, of course, about the picture, saying he hoped to be its possessor, etc., etc., and he asked me how I had got the correct details for the uniforms, and so on, having quite a little chat. He spoke very frankly, and has a most clear, audible voice."

Of course, the photographers began bothering. The idea of my portraits being published in the shop windows was repugnant to me. Nowadays one is snapshotted whether one likes it or not, but it wasn't so bad in those days; one's own consent was asked, at any rate. I refused. However, it had to come to that at last. My grandfather simply walked into the shop of the first people that had asked me, in Regent Street, and calmly made the appointment. I was so cross on being dragged there that the result was as I expected—a rather harassed and coerced young woman, and the worst of it was that this particular photograph was the one

Crimea

CRIMEAN IDEAS.

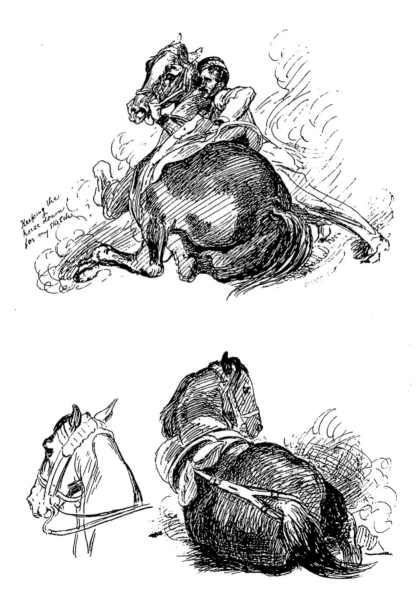

Keeping the
horse down
for my sketch

PRACTISING FOR "QUATRE BRAS."

most widely published. Indeed, one of my Aunts, passing
along a street in Chelsea, was astonished to see her rueful
niece on a costermonger's barrow amongst some bananas!

CHAPTER NINE

ECHOES OF "THE ROLL CALL"

ON May 14th I lunched at Lady Raglan's. Kinglake was
there to meet me, and we talked Crimea. I had read
and re-read his much too prolix history, which I thought
overburdened with detail, giving one an impression of the
two Balaclava charges as lasting hours rather than minutes.
But I had learnt much that was of the utmost value from
this very superabundance of detail. Then on the very next
day I rose early, and was off by seven with the Horsleys to
Aldershot at the invitation of Sir Hope Grant, of Indian
celebrity, commanding, who travelled down with us. "Lady
Grant received us at the house, where we found a nice
breakfast, and where I got dried, being drenched by a tor-
rential downpour. Would that it had continued longer, if
only to lay the hideous sand in the Long Valley, which
made the field day something very like a fiasco. I tried to
sketch, but my book was nearly blown out of my hand, my
umbrella was turned inside out and my arms benumbed by
the cold. M., most luckily, was on the field, and Mrs. Horsley and I were soon comfortably ensconced in his hansom
cab and trying to feel more comfortable and jolly. When
the sham fight began we had to keep shifting our stand-
point, and Mrs. H. and I had repeatedly to jump out of the
hansom, as we were threatened by an upset every minute
over those sandhills. As to the two charges of cavalry,
which Sir Hope had on purpose for me, I could hardly see
them, what with the dust storms half swallowing them up
in dense dun-coloured sheets and my eyes being full of
sand. However, I made the most of the situation, and hope I
have got some good hints. I ought to have so much of this

sort of thing, and hope to now, with all those 'friends in court!' When the march past began Sir Hope sent to ask me if I would like to stand by his charger at the saluting base, which I did, and saw, of course, beautifully. I felt extraordinarily situated, standing there, half liking and half not liking the situation, with an enormous mounted staff of utterly unknown, gorgeous officers curvetting and jingling behind me and the general. As one regiment passed, marching, as I thought, just as splendidly as the others, I heard Sir Hope snap at them 'Very bad, very bad. Don't, don't!' And I felt for them so much, trusting they didn't see me or mind my having heard."

Three days later, at a charming lunch at Lady Herbert's, I met her son, Lord Pembroke, and Dr. Kingsley, Charles's brother—"The Earl and the Doctor." It was interesting to see the originals of the title they gave their book. The next day people came to the Academy to find, in place of *The Roll Call*, a placard—"This picture has been temporarily removed by command of Her Majesty." She had it taken to Windsor to look at before her departure for Scotland, and to show to the Czar, who was on a visit.

Calderon, the R.A., whom I met that evening, told me the Academy had never been receiving so many daily shillings before, and that it ought to present me with a diamond necklace. And so forth, and so forth—all noted in the faithful Diary, wherein many extravagances of the moment in my regard are safely tucked away. Two days later I see: "*May 20th.*—The Woolwich review was quite glorious. I went with Lady Herbert, the Lane Foxes, Lord Denbigh and Capt. Slade. We posted there and back with two jolly greys and a postboy in a sky-blue jacket. This was quite after my own heart. Lord Denbigh talked art and war all the way, interesting me beyond expression. We were in the forefront of everything on arrival, next the Saluting Point, round which were grouped the most brilliant sons of Mars I ever saw gathered together, and of various nations. The Czar Alexander II. headed these, flanked by my two friends, the Prince of Wales and the Duke of Cambridge. The artillery manœuvres were effective, and I sketched as much as I could, getting up on the box, Lord Denbigh holding my parasol over my head, as the sun was strong. I suppose people like spoiling me just now, or *trying* to."

Then, two days later, I note that I dined at Lady Rose Weigall's, my left-hand neighbour at table the Archbishop of York, Dr. Thomson, who took in the hostess. He and I seem to have talked an immense deal about all sorts of things. He confided to me that his private opinion was that the Irish Church should never have been disestablished. In the course of further conversation I thought it better to let him know I was a Catholic by a passing remark. I said I thought the Neapolitans did not make such solid Catholics as the English. He stared, none too pleased! The next night I met at the Westmorelands', at dinner, Lord George Paget, Colonel Kingscote, and Henry Weigall, my host of the previous evening. Lord George was drawn out during dinner about Balaclava, and I listened to his loud cavalry soldier's talk with the keenest interest. He protested that we were making him say too much, but we were insatiable. Lord George was a man I had tried to picture; he was almost the last to ride back from the light cavalry charge. His manner and speech were *soldatesque*, his expressions requiring at times a "saving your presence" to the ladies, as a prefix. For me time flew in listening to this interesting Balaclava hero, and it was very late when I made up my mind to go, a wiser but by no means a sadder girl.

At a dinner at Lady Georgiana Fullerton's my sister and I met Aubrey de Vere, who delighted Alice with his conversation. The general company, however, seem to have chiefly amused themselves with the long and, on the whole, silly controversy which was appearing in *The Times* regarding the sequence of the horse's steps as he walks. It began by my horse's walk in *The Roll Call* having been criticised by those who held to the old conventional idea. How many hours I had moved alongside horses to see for myself exactly how a horse puts his feet down in the walk! I had told many people to go down on all fours themselves and walk, noting the sequence with their own hands and knees, which was sure to be correct instinctively. At this same dinner Lady Lothian told me she had followed my advice, and the idea of that sedate *grande dame*, with grey hair combed under a white lace cap, pacing round her room on all fours I thought delightful. Since those days I have been vindicated by the snap-shot.

I find many Diary pages chiefly devoted to preparations for *Quatre Bras* and the doing of several pen-and-ink reminiscences of what I had seen at Woolwich and Aldershot, and exhibited at the "Dudley." Some were bought by the picture dealer Gambart, and some by Agnew. One of those pen-and-inks was the *"Halt!"*—those Scots Greys I only half saw through the dust storm at Aldershot pulling up in the midst of a tremendous charge, very close to us. Gambart had come to my studio to see if he could get anything, and when I told him of this *"Halt!"* which I had just sent to the "Dudley," he there and then wrote me a cheque for it, without seeing it. When he went there to claim it, behold! it had already been sold, before the opening. He was very angry, and threatened law against the "Dudley" for what he called "skimming" the show before the public got a chance. But the possessor was, like Mr. Galloway, a *Manchester maan*, and these are very firm on what they call "our rights." It was no use. I had to make Gambart a compensation drawing. This introduces Mr. Whitehead, for whom I was to paint *Balaclava*. He had the *"Halt!"* tight.

On Corpus Christi Day that year Alice and I, having received our invitations from the Bishop of Salford, of happy pilgrimage memory, to join in the services and procession in honour of the Blessed Sacrament at the Missionary College, Mill Hill, we went thither that glorious midsummer day. At page 127 of the Diary I have put down certain sentiments about the practice of the Catholic faith in England, and I express a longing to see the Host carried through English fields. I little thought in one year to see my hope realised; yet so it was at Mill Hill. After vespers in the little church, the procession was formed, and I shall long remember the choristers, in their purple cassocks, passing along a field of golden buttercups and the white and gold banners at the head of the procession floating out against a typical English sky as their bearers passed over a little hillock which commands a lovely view of the rich land-scape. The bishop bore the Host, and six favoured men held the canopy. Franciscan nuns in the procession sang the hymns.

The early days of that July had their pleasant festivities, such as a dinner, with Alice, at Lady Londonderry's (she who was our mother's godmother on the occasion of her reception into the Catholic Church) and the Academy *soirée*, where Mrs. Tait invited me and Dr. Pollard to a large garden party at Lambeth Palace. There I note: "The Royal-ties were in full force, the *Waleses*, as I have heard the Prince and Princess called, and many others. It was amusing and very pleasant in the gardens, though provokingly windy. I had a curiously uncomfortable and oppressed feel-ing, though, in that headquarters of the—what shall I call it?—Opposition? The Archbishop and Mrs. Archbishop, particularly Mrs., rather appalled me. But dear Dr. Pollard, that stout Protestant, must have been very gratified."

On July 4th Colonel Browne, C.B., R.E., who took the keenest interest in my *Quatre Bras*, and did all in his power to help me with the military part of it, had a day at Chatham for me. He, Mrs. B. and daughters called for me in the morning, and we set forth for Chatham, where some 300 men of the Royal Engineers were awaiting us on the "Lines." Colonel Browne had ordered them beforehand, and had them in full dress, with knapsacks, as I desired.

They first formed the old-fashioned four-deep square for me, and not only that, but the beautiful parade dressing was broken and *accidenté* by my directions, so as to have a little more the appearance of the real thing. They fired in sections, too, as I wished, but, unfortunately, the wind was so strong that the smoke was whisked away in a twinkling, and what I chiefly wished to study was unobtainable, *i.e.*, masses of men seen through smoke. After they had fired away all their ammunition, the whole body of men were drawn up in line, and, the rear rank having been distanced from the front rank, I, attended by Colonel Browne and a sergeant, walked down them both, slowly, picking out here and there a man I thought would do for a *Quatre Bras* model (beardless), and the sergeant took down the name of each man as I pointed him out very unobtrusively, Colonel Browne promising to have these men up at Brompton, quartered there for the time I wanted them. So I write: "I shall not want for soldierly faces, what with those sappers and the Scots Fusilier Guards, of whom I am sure I can have the pick, through Colonel Hepburn's courtesy. After this interesting 'choosing a model' was ended, we all repaired to Colonel Galway's quarters, where we lunched. After that I went to the guard-room to see the men I had chosen in the morning, so as to write down their personal descriptions in my book. Each man was marched in by the sergeant and stood at attention with every vestige of expression discharged from his countenance whilst I wrote down his personal peculiarities. I had chosen eight out of the 300 in the morning, but only five were brought now by the sergeant, as I had managed to pitch upon three bad characters out of the eight, and these could not be sent me. We spent the rest of the day very pleasantly listening to the band, going over the museum, etc. I ought to see as much of military life as possible, and I must go down to Aldershot as often as I can.

"*July 16th.*—Mamma and I went to Henley-on-Thames in search of a rye field for my *Quatre Bras*. Eagerly I looked at the harvest fields as we sped to our goal to see how advanced they were. We had a great difficulty in finding any rye at Henley, it having all been cut, except a little patch which we at length discovered by the direction of a farmer. I bought a piece of it, and then immediately trampled it down with the aid of a lot of children. Mamma and I then went to work, but oh! horror, my oil brushes were missing. I had left them in the chaise, which had returned to Henley. So Mamma went frantically to work with two slimy water-colour brushes to get down tints whilst I drew down forms in pencil. We laughed a good deal and worked on into the darkness, two regular 'Pre-Raphaelite Brethren,' to all appearances, bending over a patch of trampled rye."

I seem to have felt to the utmost the exhilaration produced by the following episode. Let the young Diary speak: "The grand and glorious Lord Mayor's banquet to the stars of literature and art came off to-day, July 21st, and it was to me such a delightful thing that I felt all the time in a pleasant sort of dream. I was mentioned in two speeches, Lord Houghton's ('Monckton Milnes') and Sir Francis Grant's, P.R.A. As the President spoke of me, he said his eye rested with pleasure on me at that moment! Papa came with me. Above all the display of civic splendour one felt the dominant spirit of hospitality in that ever-to-me-delightful Mansion House. It was a unique thing because such aristocrats as were there were those of merit and genius. The few lords were only there because they represented literature, being authors. Patti was there. She wished to have a talk with me, and went through little Italian dramatic compliments, like Neilson. Old Cruickshank was a strange-looking old man, a wonder to me as the illustrator of *Oliver Twist* and others of Dickens's works—a unique genius. He said many nice things about me to Papa. I wished the evening could have lasted a week."

The next entries are connected with the *Quatre Bras* cartoon: "Dreadful misgivings about a vital point. I have made my front rank men sitting on their heels in the kneeling position. Not so the drill book. After my model went, most luckily came Colonel Browne. Shakes his head at the attitudes. Will telegraph to Chatham about the heel and let me know in the morning.

"*July 23rd.*—Colonel Browne came, and with him a smart sergeant-major, instructor of musketry. Alas! this man and telegram from Chatham dead against me. Sergeant says the men at Chatham must have been sitting on their heels to rest and steady themselves. He showed me the exact position when at the 'ready' to receive cavalry. To my delight I may have him to-morrow as a model, but it is no end of a bore, this wasted time.

"*July 24th.*—The musketry instructor, contrary to my sad expectations, was by no means the automaton one expects a soldier to be, but a thoroughly intelligent model, and his attitudes combined perfect drill-book correctness with great life and action. He was splendid. I can feel certain of everything being right in the attitudes, and will have no misgivings. It is extraordinary what a well-studied position that kneeling to resist cavalry is. I dread to think what blunders I might have committed. No civilian would have detected them, but the military would have been down upon me. I feel, of course, rather fettered at having to observe rules so strict and imperative concerning the poses of my figures, which, I hope, will have much action. I have to combine the drill book and the fierce fray! I told an artist the other day, very seriously, that I wished to show what an English square looks like viewed quite close at the end of two hours' action, when about to receive a last charge. A cool speech, seeing I have never seen the thing! And yet I seem to have seen it—the hot, blackened faces, the set teeth or gasping mouths, the bloodshot eyes and the mocking laughter, the stern, cool, calculating look here and there; the unimpressionable, dogged stare! Oh! that I could put on canvas what I have in my mind!

"*July 25th.*—A glorious day at Chatham, where again the Engineers were put through field exercises, and I studied them with all my faculties. I got splendid hints to-day. Went with Colonel Browne and Papa.

"*July 28th.*—My dear musketry instructor for a few more attitudes. He has put me through the process of loading the

'Brown Bess'—a flint-lock—so that I shall have my soldiers handling their arms properly. Galloway has sold the copyright of this picture to Messrs. Dickenson for £2,000! They must have faith in my doing it well."

On August 11th I see I took a much-needed holiday at home, at Ventnor; and, as I say, "gave myself up to fresh air, exercise, a little out-of-door painting, and Napier's *Peninsular War*, in six volumes." Shortly before I left for home I received from Queen Victoria a very splendid bracelet set with pearls and a large emerald. My mother and good friend Dr. Pollard were with me in the studio when the messenger brought it, and we formed a jubilant trio.

It was pleasant to be amongst my old Ventnor friends who had known me since I was little more than a child. But on September 10th I had to bid them and the old place goodbye, and on September 11th I re-entered my beloved studio.

"*September 12th.*—An eventful day, for my *Quatre Bras* canvas was tackled. The sergeant-major and Colonel Browne arrived. The latter, good man, has had the whole Waterloo uniform made for me at the Government clothing factory at Pimlico. It has been made to fit the sergeant-major, who put on the whole thing for me to see. We had a dress rehearsal, and very delighted I was. They have even had the coat dyed the old 'brick-dust' red and made of the baize cloth of those days! Times are changed for me. It will be my fault if the picture is a fiasco."

During the painting of *Quatre Bras* I was elected a member of the Royal Institute of Painters in Water Colour, and I contributed to the Winter Exhibition that large sketch of a sowar of the 10th Bengal Lancers which I called "*Missed!*" and which the *Graphic* bought and published in colours. This reproduction sold to such an extent that the *Graphic* must have been pleased! The sowar at "tent-pegging" has missed his peg and pulls at his horse at full gallop. I had never seen tent-pegging at that time, but I did this from description, by an Anglo-Indian officer of the 10th, who put the thing vividly before me. How many, many tent-peg-gings I have seen since, and what a number of subjects they have given me for my brush and pencil! Those captivating and pictorial movements of men and horses are inex-haustible in their variety.

I had more models sent to me than I could put into the big picture— Guardsmen, Engineers and Policemen—the latter being useful as, in those days, the police did not wear the moustache, and I had difficulty in finding heads suitable for the Waterloo time. Not a head in the picture is repeat-ed. I had a welcome opportunity of showing varieties of types such as gave me so much pleasure in the old Floren-tine days when I enjoyed the Andrea del Sartos, Masaccios, Francia Bigios, and other works so full of characteristic heads.

On November 7th my sister and I went for a weekend to Birmingham, where the people who had bought *The Roll Call* copyright were exhibiting that picture. They particu-larly wished me to go. We were very agreeably entertained at Birmingham, where I was curious to meet the buyer of my first picture sold, that *Morra* which I painted in Rome. Unfortunately I inquired everywhere for "Mr. Glass," and had to leave Birmingham without seeing him and the early work. No one had heard of him! His name was Chance, the great Birmingham *glass* manufacturer.

"*November 27th.*—In the morning off with Dr. Pollard to Sanger's Circus, where arrangements had been made for me to see two horses go through their performances of lying down, floundering on the ground, and rearing for my *Quatre Bras* foreground horses. It was a funny experience behind the scenes, and I sketched as I followed the horses in their movements over the arena with many members of the troupe looking on, the young ladies with their hair in curl-papers against the evening's performance. I am now ripe to go to Paris."

So to Paris I went, with my father. We were guests of my father's old friends, Mr. and Mrs. Talmadge, Boulevard

Haussmann, and a complete change of scene it was. It gave my work the desired fillip and the fresh impulse of emulation, for we visited the best studios, where I met my most admired French painters. The Paris Diary says:

"*December 3rd.*—Our first lion was Bonnat in his studio. A little man, strong and wiry; I didn't care for his pictures. His colouring is dreadful. What good light those Parisians get while we are muddling in our smoky art centre. We next went to Gérôme, and it was an epoch in my life when I saw him. He was at work but did not mind being interrupted. He is a much smaller man than I expected, with wide open, quick black eyes, yet with deep lids, the eyes opening wide only when he talks. He talked a great deal and knew me by name and *l'Appel*, which he politely said he heard was '*digne*' of the celebrity it had gained. We went to see an exhibition of horrors—Carolus Duran's productions, now on view at the *Cercle Artistique*. The talk is all about this man, just now the vogue. He illustrates a very disagreeable present phase of French Art. At Goupil's we saw De Neuville's *Combat on the Roof of a House*, and I feasted my eyes on some pickings from the most celebrated artists of the Continent. I am having a great treat and a great lesson.

"*December 4th.*—Had a *supposed* great opportunity in being invited to join a party of very *mondaines Parisiennes* to go over the Grand Opera, which is just being finished. Oh, the chatter of those women in the carriage going there! They vied with each other in frivolous outpourings which continued all the time we explored that dreadful building. It is a pile of ostentation which oppressed me by the extravagant display of gilding, marbles and bronze, and silver, and mosaic, and brocade, heaped up over each other in a gorged kind of way. How truly weary I felt; and the bedizened dressing-rooms of the actresses and *danseuses* were the last straw. Ugh! and all really tasteless."

However, I recovered from the Grand Opera, and really enjoyed the lively dinners where conversation was not limited to couples, but flowed with great *ésprit* across the table

and round and round. Still, in time, my sleep suffered, for I
seemed to hear those voices in the night. How graceful
were the French equivalents to the compliments I received
in London. They thought I would like to know that the
fame of *l'Appel* had reached Paris, and so I did.

We visited Détaille's beautiful studio. He was my greatest
admiration at that time. Also Henriette Browne's and others, and, of course, the Luxembourg, so I drew much profit
from my little visit. But what a change I saw in the army! I
who could remember the Empire of my childhood, with its
endless variety of uniforms, its buglings, and drummings,
and trumpetings; its *chic* and glitter and swagger: 1870 was
over it all now. Well, never mind, I have lived to see it in
the "*bleu d'horizon*" of a new and glorious day. My Paris
Diary winds up with: "*December 14th.*—Papa and I returned
home from our Paris visit. My eye has been very much
sharpened, and very severe was that organ as it rested on
my *Quatre Bras* for the first time since a fortnight ago. Ye
Gods! what a deal I have to do to that picture before it will
be fit to look at! I continue to receive droll letters and
poems(!). One I must quote the opening line of:

> 'Go on, go on, thou glorious girl!'

Very cheering."

CHAPTER TEN

MORE WORK AND PLAY

SO I worked steadily at the big picture, finding the red
coats very trying. What would I have thought when
studying at Florence, if I had been told to paint a mass of
men in one colour, and that "brick-dust". However, my
Aldershot observations had been of immense value in
showing me how the British red coat becomes blackish-pur-
ple here, pale salmon colour there, and so forth, under the
influence of the weather and wear and tear. I have all the

days noted down with the amount of work done, for future
guidance and lamentations over the fogs of that winter of
1874-5. I gave nicknames in the Diary to the figures in my
picture, which I was amused to find later on, was also the
habit of Meissonier; one of my figures I called the "Gamin,"
and he, too, actually had a "Gamin." Those fogs retarded
my work cruelly and towards the end I had to begin at the
studio at 9.30 instead of 10, and work on till very late. The
porter at No. 76 told me mine was the first fire to be lit in
the morning of all in The Avenue.

One day the Horse Guards, directed by their surgeon,
had a magnificent black charger thrown down in the riding
school at Knightsbridge (on deep sawdust) for me to see,
and get hints from, for the fallen horse in my foreground.
The riding master strapped up one of the furious animal's
forelegs and then let him go. What a commotion before he
fell! How he plunged and snorted in clouds of dust till the
final plunge, when the riding master and a trooper threw
themselves on him to keep him down while I made a frantic sketch. "What must it be," I ask, "when a horse is
wounded in battle, if this painless proceeding can put him
into such a state?"

The spring of 1875 was full of experiences for me. I note
that "at the Horse Guards' riding school a charger was again
'put down' for me, but more gently this time, and without
the risk, as the riding master said, of breaking the horse's
neck, as last time. I was favoured with a charge, two troopers riding full tilt at me and pulling up at within two yards
of where I stood, covering me with the sawdust. I stood it
bravely the second time, but the first I got out of the way.
With Quatre Bras in my head, I tried to fancy myself one of
my young fellows being charged, but I fear my expression
was much too feminine and pacific." March 22nd gave me a
long day's tussle with the grey, bounding horse shot in mid-
career. I say: "This is a teaser. I was tired out and faint when
I got home." If that was a black day, the next was a white
one: "The sculptor, Bœhm, came in, and gave me the very

hints I wanted to complete my bounding horse. Galloway also came. He says *Quatre Bras* beats *The Roll Call* into a cocked hat! He gave me £500 on account. Oh! the nice and strange feeling of easiness of mind and slackening of speed; it is beginning to refresh me at last, and my seven months' task is nearly accomplished." Another visitor was the Duke of Cambridge, who, it appears, gave each soldier in my square a long scrutiny and showed how well he understood the points.

On "Studio Monday" the crowds came, so that I could do very little in the morning. The novelty, which amused me at first, had worn off, and I was vexed that such numbers arrived, and tried to put in a touch here and there whenever I could. Millais' visit, however, I record as "nice, for he was most sincerely pleased with the picture, going over it with great gusto. It is the drawing, character, and expression he most dwells on, which is a comfort. But I must now try to improve my *tone*, I know. And what about *quality?* To-day, Sending-in Day, Mrs. Millais came, and told me what her husband had been saying. He considers me, she said, an even stronger artist than Rosa Bonheur, and is greatly pleased with my *drawing. That* (the 'drawing') pleased me more than anything. But I think it is a pity to make comparisons between artists. I *may* be equal to Rosa Bonheur in power, but how widely apart lie our courses! I was so put out in the morning, when I arrived early to get a little painting, to find the wretched photographers in possession. I showed my vexation most unmistakably, and at last bundled the men out. They were working for Messrs. Dickinson. So much of my time had been taken from me that I was actually dabbling at the picture when the men came to take it away; I dabbing in front and they tapping at the nails behind. How disagreeable!"

After doing a water colour of a Scots Grey orderly for the "Institute," which Agnew bought, I was free at last to take my holiday. So my Mother and I were off to Canterbury to be present at the opening of St. Thomas's Church there.

"April 11th, Canterbury.—To Mass in the wretched barn over a stable wherein a hen, having laid an egg, cackled all through the service. And this has been our only church since the mission was first begun six years ago, up till now, in the city of the great English Martyr. But this state of things comes to an end on Tuesday."

This opening of St. Thomas's Church was the first public act of Cardinal Manning as Cardinal, and it went off most successfully. There were rows of Bishops and Canons and Monsignori and mitred Abbots, and monks and secular priests, all beautifully disposed in the Sanctuary. The sun shone nearly the whole time on the Cardinal as he sat on his throne. After Mass came the luncheon at which much cheering and laughter were indulged in. Later on Benediction, and a visit to the Cathedral. I rather winced when a group of men went down on their knees and kissed the place where the blood of St. Thomas à Becket is supposed to still stain the flags. The Anglican verger stared and did *not* understand.

On Varnishing Day at the Academy I was evidently not enchanted with the position of my picture. "It is in what is called 'the Black Hole'—the only dark room, the light of which looks quite blue by contrast with the golden sun-glow in the others. However, the artists seemed to think it a most enviable position. The big picture is conspicuous, forming the centre of the line on that wall. One academician told me that on account of the rush there would be to see it they felt they must put it there. This 'Lecture Room' I don't think was originally meant for pictures and acts on the principle of a lobster pot. You may go round and round the galleries and never find your way into it! I had the gratification of being told by R.A. after R.A. that my picture was in some respects an advance on last year's, and I was much congratulated on having done what was generally believed more than doubtful—that is, sending any important picture this year with the load and responsibility of my 'almost overwhelming success,' as they called it, of last year on my mind. And that I should send such a difficult one, with so much more in it than the other, they all consider 'very plucky.' I was not very happy myself, although I know *Quatre Bras* to be to *The Roll Call* as a mountain to a hill. However, it was all very gratifying, and I stayed there to the end. My picture was crowded, and I could see how it was being pulled to pieces and unmercifully criticised. I returned to the studio, where I found a champagne lunch spread and a family gathering awaiting me, all anxiety as to the position of my *magnum opus*. After that hilarious meal I sped back to the fascination of Burlington House. I don't think, though, that Mamma will ever forgive the R.A.'s for the 'Black Hole.'

"*April 30th.*—The private view, to which Papa and I went. It is very seldom that an 'outsider' gets invited, but they make a pet of me at the Academy. Again this day con-trasted very soberly with the dazzling P.V. of '74. There were fewer great guns, and I was not torn to pieces to be intro-duced here, there, and everywhere, most of the people being the same as last year, and knowing me already. The same *furore* cannot be repeated; the first time, as I said, can never be a second. Papa and I and lots of others lunched over the way at the Penders' in Arlington Street, our hosts of last night, and it was all very friendly and nice, and we returned in a body to the R.A. afterwards. I was surprised, at the big 'At Home' last night, to find myself a centre again, and people all so anxious to hear my answers to their questions. Last year I felt all this more keenly, as it had all the fascination of novelty. This year just the faintest atom of zest is gone.

"*May 3rd.*—To the Academy on this, the opening day. A dense, surging multitude before my picture. The whole place was crowded so that before *Quatre Bras* the jammed people numbered in dozens and the picture was most com-pletely and satisfactorily rendered invisible. It was chaos, for there was no policeman, as last year, to make people move one way. They clashed in front of that canvas and, in struggling to wriggle out, lunged right against it. Dear little Mamma, who was there nearly all the time of our visit, told me this, for I could not stay there as, to my regret, I find I get recognised (I suppose from my latest photos, which are more like me than the first horror) and the report soon spreads that I am present. So I wander about in other rooms. I don't know why I feel so irritated at starers. One can have a little too much popularity. Not one single thing in this world is without its drawbacks. I see I am in for minute and severe criticism in the papers, which actually gave me their first notices of the R.A.. *The Telegraph* gives me its entire article. *The Times* leads off with me because it says *Quatre Bras* will be the picture the public will want to hear about most. It seems to be discussed from every point of view in a way not usual with battle pieces. But that is as it should be, for I hope my military pictures will have moral and artistic qualities not generally thought necessary to military genre.

"*May 4th.*—All of us and friends to the Academy, where we had a lively lunch, Mamma nearly all the time in 'my crowd,' half delighted with the success and half terrified at the danger the picture was in from the eagerness of the curious multitude. I just furtively glanced between the people, and could only see a head of a soldier at a time. A nice notion the public must have of the *tout ensemble* of my production!"

I was afloat on the London season again, sometimes with my father, or with Dr. Pollard. My dear mother did not now go out in the evenings, being too fatigued from her most regrettable sleeplessness. There was a dinner or At Home nearly every day, and occasionally a dance or a ball. At one of the latter my partner informed me that Miss Thompson was to be there that evening. All this was fun for the time. At a crowded afternoon At Home at the Campanas', where all the singers from the opera were herded, and nearly cracked the too-narrow walls of those tiny rooms by the concussion of the sound issuing from their wonderful throats, I met Salvini. "Having his *Otello,* which we saw the other night, fresh in my mind, I tried to enthuse about it to him, but became so tongue-tied with nervousness that I could only feebly say '*Quasi, quasi piangevo!*' '*O! non bisogna piangere,*' poor Salvini kindly answered. To tell him I nearly cried! To tell the truth, I was much too painfully impressed by the terrific realism of the murder of Desdemona and of Othello's suicide to cry. I have been told that, when Othello is chasing Desdemona round the room and finally catches her for the murder, women in the audience have been known to cry out 'Don't!' And I told him I *nearly* cried! Ugh!"

After this I went to Great Marlow for fresh air with my mother, and worked up an oil picture of a scout of the 3rd Dragoon Guards whom I saw at Aldershot, getting the landscape at Marlow. It has since been engraved.

By the middle of June I was at work in the studio once more. The evenings brought their diversions. Under Mrs. Owen Lewis's chaperonage I went to Lady Petre's At Home one evening, where 600 guests were assembled "to meet H.E. the Cardinal."[6] I record that "I enjoyed it very much, though people did nothing but talk at the top of their voices as they wriggled about in the dense crowd which they helped to swell. They say it is a characteristic of these Catholic parties that the talk is so loud, as everybody knows everybody intimately! I met many people I knew, and my dear chaperon introduced lots of people to me. I had a longish talk with H.E., who scolded me, half seriously, for not having come to see him. I was aware of an extra interest in me in those orthodox rooms, and was much amused at an enthusiastic woman asking, repeatedly, whether I was there. These fleeting experiences instruct one as they fly. Now I know what it feels like to be 'the fashion.'" Other festivities have their record: "I went to a very nice garden party at the house of the great engineer, Mr. Fowler, where the usual sort of thing concerning me went on—introductions of 'grateful' people in large numbers who, most of them, poured out their heartfelt (!) feelings about me and my work. I can stand a surprising amount of this, and am by no means *blasée* yet. Mr. Fowler has a choice collection of modern pictures, which I much enjoyed." Again: "The dinner at the Millais' was nice, but its great attraction was Heilbuth's being there, one of my greatest admirations as regards his particular line—characteristic scenes of Roman ecclesiastical life such as I so much enjoyed in Rome. I told Millais I had had Heilbuth's photograph in my album for years. 'Do you hear that, Heilbuth?' he shouted. To my disgust he was portioned off to some one else to go in for dinner, but I had de Nittis, a very clever Neapolitan artist, and, what with him and Heilbuth and Hallé and Tissot, we talked more French and Italian than English that evening. Millais was so genial and cordial, and in seeing me into the carriage he hinted very broadly that I was soon to have what I 'most *t'*oroughly deserved'—that is, my election as A.R.A. He pronounced the '*th*' like that, and with great emphasis. Was that the Jersey touch?"

In July I saw de Neuville's remarkable *Street Combat,* which made a deep impression on me. I went also to see the field day at Aldershot, a great success, with splendid weather. After the "battle," Captain Cardew took us over several camps, and showed us the stables and many things which interested me greatly and gave me many ideas. The entry for July 17th says:

"Arranging the composition for my *Balaclava* in the morning, and at 1.30 came my dear hussar,[7] who has sat on his fiery chestnut for me already, on a fine bay, for my left-hand horse in the new picture. I have been leading such a life amongst the jarring accounts of the Crimean men I have had in my studio to consult. Some contradict each other flatly. When Col. C. saw my rough charcoal sketch on the wall, he said *no* dress caps were worn in that charge, and coolly rubbed them off, and with a piece of charcoal put mean little forage caps on all the heads (on the wrong side, too!), and contentedly marched out of the door. In comes an old 17th Lancer sergeant, and I tell him what has been done to my cartoon. 'Well, miss,' says he, 'all I can tell you is that my dress cap went into the charge and my dress cap came out of it!' On went the dress caps again and up went my spirits, so dashed by Col. C. To my delight this lancer veteran has kept his very uniform—somewhat moth-eaten, but the real original, and he will lend it to me. I can get the splendid headdress of the 17th, the 'Death or Glory Boys,' of that period at a military tailor's."

The Lord Mayor's splendid banquet to the Royal Academicians and distinguished "outsiders" was in many respects a repetition of the last but with the difference that the assembly was almost entirely composed of artists. "I went with Papa, and I must say, as my name was shouted out and we passed through the lane of people to where the Lord Mayor and Lady Mayoress were standing to receive their guests, I felt a momentary stroke of nervousness, for people were standing there to see who was arriving, and every eye was upon me. I was mentioned in three or four speeches. The Lord Mayor, looking at me, said that he was honoured to have amongst his guests Miss Thompson (cheers), and Major Knollys brought in *The Roll Call* and *Quatre Bras* amidst clamour, while Sir Henry Cole's allusion to my possible election as an A.R.A. was equally well received. I felt very glad as I sat there and heard my present work cheered; for in that hall, last year, I had still the great ordeal to go through of painting, and painting successfully, my next picture, and that was now a *fait accompli*."

A rainy July sadly hindered me from seeing as much as I had hoped to see of the Aldershot manoeuvres. On one lovely day, however, Papa and I went down in the special train with the Prince of Wales, the Duke of Cambridge, and all the "cocked hats." In our compartment was Lord Dufferin, who, on hearing my name asked to be introduced and proved a most charming companion, and what he said about *Quatre Bras* was nice. He was only in England on a short furlough from Canada, and did not see my *Roll Call*.

"At the station at Farnborough the picturesqueness
began with the gay groups of the escort, and other soldiers
and general officers, all in war trim, moving about in the
sunshine, while in the background slowly passed, heavily
laden, the Army on the march to the scene of action. Papa
and I and Major Bethune took a carriage and slowly followed the march, I standing up to see all I could.

"We were soon overtaken by the brilliant staff, and saluted as it flashed past by many of its gallant members,
including the dashing Baron de Grancey in his sky blue
Chasseurs d'Afrique uniform. Poor Lord Dufferin in civilian
dress—frock coat and tall hat—had to ride a rough-trotting
troop horse, as his own horse never turned up at the station. A trooper was ordered to dismount, and the elegant
Lord Dufferin took his place in the black sheepskin saddle.
He did all with perfect grace, and I see him now, as he
passed our carriage, lift his hat with a smiling bow, as
though he was riding the smoothest of Arabs. The country
was lovely. All the heather out and the fir woods aromatic.
In one village regiments were standing in the streets, others
defiling into woods and all sorts of artillery, ambulance, and
engineer waggons lumbering along with a dull roll very suggestive of real war. At this village the two Army Corps
separated to become enemies, the one distinguished from
the other by the men of one side wearing broad white bands
round their headdresses. This gave the wearers a rather savage look which I much enjoyed. It made their already
brown faces look still grimmer. Of course, our driver took
the wrong road and we saw nothing of the actual battle, but
distant puffs of smoke. However, I saw all the march back
to Aldershot, and really, what with the full ambulances, the
men lying exhausted (*sic*) by the roadside, or limping along,
and the cheers and songs of the dirty, begrimed troops, it
was not so unlike war. At the North Camp Sir Henry de
Bathe was introduced, and Papa and I stood by him as the
troops came in." A day or two later I was in the Long Valley
where the most splendid military spectacle was given us,

some 22,000 being paraded in the glorious sunshine and
effective cloud shadows in one of the most striking landscapes I have seen in England. "It was very instructive to
me," I write, "to see the difference in the appearance of the
men to-day from that which they presented on Thursday.
Their very faces seemed different; clean, open and good-
looking, whereas on Thursday I wondered that British
soldiers could look as they did. The infantry in particular,
on that day, seemed changed; they looked almost savage, so
distorted were their faces with powder and dirt and deep
lines caused by the glare of the sun. I was well within the
limits when I painted my 28th in square. I suppose it would
not have done to be realistic to the fullest extent. The
lunch at the Welsh Fusiliers' mess in a tent I thought very
nice. Papa came down for the day. It is very good of him. I
don't think he approves of my being so much on my own
hook. But things can't help being rather abnormal."

Here follows another fresh air holiday at my grandpar-
ents' at Worthing (where I rode with my grandfather),
finishing up with a visit which I shall always remember with
pleasure—I ought to say gratitude—not only for its own
sake, but for all the enjoyment it obtained for me in Italy.
That August I was a guest of the Higford-Burrs at Aldermaston Court, an Elizabethan house standing in a big
Berkshire park. "I arrived just as the company were finishing dinner. I was welcomed with open arms. Mrs.
Higford-Burr embraced me, although I have only seen her
twice before, and I was made to sit down at table in my
travelling dress, positively declining to recall dishes, hating
a fuss as I do. The dessert was pleasant because every one
made me feel at home, especially Mrs. Janet Ross, daughter
of the Lady Duff Gordon whose writings had made me long
to see the Nile in my childhood. There are five lakes in the
Park, and one part is a heather-covered Common, of which
I have made eight oil sketches on my little panels, so that I
have had the pleasure of working hard and enjoying the
society of most delightful people. There were always other

guests at dinner besides the house party, and the average number who sat down was eighteen. Besides Mrs. Ross were Mr. and Mrs. Layard, he the Nineveh explorer, and now Ambassador at Madrid, the Poynters, R.A., the Misses Duff Gordon, and others, in the house. Mrs. Burr with her great tact allowed me to absent myself between breakfast and tea, taking my sandwiches and paints with me to the moor."

Days at Worthing followed, where my mother and I painted all day on the Downs, I with my *Balaclava* in view, which required a valley and low hills. My mother's help was of great value, as I had not had much time to practise landscape up to then. Then came my visit, with Alice, to Newcastle, where *Quatre Bras* was being exhibited, to be followed by our visit at Mrs. Ross's Villa near Florence, whither she had invited us when at Aldermaston, to see the *fêtes* in honour of Michael Angelo.

"We left for Newcastle by the 'Flying Scotchman' from King's Cross at 10 a.m., and had a flying shot at Peterborough and York Cathedrals, and a fine flying view of Durham. Newcastle impressed us very much as we thundered over the iron bridge across the Tyne and looked down on the smoke-shrouded red-roofed city belching forth black and brown smoke and jets of white steam in all directions. It rises in fine masses up from the turbid flood of the dark river, and has a lurid grandeur quite novel to us. I could not help admiring it, though, as it were, under protest, for it seems to me something like a sin to obscure the light of Heaven when it is not necessary. The laws for consuming factory smoke are quite disregarded here. Mrs. Mawson, representing the firm at whose gallery *Quatre Bras* is being exhibited, was awaiting our arrival, and was to be our hostess. We were honoured and fêted in the way of the warm-hearted North. Nothing could have been more successful than our visit in its way. These Northerners are most hospitable, and we are delighted with them. They have quite a *cachet* of their own, so cultured and well read on the top of their intense commercialism—far more responsive in conversation than many society people I know 'down South.' We had a day at Durham under Mrs. Mawson's wing, visiting that finest of all English Cathedrals (to my mind), and the Bishop's palace, etc. We rested at the Dean's, where, of course, I was asked for my autograph. I already find how interested the people are about here, more even than in other parts where I have been. Durham is a place I loved before I saw it. The way that grand mass of Norman architecture rises abruptly from the woods that slope sheer down to the calm river is a unique thing. Of course, the smoky atmosphere makes architectural ornament look shallow by dimming the deep shadows of carvings, etc.—a great pity. On our return we took another lion *en passant*—my picture at Newcastle, and most delighted I was to find it so well lighted. I may say I have never seen it properly before, because it never looked so well in my studio, and as to the Black Hole—! What people they are up here for shaking hands! When some one is brought up to me the introducer puts it in this way: 'Mr. So-and-So wishes very much to have the honour of shaking hands with you, Miss Thompson.' There is a straightforward ring in their speech which I like."

We were up one morning at 4.30 to be off to Scotland for the day. At Berwick the rainy weather lifted and we were delighted by the look of the old Border town on its promontory by the broad and shining Tweed. Passing over the long bridge, which has such a fine effect spanning the river, we were pleased to find ourselves in a country new to us. Edinburgh struck us very much, for we had never quite believed in it, and thought it was "all the brag of the Scotch," but we were converted. It is so like a fine old Continental city—nothing reminds one of England, and yet there is a *Scotchiness* about it which gives it a sentiment of its own. Our towns are, as a rule, so poorly situated, but Edinburgh has the advantage of being built on steep hills and of being back-grounded by great crags which give it a most majestic look. The grey colour of the city is fine, and the houses, nearly all gabled and very tall, are exceedingly picturesque, and none have those vile, black, wriggling chimney pots which disfigure what sky lines our towns may have. I was delighted to see so many women with white caps and tartan shawls and the children barefoot; picturesque horse harness; plenty of kilted soldiers.

We did all the lions, including the garrison fortress where the Cameron Highlanders were, and where Colonel Miller, of Parkhurst memory, came out, very pleased to speak to me and escort us about. He had the water colour I gave him of his charger, done at Parkhurst in the old Ventnor days. Our return to Newcastle was made in glorious sunshine, and we greedily devoured the peculiarly sweet and remote-looking scenes we passed through. I shall long remember Newcastle at sunset on that evening. Then, I will say, the smoke looked grand. They asked me to look at my picture by gas light. The sixpenny crowd was there, the men touching their caps as I passed. In the street they formed a lane for me to pass to the carriage. "What nice people!" I exclaim in the Diary.

All the morning of our departure I was employed in sitting for my photograph, looking at productions of local artists and calling on the Bishop and the Protestant Vicar. One man had carved a chair which was to be dedicated to me. I was quaintly enthroned on it. All this was done on our way to the station, where we lunched under dozens of eyes, and on the platform a crowd was assembled. I read: "Several local dignitaries were introduced and 'shook hands,' as also the 'Gentlemen of the local Press.' As I said a few words to each the crowd saw me over the barriers, which made me get quite hot and I was rather glad when the train drew up and we could get into our carriage. The farewell handshakings at the door may be imagined. We left in a cloud of waving handkerchiefs and hats. I don't know that I respond sufficiently to all this. Frankly, my picture being made so much of pleases me most satisfactorily, but the *personal* part of the tribute makes me curiously uncomfortable when coming in this way."

Ruskin wrote a pamphlet on that year's Academy in which he told the world that he had approached *Quatre Bras* with "iniquitous prejudice" as being the work of a woman. He had always held that no woman could paint, and he accounted for my work being what he found it as being that of an Amazon. I was very pleased to see myself in the character of an Amazon.

CHAPTER ELEVEN

TO FLORENCE AND BACK

WE started on our most delightful journey to Florence early in September of that year to assist at the Michael Angelo fêtes as the guests of dear Mrs. Janet Ross and the Marchese della Stufa, who, with Mr. Ross, inhabited in the summer the delicious old villa of Castagnolo, at Lastra a Signa, six miles on the Pisan side of my beloved Florence. Of course, I give page after page in the Diary to our journey across Italy under the Alps and the Apennines. To the modern motorist it must all sound slow, though we did travel by rail! Above all the lovely things we saw on our way by the Turin-Bologna line, I think Parma, rising from the banks of a shallow river, glowing in sunshine and palpitating jewel-like shade, holds pride of place for noontide beauty. After Modena came the deeper loveliness of the afternoon, and then Bologna, mellowed by the rosy tints of early evening. Then the sunset and then the tender moon.

By moonlight we crossed the Apennines, and to the sound of the droning summer beetle—an extraordinarily penetrating sound, which I declared makes itself heard above the railway noises, we descended into the Garden of Italy, slowly, under powerful brakes. At ten we reached Florence, and in the crowd on the platform a tall, distinguished-looking man bowed to me. "Miss Thompson?" "Yes." It was the Marchese, and lo! behind him, who should there be but my old master, Bellucci. What a warm welcome they gave us. Of course, our luggage had stuck at the *douane* at Modane, and was telegraphed for. No help for it; we must do without it for a day or two. We got into the carriage which was awaiting us, and the Marchese into his little pony trap, and off we went flying for a mysterious, dream-like drive in misty moonlight, we in front and our host behind, jingle-jingling merrily with the pleasant monotony of his lion-maned little pony's canter. We could not believe the drive was a real one. It was too much joy to be at Florence—too good to be true. But how tired we were!

At last we drove up to the great towered villa, an old-fashioned Florentine ancestral place, which has been the home of the Della Stufas for generations, and there, in the great doorway, stood Mrs. Ross, welcoming us most cordially to "Castagnolo." We passed through frescoed rooms and passages, dimly lighted with oil lamps of genuine old Tuscan patterns, and were delighted with our bedrooms—enormous, brick-paved and airy. There we made a show of tidying ourselves, and went down to a fruit-decked supper, though hardly able to sit up for sleep. How kind they were to us! We felt quite at home at once.

"*September 12th.*—After Mass at the picturesque little chapel which, with the *vicario's* dwelling, abuts on the *fattoria* wing of the villa, we drove into Florence with Mrs. Ross and the Marchese, whom we find the typical Italian patrician of the high school. We were rigged out in Mrs. Ross's frocks, which didn't fit us at all. But what was to be done? Provoking girls! It was a dear, hot, dusty, dazzling old Florentine drive, bless it! and we were very pleased. Florence was *en fête* and all *imbandierata* and hung with the usual coloured draperies, and all joyous with church bells and military bands. The concert in honour of Michael Angelo (the fêtes began to-day) was held in the Palazzo Vecchio, and very excellent music they gave us, the audience bursting out in applause before some of the best pieces were quite finished in that refreshingly spontaneous way Italians have. After the concert we loitered about the piazza looking at the ever-moving and chattering crowd in the deep, transparent shade and dazzling sunshine. It was a glorious sight, with the white statues of the fountain rising into the sunlight against houses hung mostly with very beautiful yellow draperies. I stood at the top of the steps of the Loggia de' Lanzi, and, resting my book on the pedestal of one of the lions, I made a rough sketch of the scene, keeping the *Graphic* engagement in view. I subsequently took another of the Michael Angelo procession passing the Ponte alle Grazie on its way from Santa Croce to the new 'Piazzale Michel Angelo,' which they have made since we were here before, on the height of San Miniato. It was a pretty procession on account of the rich banners. A day full of charming sights and melodious sounds."

The great doings of the last day of the fêtes were the illuminations in the moonlit evening. They were artistically done, and we had a feast of them, taking a long, slow drive to the piazzale by the new zigzag. Michael Angelo was remembered at every turn, and the places he fortified were especially marked out by lovely lights, all more or less soft and glowing. Not a vile gas jet to be seen anywhere. The city was not illuminated, nor was anything, with few exceptions, save the lines of the great man's fortifications. The old white banner of Florence, with the *Giglio*, floated above the tricolour on the heights which Michael Angelo defended in person. The effect, especially on the church of San Miniato, of golden lamps making all the surfaces aglow, as if the walls were transparent, and of the green-blue moonlight above, was a thing as lovely as can be seen on this earth. It was a thoroughly Italian festival. We were charmed with the people; no pushing in the crowds, which enjoyed themselves very much. They made way for us when they saw we were foreigners.

We stayed at Castagnolo nearly all through the vintage, pressed from one week to another to linger, though I made many attempts to go on account of beginning my *Balaclava*. The fascination of Castagnolo was intense, and we had certainly a happy experience. I sketched hard every day in the garden, the vineyards, and the old courtyard where the most picturesque vintage incidents occurred, with the white oxen, the wine pressing, and the bare-legged, merry *contadini*, all in an atmosphere scented with the fermenting grapes. Everything in the *Cortile* was dyed with the wine in the making. I loved to lean over the great vats and inhale that wholesome effluence, listening to the low sea-like murmur of the fermentation. On the days when we helped to pick the grapes on the hillside (and "helping ourselves" at the same time) we had *collazione* there, a little picnic, with the indispensable guitar and post-prandial cigarette. Every one made the most of this blessed time, as such moments should be made the most of when they are given us, I think. Young Italians often dined at the villa, and the evenings were spent in singing *stornelli* and *rispetti* until midnight to the guitar, every one of these young fellows having a nice voice. They were merry, pleasant creatures.

Nothing but the stern necessity of returning to work could have kept me from seeing the vintage out. We left most regretfully on October 4th, taking Genoa and our dear step-sister on the way. Even as it was our lingering in Italy made me too late, as things turned out, for the Academy!

October 19th has this entry: "Began my *Balaclava* cartoon to-day. Marked all the positions of the men and horses. My trip to Italy and the glorious and happy and healthy life I have led there, and the utter change of scene and occupation, have done me priceless good, and at last I feel like going at this picture *con amore*. I was in hopes this happy result would be obtained." *Balaclava* was painted for Mr. Whitehead, of Manchester. I had owed him a picture from the time I exhibited *Missing*. It was to be the same size, and for the same price as that work, and I was in honour bound to fulfil my contract! So I again brought forward the *Dawn of Sedan*, although my prices were now so enlarged that £80 had become quite out of proportion, even for a simple subject like that. However, after long parleys, and on account of Mr. Whitehead's repudiation of the Sedan subject, it was agreed that *Balaclava* should be his, at the new scale altogether. The Fine Art Society (late Dickenson & Co.) gave Mr. Whitehead £3,000 for the copyright, and engaged the great Stacpoole, as before, to execute the engraving.

I was very sorry that the picture was not ready for Sending-in Day at the Academy. No doubt the fuss that was made about it, and my having begun a month too late, put me off; but, be that as it may, I was a good deal disturbed towards the end, and had to exhibit *Balaclava* at the private gallery of the purchasers of the copyright in Bond Street. This gave me more time to finish. I had my own Private View on April 20th, 1876: "The picture is disappointing to me. In vain I call to mind all the things that judges of art have said about this being the best thing I have yet painted. Can one *never* be happy when the work is done? This day was only for our friends and was no test. Still, there was what may be called a sensation. Virginia Gabriel, the composer, was led out of the room by her husband in tears! One officer who had been through the charge told a friend he would never have come if he had known how like the real thing it was. Curiously enough, another said that after the stress of Inkermann a soldier had come up to his horse and leant his face against it exactly as I have the man doing to the left of my picture.

"*April 22nd.*—An enormous number of people at the Society's Private View and some of the morning papers blossoming out in the most beautiful notices, ever so long, and I getting a little reassured." A day later: "Went to lunch at Mrs. Mitchell's, who invited me at the Private View, next door to Lady Raglan's, her great friend. Two distinguished officers were there to meet me, and we had a pleasant chat." And this is all I say! One of the two was Major W.F. Butler, author of *The Great Lone Land.*

The London season went by full of society doings. Our mother had long been "At Home" on Wednesdays, and much good music was heard at "The Boltons," South Kensington. Ruskin came to see us there. He and our mother were often of the same way of thinking on many subjects, and I remember seeing him gently clapping his hands at many points she made. He was displeased with me on one occasion when, on his asking me which of the Italian masters I had especially studied, I named Andrea del Sarto. "Come into the corner and let me scold you," were his disconcerting words. Why? Of course, I was crestfallen, but, all the same, I wondered what could be the matter with Andrea's *Cenacolo* at San Salvi, or his frescoes at the SS. Annunziata, or his *Madonna with St. Francis and St. John,* in the Tribune of the Uffizi. The figure of the St. John is, to me, one of the most adorable things in art. That gentle, manly face; that dignified pose; the exquisite modelling of the hand, and the harmonious colours of the drapery— what *could* be the matter with such work? I remember, at one of the artistic London "At Homes," Frith, R.A., coming up to me with a long face to say, if I did not send to the Academy, I should lose my chance of election. But I think the difficulties of electing a woman were great, and much discussion must have been the consequence amongst the R.A.'s. However, as it turned out, in 1879 I lost my election by *two* votes only! Since then I think the door has been closed, and wisely. I returned to the studio on May 18th, for I could not lay down the brush for any amount of society doings. Besides, I soon had to make preparations for *Inkermann.*

"*Saturday, June 10th.*—Saw Genl. Darby-Griffith, to get information about Inkermann. I returned just in time to dress for the delightful Lord Mayor's Banquet to the Representatives of Art at the Mansion House, a place of delightful recollections for me. Neither this year's nor last year's banquet quite came up to the one of *The Roll Call* year in point of numbers and excitement, but it was most delightful and interesting to be in that great gathering of artists and hear oneself gracefully alluded to in The Lord Mayor's speech and others. Marcus Stone sat on my left, and we had really a thoroughly good conversation all through dinner such as I have seldom embarked on, and I found, when I tried it, that I could talk pretty well. He is a fine fellow, and simple-minded and genuine. My *vis-à-vis* was Alma Tadema, with his remarkable-looking wife, like a lady out of one of his own pictures; and many well-known heads wagged all around me. After dinner and the speeches, Du Maurier, of *Punch*, suggested to the Lord Mayor that we should get up a quadrille, which was instantly done, and the friskier spirits amongst us had a nice dance. Du Maurier was my partner; and on my left I had John Tenniel, so that I may be said to have been supported by Punch both at the beginning and end of dinner, this being Du Maurier's simple and obvious joke, *vide* the post-turtle indulgence peculiar to civic banquets. After a waltz we laggards at last took our departure in the best spirits."

I remember that in June we went to a most memorable High Mass, to wit, the first to be celebrated in the Old Saxon Church of St. Etheldreda since the days of the Reformation. This church was the second place of Christian worship erected in London, if not in England, in the old Saxon times. We were much impressed as the Gregorian Mass sounded once more in the grey-stoned crypt. The upper church was not to be ready for years. Those old grey stones woke up that morning which had so long been smothered in the London clay.

Here follow too many descriptions in the Diary of dances, dinners and other functions. They are superfluous. There were, however, some *Tableaux Vivants* at an interesting house—Mrs. Bishop's, a very intellectual woman, much appreciated in society in general, and Catholic society in particular—which may be recorded in this very personal narrative, for I had a funny hand in a single-figure tableau which showed the dazed 11th Hussar who figures in the foreground of my *Balaclava*. The man who stood for him in the tableau had been my model for the picture, but to this day I feel the irritation caused me by that man. In the picture I have him with his busby pushed back, as it certainly would and should have been, off his heated brow. But, while I was posing him for the tableau, every time I looked away he rammed it down at the becoming "smart" angle. I got quite cross, and insisted on the necessary push back. The wretch pretended to obey, but, just before the curtain rose, rammed the busby down again, and utterly destroyed the meaning of that figure! We didn't want a representation of Mr. So-and-so in the becoming uniform of a hussar, but my battered trooper. The thing fell very flat. But tableaux, to my mind, are a mistake, in many ways.

I often mention my pleasure in meeting Lord and Lady Denbigh, for they were people after my own heart. Lady Denbigh was one of those women one always looks at with a smile; she was so *simpatica* and true and unworldly.

July 18th is noted as "a memorable day for Alice, for she and I spent the afternoon at *Tennyson's!* I say 'for Alice' because, as regards myself, the event was not so delightful as a day at Aldershot. Tennyson has indeed managed to shut himself off from the haunts of men, for, arrived at Haslemere, a primitive little village, we had a six-mile drive up, up, over a wild moor and through three gates leading to narrow, rutty lanes before we dipped down to the big Gothic, lonely house overlooking a vast plain, with Leith Hill in the distance. Tennyson had invited us through Aubrey de Vere, the poet, and very apprehensive we were, and nervous, as we neared the abode of a man reported to be such a bear to strangers. We first saw Mrs. Tennyson, a gentle, invalid lady lying on her back on a sofa. After some time the poet sent down word to ask us to come up to his sanctum, where he received us with a rather hard stare, his clay pipe and long, black, straggling hair being quite what I expected. He got up with a little difficulty, and when we had sat down—he, we two and his most deferential son—

he asked which was the painter and which was the poet. After our answer, which struck me as funny, as though we ought to have said, with a bob, 'Please, sir, I'm the painter,' and 'Please sir, I'm the poet,' he made a few common-place remarks about my pictures in a most sepulchral bass voice. But he and Alice, in whom he was more interested, naturally, did most of the talking; there was not much of that, though, for he evidently prefers to answer a remark by a long look, and perhaps a slightly sneering smile, and then an averted head. All this is not awe-inspiring, and looks rather put on. We ceased to be frightened.

"There is no grandeur about Tennyson, no melancholy abstraction; and, if I had made a demi-god of him, his personality would have much disappointed me. Some of his poetry is so truly great that his manner seems below it. The pauses in the conversation were long and frequent, and he did not always seem to take in the meaning of a remark, so that I was relieved when, after a good deal of staring and smiling at Alice in a way rather trying to the patience, he acceded to her request and read us 'The Passing of Arthur.' He was so long in finding the place, when his son at last found him a copy of the book which suited him, and the tone he read in so deep and monotonous, that I was much bored and longed for the hour of our departure. He was vexed with Alice for choosing that poem, which he seemed to think less of than of his later works, and he took the poor child to task in a few words meant to be caustic, though they made us smile. But the ice was melting. He seemed amused at us and we gratefully began to laugh at some quaint phrases he levelled at us. Then he dropped the awe-inspiring tone, and took us all over the grounds and gave us each a rose. He pitched into us for our dresses which were too fashionable and tight to please him. He pinned Alice against a pillar of the entrance to the house on our re-entry from the garden to watch my back as I walked on with his son, pointing the *walking-stick* of scorn at my skirt, the trimming of which particularly roused his ire. Altogether I felt a great relief when we said goodbye to our curious host with whom it was so difficult to carry on conversation, and to know whether he liked us or not. Away, over the windy, twilight heath behind the little ponies—away, away!"

At the beginning of August I began my studies for *The Return from Inkermann*. The foreground I got at Worthing; and I had another visit to Aldershot and many further conversations with Inkermann survivors—officers of distinction. I am bound to say that these often contradicted each other, and the rough sketches I made after each interview had to be re-arranged over and over again. I read Dr. Russell's account (*The Times* correspondent) and sometimes I returned to my own conception, finding it on the whole the most likely to be true.

I laugh even now at the recollection of two elderly *sabreurs*, one of them a General in the Indian Army, who had a hot discussion in my studio, à propos of my *Balaclava*, about the best use of the sabre. The Indian, who was for slashing, twirled his umbrella so briskly, to illustrate his own theory, that I feared for the picture which stood close by his sword arm. The opposition umbrella illustrated "the point" theory.

Having finally clearly fixed the whole composition of *Inkermann*, in sepia on tinted paper the size of the future picture I closed the studio on August 25th and turned my face once more to Italy.

CHAPTER TWELVE

AGAIN IN ITALY

MY sister and I tarried at Genoa on our way to Castagnolo where we were to have again the joys of a Tuscan vintage. But between Genoa and Florence lay our well-loved Porto Fino and, having an invitation from our old friend Monty Brown, the English Consul and his young wife, to stay at their castello there, we spent a week at that Eden. We were alone for part of the time and thoroughly relished the situation, with only old Caterina, the cook, and the dog, "Bismarck," as company. Two Marianas in a moated grange, with a difference. "He" came not, and so allowed us to clasp to our hearts our chief delights—the sky, the sea, the olives and the joyous vines. In those early days many of the deep windows had no glass, and one night, when a staggering Mediterranean thunderstorm crashed down upon us, we really didn't like it and hid the knives under the table at dinner. Caterina was saying her Rosary very loud in the kitchen. As we went up the winding stairs to bed I carried the lamp, and was full of talk, when a gust of wind blew the lamp out, and Alice laughed at my complete silence, more eloquent than any words of alarm. We had every evening to expel curious specimens of the lizard tribe that had come in, and turn over our pillows, remembering the habits of the scorpion.

But that storm was the only one, and as to the sea, which three-parts enveloped our little Promontory its blue utterly baffled my poor paints. But paint I did, on those little panels that we owe to Fortuny, so nicely fitting into the box he invented. There was a little cape, crowned with a shrine to Our Lady—"the Madonetta" it was called—where I used to go daily to inhale the ozone off the sea which thundered down below amongst the brown "pudding-stone" rocks, at the base of a sheer precipice. The "sounding deep." Oh, the freshness, the health, the joy of that haunt of mine! Our walks were perilous sometimes, the paths which almost overhung the deep foaming sea being slippery with the sheddings of the pines. At the "nasty bits" we had to hold on by shrubs and twigs, and haul ourselves along by these always aromatic supports.

Admirable is the industry of the peasants all over Italy. Here on the extreme point of Porto Fino wherever there was a tiny "pocket" of clay, a cabbage or two or a vine with its black clusters of grapes toppling over the abyss found foot-hold. We came one day upon a pretty girl on the very verge of destruction, "holding on by her eyelids," gathering figs with a hooked stick, a demure pussy keeping her company by dozing calmly on a branch of the fig tree. The walls built to support these handfuls of clay on the face of the rock are a puzzle to me. Where did the man stand to build them? It makes me giddy to think of it.

Paragi, the lovely rival of Monty's robber stronghold, belonged to his brother, and a fairer thing I never saw than Fred's loggia with the slender white marble columns, between which one saw the coast trending away to La Spezzia. But "goodbye," Porto Fino! On our way to Castagnolo, at lovely Lastre a Signa, we paused at Pisa for a night.

"Pisa is a *bald Florence*, if I may say so; beautiful, but so empty and lifeless. There are houses there quite peculiar, however, to Pisa, most interesting for their local style. Very broad in effect are those flat blank surfaces without mouldings. The frescoes on them, alas! are now merely very beautiful blotches and stains of colour. We had ample time for a good survey of the Duomo, Baptistery, Camposanto and Leaning Tower, all vividly remembered from when I saw them as a little child. But I get very tired by sight-seeing and don't enjoy it much. What I like is to sit by the hour in a place, sketching or meditating. Besides, I had been kept nearly all night awake at the Albergo Minerva by railway whistles, ducks, parrots, cats, dogs, cocks and hens, so that I was only at half power and I slept most of the way to Signa.

"At the station a carriage fitted, for the heat, with

cool-looking brown holland curtains was awaiting us on the chance of our coming, and we were soon greeted at dear Castagnolo by Mrs. Ross. Very good of her to show so much happy welcome seeing we had been expected the evening before, not to say for many days, and only our luggage had turned up! The Marchese, who had to go into Florence this morning for the day, had gone down to meet us last evening, and returned with the disconcerting announcement that, whereas we had arrived last year without our luggage, this year the luggage had arrived without us. 'I *bauli sono giunti ma le bambine—Chè!*'"

Here follows the record of the same delights as those of the year before. We had been long expected, and Mrs. Ross told me that the peaches had been kept back for us in a most tantalising way by the *padrone*, that everything was threatening over-ripeness by delay. The light-hearted life was in full force. There were great numbers of doves and pigeons at Castagnolo which shared in the general hilarity, swirling in the sunshine and swooping down on the grain scattered for them with little cries of pleasure. I don't know whether I should find a socialistic blight appearing here and there, if I returned to those haunts of my youth, over that patriarchal life, but it seemed to me that the relations between the *padrone* and his splendid *contadini* showed how suitable the system obtaining in Tuscany was then. The labourers were the *fanciulli* (the children) of the master, and without the least approach to servility these men stood up to him in all the pride of their own station. But what deference they showed to him! Always the uncovered head and the respectful and dignified attitude when spoken to or speaking. I mustn't forget the frank smile and the pleasant white teeth. It was a smiling life; every one caught the smiling habit. Oh, that we could keep it up through a London winter! And to a London winter we returned, for my friends in England were getting fidgety about *Inkermann*. One more extract, however, from the Castagnolo Diary must find a place before the veil is drawn. The Marchese took us to

Siena for two days.

"*September 29th.*—We got up by candlelight at 5 a.m. and had a fresh drive in the phaeton to the station, whence we took train to the fascinating Etruscan city, whose very name is magic. The weather, as a matter of course, was splendid, and Siena dwells in my mind all tender brown-gold in a flood of sunshine. Small as the city is, and hard as we worked for those two days, we could only see a portion of its treasures. The result of my observation in the churches and picture galleries shows me that the art there, as regards painting, is very inferior; and, indeed, after Florence, with its most exquisite examples of painting and drawing, these works of art are not taking. I suppose Florence has spoilt me. Here and there one picks out a plum, such as the *Svenimento of St. Catherine* in San Domenico, by Sodoma, the only thing by him that I could look at with pleasure; also, of course, the famous Perugino in Sant' Agostino, which I beheld with delight, and a lovely gem of a Holy Family by Palma Vecchio in the Academy—such a jewel of Venetian colour.

"The frescoes, however, in the sacristy of the cathedral are things apart, and such as I have never seen anywhere else, for the very dry air of Siena has preserved them since Pintoricchio's time quite intact, and there one sees, as one can see nowhere else, ancient frescoes as they were when freshly painted. And very different they are from one's notions of old frescoes; certainly not so pleasing if looked at as bits of colour staining old walls in mellow broken tints, but intensely interesting and beautiful as pictures. Here one sees what frescoes were meant to be: deep in colour, exceedingly forcible, with positive illusion in linear and aërial perspective, the latter being most unexpected and surprising. One's usual notion of frescoes is that they must be flat and airless, and modern artists who go in for fresco decorative art paint accordingly, judging from the faded examples of what were once evidently such as one sees here—forcible pictures.

"Certainly these wall spaces, looking like apertures through which one sees crowds of figures and gorgeous halls or airy landscapes, do not please the eye when looking at the room *as* a room. One would prefer to feel the solidity of the walls; but taking each fresco and looking at it for its own sake only, one feels the keenest pleasure. They are magnificent pictures, full of individual character and realistic action, unsurpassable by any modern.

"I cannot attempt to put into words my impression of the cathedral itself. Certainly, I never felt the beauty of a church more. It being St. Michael's Day, we heard Mass in the midst of our wanderings, and we were much struck by the devotion of the people, the men especially—very unlike what we saw in Genoa. In the afternoon we had a glorious drive through a perfect pre-Raphaelite landscape to Belcaro, a fortress-villa about six miles outside Siena, every turn in the road giving us a new aspect of the golden-brown city behind us on its steep hill. Perhaps the most beautiful view of Siena is from near Belcaro, where you get the dark pine trees in the immediate foreground. The owner of the villa took us all over it, the Marchese gushing outrageously to him about the beauties of the dreadful frescoes on walls and ceilings, painted by the man himself. We had been warned, Alice and I, to express our admiration, but I regret to say we had our hearts so scooped out of us on seeing those things in the midst of such true loveliness that we couldn't say a thing, but only murmured. So the poor Marchese had to do triple-distilled gush to serve for three, and said everything was 'portentoso.'

"In the evening we all three went out again and, in the bright moonlight, strolled about the streets, the piazza, and round the cathedral, which shone in the full light which fell upon it. The deep sky was throbbing with stars, and all the essence of an Italian September moonlight night was there. Oh, sweet, restful Siena dream! Like a dream, and yet such a precious reality, to be gratefully kept in memory to the end."

Back at Castagnolo on October 1st. "Went for my *solita passeggiata* up to the hill of lavender and dwarf oak and other mountain shrubs, where I made a study of an oak bush on the only wet day we have had, for my *Inkermann* foreground. Mrs. Ross, a fearless rider, went on with the breaking in of the Arab colt 'Pascià' to-day. Old Maso, one of the *habitués* of the villa, whooped and screamed every time the colt bucked or reared, and he waddled away as fast as he could, groaning in terror, only to creep back again to venture another look. And he had been an officer in the army! I have secured some water-colour sketches of the vintage for the 'Institute' and knocked off another panel or two, and sketched Mrs. Ross in her Turkish dress, so I have not been idle." Janet Ross seemed to have assimilated the sunshine of Egypt and Italy into her buoyant nature, and to see the vigour with which she conducted the vintage at Castagnolo acted as a tonic on us all; so did the deep contralto voice and the guitar, and the racy talk.

We left on October 14th, on a golden day, with the thermometer at 90 degrees in the shade, to return to the icy smoke-twilight of London, where we groped, as the Diary says, in sealskins and ulsters. Castagnolo has our thanks. How could we have had the fulness of Italian delights which our kind hosts afforded us in some pension or hotel in Florence? And what hospitality theirs was! We tried to sing some of the "*Stornelli*" in the hansom that took us home from Victoria Station. One of our favourites, "*M'affacio alla finestra e vedo Stelle*," had to be modified, as we looked through the glass of the cab, into "*Ma non vedo Stelle*," sung in the minor, for nothing but the murk of a foggy night was there. What but the stern necessity of beginning *Inkermann* could have brought me back! My dear sister cannot have rejoiced, and may have wished to tarry, but when did she ever "put a spoke in my wheel"?

Balaclava
The Start

The finish

ONE OF THE BALAKLAVA SIX-HUNDRED.

Sowar 10th Bengal Lancers
Tentpegging
For "The Rivals."

"GOT IT. BRAVO!"

CHAPTER THIRTEEN
A SOLDIER'S WIFE

THOUGH the London winter was gloomy, on the whole, and I was handicapped in the middle of my work by a cold which retarded the picture so much that, to my deep disappointment, I had again to miss the Academy, the brightest spring of my life followed, for on March 3rd I was engaged to be married to the author of *The Great Lone Land*. It may not be out of place to give a little sketch of our rather romantic meeting.

When the newly-promoted Major Butler was lying at Netley Hospital, just beginning to recover from the Ashanti fever that had nearly killed him at the close of that campaign, his sister Frances used to read to him the papers, and they thus learnt together how, at the Royal Academy banquet of that spring, the Prince of Wales and the Duke of Cambridge had spoken as they did of Miss Elizabeth Thompson. As paper after paper spoke of me and of my work, he said one day to his sister, in utter fun under his slowly reviving spirits, "I wonder if Miss Thompson would marry me?" Two years after that he met me for the first time, and yet another year was to go by before the Fates said "Now!"

When *Inkermann* was carted off to Bond Street on April 19th, what a relief and delight it was to tell the model "Time is up." "Mamma and I danced about the studio when the picture was gone, revelling in our freedom to make as much dust as we liked, when hitherto one had had to be so careful about dust." We always did this on such occasions.

The Fine Art Society, at whose galleries in Bond Street the picture was exhibited, bought it and the copyright together. No doubt for some the subject of this work is too sad, but my dominant feeling in painting it was that which Wellington gave expression to in those memorable words on leaving the field of battle at Waterloo: "There is nothing sadder than a victory, except a defeat." It shows the remnants of the Guards and the 20th Regiment and odds and ends of infantry returning in the grey of a November evening from the "Soldiers' Battle," most of the men very weary. The A.D.C. on horseback I painted from a fine young soldier, Rupert Carrington, who kindly gave me a sitting. His mother, Lady Carrington, sent me as a wedding present a medal taken from a dead Russian on the field of Inkermann, set in a gold bracelet, which is one of my treasures, her name and mine engraved on it.

"*April 20th.*—The first Private View of *Inkermann*. I was there a short time, and was quite happy at the look of my picture. The other three are in the same gallery, and very popular the whole exhibition seems to be. They have even got my 1873 venture, *Missing*, by itself upstairs, and remarkably well it looks, too. The crowd was dense and I left the good people wriggling in a cloud of dust."

June 11th of that year, 1877, was my wedding day. Cardinal Manning married us in the Church of the Servite Fathers; our guests were chiefly that gallant group of soldiers who, with my husband, had won the Ashanti War, Sir Garnet Wolseley, Redvers Buller and their comrades. My "Red Cross" fellow students of old South Kensington days gave me the very touching surprise of strewing our path down the church, as we came out, with flowers. I had not known they were there.

And now a new country opened out for my admiration and delight in days so long before the dreadful cloud had fallen on it under which I am now writing these Recollections—so long, so long before. It looks like another world to me now. One might say I had had already a sufficiently large share of the earth's beauties to enjoy, yet here opened out an utterly new and unique experience—Ireland. Our wedding tour was chiefly devoted to the Wild West, with a pause at Glencar, in Kerry. I have tried in happier political times to convey to my readers in another place[8] my impression of that Western country—its freshness, its wild beauty, its entrancing poetry, and that sadness which, like the

minor key in music, is the most appealing quality in poetry.
That note is utterly absent from the poetry of Italy; there all
is in the major, like its national music, so that my mind
received, with strange delight, a new sensation, surprising,
heart-stirring, appealing. My husband had given me the
choice of a *local* for the wedding tour between Ireland and
the Crimea. How could I hesitate?

My first married picture was the one I made studies for in
Glencar—'*Listed for the Connaught Rangers*. I had splendid
models for the two Irish recruits who are being marched out
of the glen by a recruiting sergeant, followed by the "decoy"
private and two drummer boys of that regiment, the old
88th, with the yellow facings of that time. The men were
cousins, Foley by name, and wore their national dress, the
jacket with the long, white homespun sleeves and the picturesque black hat which I fear is little worn now, and is
largely replaced by that quite cosmopolitan peaked cap I
loathe. The deep richness of those typical Irish days of
cloud and sunshine had so enchanted me that I was deter-
mined to try and represent the effect in this picture, which
was a departure from my former ones, the landscape occu-
pying an equal share with the figures, and the civilian
peasant dress forming the centre of interest. Its black, white
and brown colouring, the four red coats and the bright
brass of the drum, gave me an enjoyable combination with
the blue and red-purple of the mountains in the background, and the sunlight on the middle distance of the
stony Kerry bog-land. Here was that variety as to local
colour denied me in the other works. It was a joy to realise
this subject. The picture was for Mr. Whitehead, the owner
of *Balaclava*.

The opening day of my introduction to the Wild West
was on a Sunday in that June: "From Limerick Junction to
Glencar. I had my first experience of an Irish Mass, and my
impression is deepening every day that Ireland is as much a
foreign country to England as is France or Italy. The con-
gregation was all new to me. The peasant element had

quite a *cachet* of its own, though in a way an exact equivalent to the Tuscan—the rough-looking men in homespun coats in a crowd inside and outside of the church, the women in national dress; the constabulary, equivalent to the *gendarmes*, in full dress, mixing with the people and yet not of them. This Limerick Junction was the nucleus of the Fenian nebula. In this terrible Tipperary the stalwart constabulary, whom I greatly admire, have a grave significance. I have never seen finer men than those, and they are of a type new to me. How I enjoy new types, new countries, new customs! The girls, looking so nice in their Bruges-like hoods, are very fresh and comely.

"We left at noon for the goal of our expedition, and I think I may say that I never had a more memorable little journey. The distant mountains I had looked at in the morning took clearer forms and colours by degrees, and the charm of the Irish bogs with their rich black and purple peat-earth, and bright, reedy grass, and teeming wild flowers, developed themselves to my delighted eyes as the train whirled us southwards. At Killarney we took a carriage and set off on my favourite mode of travel, soon entering upon tracts of that wild nature I was most anxious to experience. The evening was deepening, and in its solemn tones I saw for the first time the Wild West Land, whose aspect gradually grew wilder and more strange as we neared the mysterious mountains that rose ahead of us. I was content. I was beginning to taste the salt of the Wilds. What human habitations there are are so like the stone heaps that lie over the face of the land that they are scarcely distinguishable from them; but my 'contentment' was much dashed by the sight of the dwellers in this poor land which yields them so little. Very strange, wild figures came to the black doors to watch us pass, with, in some cases, half-witted looks.

"The mighty 'Carran Thual,' one of the mountain group which rises out of Glencar and dominates the whole land of Kerry, was on fire with blazing heather, its peaks sending up a glorious column of smoke which spread out at the top for miles and miles, and changed its delicate smoke tints every minute as the sun sank lower. As we reached the rocky pass that took us by the remote Lough Acoose that sun had gone down behind an opposite mountain, and the blazing heather glowed brighter as the twilight deepened, and circles of fire played weirdly on the mountain side. Our glen gave the 'Saxon bride' its grandest illumination on her arrival. Wild, strange birds rose from the bracken as we passed, and flew strongly away over lake and mountain torrent, and the little black Kerry cattle all watched us go by with ears pricked and heads inquiringly raised. The last stage of the journey had a brilliant *finale*. A herd of young horses was in our way in the narrow way, and the creatures careered before us, unable or too stupid to turn aside into the ditches by the roadside to let us through. We could not head them, and for fully a mile did those shaggy, wild things caper and jump ahead, their manes flying out wildly, with the glow from the west shining through them. Some imbecile cows soon joined them in the stampede, for no imaginable reason, unless they enjoyed the fright of being pursued, and the ungainly progress of those recruits was a sight to behold—tails in the air and horns in the dust. With this escort we entered Glencar."

Nothing that I have seen in my travels since that golden time has in the least dimmed my recollections of that Glencar existence; nor could anything jar against a thing so unique. I have fully recorded in my former book how we made different excursions, always on ponies, every day, not returning till the evening. What impressed me most during these rides was the depth and richness of the Irish landscape colouring. The moisture of the ocean air brings out all its glossy depth. Even without the help of actual sunshine, so essential to the landscape beauty of Italy, the local colour is powerful. In describing to me the same deep colouring in Scotland Millais used the simile of the wet pebble. Take a grey, dry pebble on the seashore and dip it in

the water. It will show many lovely tints. Our inn was in
the centre of the glen, delightfully rough, and impregnated
with that scent of turf smoke which has ever since been to
me the subtlest and most touching reminder of those days.
Yet with that roughness there was in the primitive little inn
a very pleasant provision of such sustenance as old cam-
paigners and fishermen know how to establish in the haunts
they visit.

The coast of Clare came next in our journey, where the
Atlantic hurls itself full tilt at the iron cliffs, and the west
wind, which I learnt to love, comes, without once touching
land since it left the coast of Labrador, to fill one with a
sense of salt and freshness and health as it rushes into one's
lungs from off the foam. I was interested in making comparisons between that sea and the other "sounding deep" that
washes the rocks of Porto Fino as I looked down on the
thundering waves below the cliffs of Moher. Here was the
simplest and severest colouring—dark green, almost
amounting to black; light green, cold and pure; foam so
pure that its whiteness had over it a rosy tinge, merely by
contrast with the green of the waves, and that was all;
whereas the sea around Porto Fino baffles both painter and
word-painter with its infinite variety of blues, purples, and
greens. These are contrasts that I delight in. How the west
wind rushed at us, full of spray! How the ocean roared! It
was a revel of wind where we stood at the very edge of
those sheer cliffs. Across their black faces sea birds incessantly circled and wheeled, crying with a shrill clamour.
That and the booming of the waves many fathoms below, as
they leap into the immense caverns, were the only sounds
that pierced the wind. The black rocks had ledges of greyer
rock, and along these ledges, tier above tier, sat myriads of
white-headed gulls, their white heads looking like illumination lamps on the faces of titanic buildings. The Isles of
Arran and the mountains of Connemara spread out before
us on the ocean, which sparkled in one place with the gold
beams of the faint, spray-shrouded sun.

Then good-bye to Erin for the present on July 15th and the establishment of ourselves in London till our return to the Land that held a magnet for us on September 21st. There we paid a visit to the Knight of Kerry, at Valentia Island. What a delightful home! The size of the fuchsia trees told of the mild climate; the scenery was of the remotest and freshest, most pleasing to the senses, and the ever-welcome scent of turf smoke would not be denied in the big house where the sods glowed in the great fireplaces. My surprise, when strolling on one of the innocent little strands by the sea, was great at seeing the Atlantic cable emerging, quite simply, from the water between the pebbles, as though it was nothing in particular. Following it, we reached a very up-to-date building, so out of keeping with the primitive scene, filled with busy clerks transmitting goodness knows what cosmopolitan corruption from the New World to the Old, and *vice versâ*.

I would not have missed the Valentia pig for anything. A taller, leaner, gaunter specimen has not his match anywhere, not even in the little black hog of Monte Cassino, whose salient hips are so unexpected. There is something particularly arresting in a pig with visible hips.[9] All the animals in the west seemed to me free-and-easy creatures that live with the peasants as members of the family, having a much better time than the humans. They frisk irresponsibly in and out of the cabins—no "by your leave" or "with your leave"—and, altogether, enjoy life to the top of their own highest level. The poorer the people, the greater appears the contrast caused by this inverted state of things.

The next time we left England was to go in the opposite direction—to the Pyrenees. Rapid travel is fast levelling down the different countries, and a carriage journey through the Pyrenean country is a bygone pleasure. We have to go to Thibet or the Great Wall of China for our trips if we want to write anything original about our travels. A flight by air to the North Pole would, at first, prove very readable and novel, if well described. This, however, does not take from the pleasure of going over the inner circle in memory. In the year 1878 we could still find much that was new and refreshing in a tour through the south of France! Some friends of mine went up to Khartoum from Cairo not long ago, with return tickets, by rail, and all they could say was that the journey was so dusty that they had to draw the blinds of their compartment and play bridge all the way. Poor dears, how arid!

This little tour of ours was well advised. The loss of our firstborn, Mary Patricia, brought our first sorrow with it, and we went to Lourdes and made a wide *détour* from there through the Pyrenees to Switzerland. There is nothing like travel for restoring the aching mind to usefulness. But, undoubtedly, the send-off from Lourdes gave me the initial impetus towards recovery of which, though I say little, I am very sensible. We drove to St. Sauveur after our visit to the Grotto where such striking cures have happened, and each day brought more fully back to me that zest for natural beauty which has been with me such an invigorator.

St. Sauveur was bracing and beautiful, but too full of invalids. It was rather saddening to see them around the Hontalade Sulphur Springs. At Lourdes they were clustering round the cascade that flows from the Grotto where the statue of Our Lady stands, exactly reproducing the figure as seen by the little Shepherdess. Poor humanity, reaching out hopeful arms in its pain, here for physical help, there for spiritual. The Gave rushes through both Lourdes and St. Sauveur, with a very sharp noise in the rocky gorge of the latter, too harsh to be a soothing sound. I looked forward to getting yet another experience of *vetturino* travel which I had never thought could be enjoyed again, and which proved to be still possible. The journey was a success, and, besides the beauty of that very majestic mountain scenery, the little incidents of the road were picturesque. Our driver was proud to tell us he was known as "*L'ancien chien des Pyrénées,*" and a characteristic "old dog" he was, one-eyed and weatherbeaten, wearing the national blue *béret* and very voluble in local *patois*. His horses' bells jingled in the old familiar way of my childhood; two absurd little dogs of his accompanied us all the way who, in the noonday heat, sat in the wayside streams for a moment to cool, and emerged little dripping rags. The first day's ascent was over the Pass of the Tourmalet, the second over that of the Col d'Aspin, and the third and final climb was that of the Col de Peyresourde. Then Bagnères de Luchon appeared deep down in the valley where our drive came to an end. What would we have seen of the Pyrenees if we had burrowed in tunnels under those *Cols?* Luchon was not embellished by the invalids there, whose principal ailment amongst the female patients was evidently a condition of *embonpoint* so remarkable that the suggestion of overfeeding could not possibly be ignored.

We had refreshing "*ascensions*" on horseback; a wide view of Spain from Super-Bagnère, wherein the backbone of the Pyrenees, with the savage "Maladetta," rising supreme, 11,000 feet above sea level, has its origin. Many very pleasant excursions we had besides. I tried a hurried sketch of one of these views from the saddle, the only precious chance I had, but a little Frenchman in tourist helmet and blue veil (and such boots and spurs!), who was riding in our direction with a party, threw himself off his pony into my foreground and, hoping to be included in the view which he was pretending to admire, posed there, right in my way, his comrades calling him in vain to rejoin them.

On leaving Luchon we journey *viâ* Toulouse to Cette, following the course of the Garonne, which famous river we had seen in its little muddy infancy near Arreau and in its culminating grandeur at Bordeaux. Toulouse looked majestic, a fair city as I remember it. There I was interested to see that famous canal which carries on the traffic from the great river to the Mediterranean. A noteworthy feature in the landscape as we journeyed on to Cette in the dreary, dun-coloured gloaming was the mediaeval city of Carcassonne. To come suddenly upon a complete restoration to life of an old-world city, full of towers and wrapped in its unbroken walls, gives one a strange sensation. One seems to be suddenly deposited in the heart of the Middle Ages. That dark evening there was something indescribably gloomy in the aspect of that cinder-coloured mass against an ashen sky, and set on a hill high above the fields cultivated in prim rows and patches, looking like a town in the background of some hunting scene, so often shown in old tapestry. All was darkening before an approaching storm. In writing of it at the time I was not aware that we owed this most precious old city to Viollet-le-Duc, who has restored it stone by stone.

Cette looked so bleared and blind the next morning in a sea mist that I have preserved a dejected impression of those low shores, grey tamarisks, and lagunes, and waste places, seen as though in a dismal dream. I was coaxed back to cheerfulness by the sunshine of Nîmes, where we spent several hours, on our way to our halt for the night, strolling in the warm-tinted Roman ruins, and I finally relaxed in the delight of our arriving once more at one of my most beloved cities, splendid Avignon. Good travelling. This closed the day. Under my parents' *régime*, and chiefly on account of my mother, who hated night travel, and on account of our general easy-going ways, we gave nearly a fortnight to reach Genoa from England, with pauses here and there.

My redundant Diary carries me on now, like the rapid Rhone itself, to my native Lake Leman. I see it now as I saw it that day, August 8th, 1878—a blue opal. There is always something sacred about a place in which one came into the world. We visited "Claremont," a lovely dwelling overlooking the lake, and facing the snowy ridges of the Dents du Midi. Looking at that house "all my mother came into my eyes" as I thought of her that November night, long ago, and of our dear, faithful nurse whom I captured there to our service till death, with a smile!

And now for the dear old Rhine once more. We got to

Bâle next day, and very scenic the old town looked on our arrival in the evening. On either side of the swift-flowing river the gabled houses were full of lights, which were reflected in the water, all looking red-gold by contrast with the green-gold of the moon. On August 10th from Bâle to Heidelberg, the rose-coloured city of the great Tun! Other tuns are also shown, not quite so capacious; but what swilling they suggest on the part of the old electors, who gathered all that hock in tithes!

I was mortified when trying to impress my husband with the charms of the Rhine as we dropped down to Cologne. My early Diary tells of my enchantment on that fondly-remembered river. But, alas! this time the weather was rainy and ugly all the way, and as we came to the best part, the romantic Gorge, he shut himself up in a deck cabin, out of which I could not entice him. I suspect the natives on board drove him in there rather than his resentment at the "come down" from the glowing descriptions one reads in travel books. These natives were a most irritating foreground to the blurred views. All day long, and into the night, meals were perpetually breaking out all over the deck and, do what one could, the feeding of those Teutons obtruded itself on one's attention *ad nauseam*. I have a sketch, taken *sub rosa*, of an obese and terrible *frau*, seated behind her rather smart officer husband at one of the little tables. She had emptied her capacious mug of beer, and was asking him for more, to which demand he was paying no attention. But "Gustav! Gustav!" she persisted, poking him in the back with her empty tankard. The "Gustav!" and the prods were getting too much to be ignored by the long-suffering back, and she got her refill. What General Gordon calls the "German visage" in contrast with the "Italian countenance" never appeared so surprisingly ugly as it did to us that day on the crowded deck of the *Queen of Prussia*.

My Diary says: "At Mayence, Will and I, always on the look-out for soldiers, had a good opportunity of seeing German infantry, as we stopped here a long time and two line battalions crossed the bridge near us. From the deck of the steamer the men looked big enough, but when Will ran on shore and overhauled them to have a nearer look, I could gauge their height by his six-foot-two. He showed a clear head and shoulders above their *pickelhauben*. They were short, chiefly by reason of the stumpy legs, which carry a long back—a very unbeautiful arrangement."

The next day we had a rather dull start from Cologne along a dismal stretch of river as far as Düsseldorf. Killing time at Düsseldorf is not lively. At the café where we had tea two young subalterns of hussars came gaily in to have their coffee, and, just as they were sitting down with a cav-alry swagger, there came in a major of some other corps, and the two immediately got up, saluted, and left the room. Here was discipline! On our returning to the steamer Will found an epauletted disciple of Bismarck in my place at sup-per. He told the epauletted one of his mistake, much to the latter's manifest astonishment, who didn't move. I suppose there came something into the British soldier's eye, but, anyway, the sabre-rattler eventually got up and went else-where: things felt electric.

August 14th found us nearly all day on board the boat. "A very interesting day, showing me a phase of Rhine scenery familiar to me in Dutch pictures by the score, but never seen by me till then in reality. The strong wind blew from the sea and tossed the green-yellow river into tumul-tuous waves, over which came bounding the blunt-bowed craft from Holland, taking merchandise up stream, and dif-fering in no way from the boats beloved of the old Dutch masters. On either side of the river were low banks waving with rushes, and beyond stretched sunken marshy meadows, and here and there quaint little towns glided by with wind-mills whirring, and clusters of ships' masts appearing above the grey willows and sedges. Dordrecht formed a perfect picture *à la* Rembrandt, with a host of windmills on the sky-line, telling dark against the brightness, at the confluence of the Maes and Rhine. Here Cuyp was born, the painter of sunlit cows. Rotterdam pleased us greatly, and we strolled about in the evening, coming upon the statue of Erasmus, which I place amongst the most admirable statues I have seen. Rotterdam possesses in rich abundance the peculiar charm of a seaport. A place of this kind has for me a very strong attraction. The varied shipping, the bustle on land and water, the colour, the noise, the mixture of human types, the bustle of men and animals; all these things have always filled me with pleasure at a great seaport." A visit to Holland ("the dustless" land, as my husband called it truly), a revel amongst the Amsterdam galleries, then Antwerp, where we embarked for Harwich, closed our trip. Invigorated and restored, I set to work on an 8-foot canvas, whereon I painted a subject which had been in my mind since childhood.

CHAPTER FOURTEEN

QUEEN VICTORIA

IT must have been at Villa de' Franchi that my father related to me a tragedy which had profoundly moved England in the year 1842, and he laughingly encouraged me to paint it when I should be grown up. The Diary says: "We are now at war with poor Shere Ali, and this new Afghan War revived for me the idea of the tragedy of '42, namely, Dr. Brydon reaching Jellalabad, weary and fainting, on his dying horse, the sole survivor, as was then thought, from our disaster in the Cabul passes...Here I am, on 1st March, 1879, not doing badly with the picture. I think it is well painted, and I hope poetical. But I have had the darkest winter I can remember, and lost nearly all January by the succession of fogs which have accompanied this long frost. Will sailed under orders for the Cape last Friday, February 28th. Our terrible defeat at Isandula has caused the greatest commotion here, and regiments are being poured out of England to Zululand in a fleet of transports; and now staff officers are being selected for posts of great responsibility out there, and amongst these is Colonel Butler, A.A.G. to General Clifford.

"*March 16th, 1879.*—I am beginning to show my picture. Scarcely anything is talked of still but the fighting in Zululand and the incapacity of that poor unfortunate Lord Chelmsford, whom Government keeps telling they will continue to trust in his supreme post of Commander-in-Chief, though he would evidently be thankful to be relieved of an anxiety which his nervous temperament and susceptible nature must make unbearable. What magnificent subjects for pictures the defence of Rorke's Drift will furnish. When we get full details I shall be much tempted to paint some episode of that courageous achievement which has shed balm on the aching wound of Isandula. But the temptation will have to be very strong to make me break my rule of not painting contemporary subjects. I like to mature my themes.

"Studio Sunday. At last, at last! After three years of disappointment another Academy Studio Show has come, and that very brightly and successfully. I have called the Afghan picture *The Remnants of an Army*. I had the Irish picture to show also, by permission of Whitehead, *'Listed for the Connaught Rangers*. From one till six to-day people poured in. My studio was got up quite charmingly with curtains and screens, and with wild beast skins disposed on the floor, and my arms and armour furbished up. The two pictures came out well, and both appeared to 'take.' However, not much value can be attached to to-day's praises to my face. But I must not let Elmore's (R.A.) tribute to the *Remnants of an Army* go unrecorded. 'It is impossible to look at that man's face unmoved,' and his eyes were positively dimmed! I have heard it said that no one was ever known to shed tears before a picture. On reading a book, on hearing music, yes, but not on seeing a painting. Well! that is not true, as I have proved more than once. I can't resist telling here of a pathetic man who came to me to say, 'I had a wet eye when

I saw your picture!' He had one eye brown and the other blue, and I almost asked, 'Which, the brown or the blue?' It is often so difficult to know what to answer appreciatively to enthusiastic and unexpected praise!

"Varnishing Day. A long and cheery day in those rooms of happy memory at Burlington House. Both my pictures are well hung and look well, and congratulations flowed in." A few days later: "Alice and I to the Private View at that fascinating Burlington House, so fascinating when one's works are well placed! The Press is treating me very well. No subsidised puffs *here*, so I enjoy these critiques. The Academy has received me back with open arms, and the members are very nice to me, some of them expressing their hope that I am pleased with the positions of my pictures, and several of them speaking quite openly about their determination to vote for me at the next election."

The Fine Art Society bought the Afghan subject of which they published a very faithful engraving, and it is now at the Tate Gallery. It is a comfort to me to know that nearly all my principal works are either in the keeping of my Sovereign or in public galleries, and not changing hands among private collectors.

I spent much of a cool, if rainy, summer at Edenbridge, in Kent, taking a rose bower of a cottage there, my parents with me. There we heard in the papers the dreadful news of the Prince Imperial's death. Then followed a hasty line from my husband, written in a fury of indignation from Natal, at the sacrifice of "the last of the Napoleons." When he returned at long last from the deplorable Zulu War, followed by the Sekukuni Campaign, the poor Empress Eugénie sent for him to Camden Place, and during a long and most painful interview she asked for all details, her tears flowing all the time, and in her open way letting all her sorrow loose in paroxysms of grief. He had managed the funeral and embarkatioon at Durban. The pall was covered with artificial violets which he had asked the nuns there to make, at high pressure, and he subsequently described to me the impressive sight of the *cortège* as it wound down the hill to the port off Durban, in the afternoon sunshine.

At little Edenbridge I was busy making studies of any grey horses I could find, as I had already begun my charge of the Scots Greys at Waterloo at my studio. That charge I called "*Scotland for Ever!*," and I owe the subject to an impulse I received that season from the Private View at the Grosvenor Gallery, now extinct. The Grosvenor was the home of the "Æsthetes" of the period, whose sometimes unwholesome productions preceded those of our modern "Impressionists." I felt myself getting more and more annoyed while perambulating those rooms, and to such a point of exasperation was I impelled that I fairly fled and, breathing the honest air of Bond Street, took a hansom to my studio. There I pinned a 7-foot sheet of brown paper on an old canvas and, with a piece of charcoal and a piece of white chalk, flung the charge of "The Greys" upon it. Dr. Pollard, who still looked in during my husband's absences as he used to do in my maiden days to see that all was well with me, found me in a surprising mood.

On returning from my *villeggiatura* in Kent with my parents I took up again the painting of this charge, and one day the Keeper of the Queen's Privy Purse, Sir Henry Ponsonby, called at the studio to ask me if I would paint a picture for Her Majesty, the subject to be taken from a war of her own reign.

Of course, I said "Yes," and gladly welcomed the honour, but being a slow worker, I saw that "*Scotland for Ever!*" must be put aside if the Queen's picture was to be ready for the next Academy.

Every one was still hurrahing over the defence of Rorke's Drift in Zululand as though it had been a second Waterloo. My friends (not my parents) urged and urged. I demurred, because it was against my principles to paint a conflict. In the "Greys" the enemy was not shown, here our men would have to be represented at grips with the foe. No, I put that subject aside and proposed one that I felt and saw in my mind's eye most vividly. I proposed this to the Queen—the finding of the dead Prince Imperial and the bearing of his body from the scene of his heroic death on the lances of the 17th Lancers. Her Majesty sent me word that she approved, to my great relief. I began planning that most impressive composition. Then I got a message to say the Queen thought it better not to paint the subject. What was to be done? The Crimea was exhausted. Afghanistan? But I was compelled by clamour to choose the popular Rorke's Drift; so, characteristically, when I yielded I threw all my energies into the undertaking.

When the 24th Regiment, now the South Wales Borderers, who in that fight saved Natal, came home, some of the principal heroes were first summoned to Windsor and then sent on to me, and as soon as I could get down to Portsmouth, where the 24th were quartered, I undertook to make all the studies from life necessary for the big picture there. Nothing that the officers of the regiment and the staff could possibly do to help me was neglected. They even had a representation of the fight acted by the men who took part in it, dressed in the uniforms they wore on that awful night. Of course, the result was that I reproduced the event as nearly to the life as possible, but from the soldier's point of view—I may say the *private's* point of view—not mine, as the principal witnesses were from the ranks. To be as true to facts as possible I purposely withdrew my own view of the thing. What caused the great difficulty I had to grapple with was the fact that the whole mass of those fighting figures was illuminated by firelight from the burning hospital. Firelight transforms colours in an extraordinary way which you hardly realise till you have to reproduce the thing in paint.

The Zulus were a great difficulty. I had them in the composition in dark masses, rather swallowed up in the shade, but for one salient figure grasping a soldier's bayonet to twist it off the rifle, as was done by many of those heroic savages. My excellent Dr. Pollard got me a sort of Zulu as model from a show in London. It was unfortunate that a fog came down the day he was brought to my studio, so that at one time I could see nothing of my dusky savage but the whites of his eyes and his teeth. I hope I may never have to go through such troubles again!

When the picture was in its pale, shallow, early stage, the Queen, who was deeply interested in its progress, wished to see it, and me. So to Windsor I took it. The Ponsonbys escorted me to the Great Gallery, where I beheld my production, looking its palest, meanest, and flattest, installed on an easel, with two lords bending over it—one of them Lord Beaconsfield.

Exeunt the two lords, right, through a dark side door. Enter the Queen, left. Prince Leopold, Duchess of Argyll, Princess Beatrice and others grouped round the easel, centre. The Queen came up to me and placed her plump little hand in mine after I had curtseyed, and I was counselled to give Her Majesty the description of every figure. She spoke very kindly in a very deep, guttural voice, and showed so much emotion that I thought her all too kind, shrinking now and then as I spoke of the wounds, etc. She told me how she had found my husband lying at Netley Hospital after Ashanti, apparently near his end, and spoke with warmth of his services in that campaign. She did not leave us until I had explained every figure, even the most distant. She knew all by name, for I had managed to show, in that scuffle, all the V.C.'s and other conspicuous actors in the drama, the survivors having already been presented to her. Majors Chard and Bromhead were sufficiently recognisable in the centre, for I had had them both for their portraits.

The Academicians put *The Defence of Rorke's Drift* in the Lecture Room of unhappy *Quatre Bras* memory, no doubt for the same reason they gave in the case of that picture. Yes, there was a great crush before it, but I was not satisfied as to its effect in that poor light. It is now with *The Roll Call* at St. James's Palace. I learnt later how very, very pleased the Queen was with her commission, and that one day at

Windsor, wishing to show it to some friends, the twilight deepening, she showed so much appreciation that she took a pair of candlesticks and held them up at the full stretch of her arms to light the picture. I like to see in my mind's eye that Rembrandtesque effect, with the principal figure in the group our Queen. She wanted me to paint her two other subjects, but, somehow, that never came off.

CHAPTER FIFTEEN

OFFICIAL LIFE—THE EAST

IN 1880 my husband was offered the post of Adjutant-General at Plymouth, and thither we went in time, with the pretty little infant Elizabeth Frances, who came to fill the place of the sister who was gone. There three more of our children were born.

I took up *"Scotland for Ever!"* again, and in the bright light of our house on the Hoe, with never a brown fog to hinder me, and with any amount of grey army horses as models, I finished that work. It was exhibited alone. It is quite unnecessary to burden my readers with the reason of this. I was very sorry, as I expected rather a bright effect with all those white and grey galloping *hippogriffes* bounding out of the Academy walls. There was a law suit in question, and there let the matter rest. Messrs. Hildesheimer bought the copyright from me, and the picture I sold, later on, to a private purchaser, who has presented it to the city of Leeds. By a happy chance I had a supply of very brilliant Spanish white (*blanco de plata*) for those horses, and though I have ever since used the finest *blanc d'argent*, made in Paris, I don't think the Spanish white has a rival. Perhaps its maker took the secret with her to the Elysian Fields. It was an old widow of Seville.

On May 11th of that year our beloved father died, comforted with the heartening rites of the Church. He had been received not long before the end.

Life at "pleasant Plymouth" was very interesting in its way, and the charm of the West Country found in me the heartiest appreciation. But the climate is relaxing, and conducive to lotus eating. One seems to live in a mental Devonshire cream of pleasant days spent in excursions on land and water, trips up the many lovely rivers, or across the beautiful Sound to various picnic rendezvous on the coast. There was much festivity: balls in the winter and long excursions in summer, frequently to the wilds of Dartmoor. Particularly pleasant were the receptions at Government House under the auspices of the Pakenhams—perfect hosts—and at the Admiralty, with its very distinguished host and hostess, Sir Houston and Lady Stewart. Over Dartmoor there spread the charm of the unbounded hospitality of the Mortimer Colliers, who lived on the verge of the moor, and this was a thing ever to be fondly remembered. No pleasanter house could offer one a welcome than "Foxhams," and how hearty a welcome that always was!

Riding was our principal pleasure. I never spent more enjoyable days in the saddle elsewhere. My husband and I had a riding tour through Cornwall—just the thing I liked most. But he was from time to time called away. To Egypt in 1882, for Tel-el-Kebir; twice to Canada, the second time on Government business; and in 1884 to the great Gordon Relief Expedition, that terrible tragedy, made possible by the maddening delays at home. I illustrated the book he wrote[10] on that colossal enterprise, so wantonly turned into failure from quite feasible success.

My next picture was on a smaller scale than its predecessors, and was exhibited at the Academy in 1882. The Boer War, with its terrible Majuba Hill disaster, had attracted all our sorrowful attention the year before to South Africa, and I chose the attack on Laing's Nek for my subject. The two Eton boys whom I show, Elwes and Monck, went forward (Elwes to his death) with the cry of *Floreat Etona!* and I gave the picture those words for its title.

Yet another Lord Mayor's Banquet at the Mansion House, in honour of the Royal Academicians, saw me late in 1881 a guest once more in those gilded halls, this time by my husband's side. He responded for the Army, and joined Arts and Arms in a bright little speech, composed *impromptu*. "We were a highly honoured couple," I read in the Diary, "and very glad that we came up. We must have sat at that festive board over three hours. The music all through was exceedingly good and, indeed, so was the fare. The homely tone of civic hospitality is so characteristic, dressed as it is with gold and silver magnificence, rivalling that of Royalty itself! One of the waiters tried to press me to have a second helping of whitebait by whispering in my ear the seductive words, '*Devilled*, ma'am.' It was a fiery edition of the former recipe. I resisted."

The departure of my husband with Lord Wolseley (then Sir Garnet) and Staff for Egypt on August 5th, 1882, to suppress poor old Arabi and his "rebels" was the most trying to me of all the many partings, because of its dramatic setting. One bears up well on a crowded railway platform, but when it comes to watching a ship putting off to sea, as I did that time at Liverpool, to the sound of farewell cheering and 'Auld Land Syne,' one would sooner read of its pathos than suffer it in person. Soldiers' wives in war time have to feel the sickening sensation on waking some morning when news of a fight is expected of saying to themselves, "I may be a widow." Not only have I gone through that, but have had a second period of trial with two sons under fire in the World War.

I gave a long period of my precious time to making preparations for a large picture representing Wolseley and his Staff reaching the bridge across the canal at the close of the battle of Tel-el-Kebir, followed by his Staff, wherein figured my husband. The latter had not been very enthusiastic about the subject. To beat those poor *fellaheen* soldiers was not a matter for exultation, he said; and he told me that the capture of Arabi's earthworks had been like "going through brown paper." He thought the theme unworthy, and hoped I would drop the idea. But I wouldn't; and, seeing me bent on it, he did all he could to help me to realise the scene I had chosen. Lord Wolseley gave me a fidgety sitting at their house in London, his wife trying to keep him quiet on her knee like a good boy. I had crowds of Highlanders to represent, and went in for the minutest rendering of the equipment then in use. Well, I never was so long over a work. Depend upon it, if you do not "see" the thing vividly before you begin, but have to build it up as you go along, the picture will not be one of your best. Nor was this one! It was exhibited in the Academy of 1885, and had a moderate success. It was well engraved.

In the September of 1884 my husband left for the Gordon Expedition, having finished his work of getting boats ready for the cataracts, boats to carry the whole Army. In the following June he came home on leave, well in health, in spite of rending wear and tear, but deeply hurt at the failure of what might have been one of the greatest campaigns in modern history. How he had urged and urged, and fumed at the delays! He told me the campaign was lost *three times over*. Gordon was simply sacrificed to ineptitude in high quarters at home. In this connection, I ask, can praise be too great for the British rank and file who did *their* best in this unparalleled effort? You saw Lifeguardsmen plying their oars in the boats, oars they had never handled before this call; marines mounted on camels—more than "horse-marines," as a camel in his movements is five horses rolled into one; everything he was called upon to do the British soldier did to the best of his capacity.

We spent most of my husband's precious leave in Glencar. What better haven to come to from the feverish toil on river and in desert, ending in bitter disappointment? We went to Court functions, also. How these functions amused me, and how I revelled in their colour, in their variety of types brought together, all these guests in national uniform or costume. And I must be allowed to add how proud I was

of my six-foot-two soldier in all his splendour. The Queen's
aide-de-camp uniform, which he wore at the time of which
I am writing, till he was promoted major-general, was particularly well designed, both for "dress" and "undress." I
frankly own I loved these Court Receptions. No, I was
never bored by them, I am thankful to say; and I don't
believe any woman is who has the luck to go there, whatever she may say.

CHAPTER SIXTEEN

TO THE EAST

I FOLLOWED my husband to Egypt, where he had
returned, in command at Wady Halfa on the expiration
of his leave, on November 14th, 1885. I went with our
eldest little boy and girl. A new experience for me—the
East! One of my longings in childhood was to see the East.
There it was for me.

Cairo in 1885 still retained much of its Oriental aspect
in the European quarter. (I don't suppose the old, true
Cairo will ever change.) I was just in time. The Shepheard's
Hotel of that day had a terrace in front of it where we used
to sit and watch the life of the street below, an occupation
very pleasing to myself. The building was overrun with a
wealth of flowering creepers of all sorts of loveliness, and
surrounded with a garden. When next we visited Cairo the
creepers were being torn down, and the terrace demolished.
Then a huge hotel was run up in avaricious haste to reap
the next season's harvest from the thronging visitors, and
now stands flush with the street to echo the trams.

It is difficult for me now to revive in memory the exquisite surprise I felt when first I saw the life of the East. I could
hardly believe the thing was real, everyday life. Though I
have often returned to Egypt since, that first-time feeling
never was renewed, though my enjoyment of Oriental
beauty and picturesqueness never, I am glad to say, faded in

the least. Oh, you who enjoy the zest of life, be thankful that you possess it! It is a thing not to be acquired, but to be born with. I think artists keep it the longest, for it enters the heart by the eye. The long letters I wrote to my mother on the spot and at the moment I incorporated later in the little book already referred to. Oh, the pleasures of memory, streaked with sadness though they must be, and with ugly things of all kinds, too! Still, how intensely precious a possession they are when *weeded*. To me, after Italy and, of course, the Holy Land, give me the Nile.

I and the children remained in Cairo till I got my husband's message from the front that the way was clear enough for our journey as far as Luxor. There I and the children remained until the fight at Giniss was won and all danger was over further up stream. At Luxor began the most enjoyable of all modes of travel—by houseboat. The *dahabiyeh Fostat* was sent down from Wady Halfa to take us up to Assouan, where my husband awaited us. We had reached Luxor from Cairo by the commonplace post boat. The Assouan Dam was, of course, not in existence, and our *dahabiyeh* had to be hauled in the old way through the first cataract, while we transferred ourselves to another *dahabiyeh* moored off the now submerged island of Philæ.

This cut-and-dried chronicle includes one of the most enchanting experiences of my life. Above Philæ we entered Nubia, before whose intensified colouring the lower desert pales. Time being very precious to my husband, our slow, dreamy sailing houseboat had to be towed by a little steamer for the rest of the way to Wady Halfa, where we lived till the heat of March warned us that I and the children must prudently go into northern coolness. And to Plymouth we returned, leaving the General to drag out the burning summer at Wady Halfa in such heat as I never had had to suffer. While at Halfa I made many sketches in oil for my picture, *A Desert Grave*, out in the desert across the river. It is very trying painting in the desert on account of the wind, which blows the sand perpetually into your eyes. With that and the glare, I took two inflamed eyes back with me to Europe. The picture should have been more poetical than it turned out to be, and I wish I could repaint it now. It was well placed at the Academy. The Upper Nile had these graves of British officers and men all along its banks during that terrible toll taken in the course of the Gordon Expedition and after, some in single loneliness, far apart, and some in twos and threes. These graves had to be made exactly in the same way as those of the enemy, lest a cross or some other Christian mark should invite desecration.

The World War has thrown a dreadful cloud between us and those old war days, but the cloud in time will spread out thinner and let us look through to those past times.

My next experience was Brittany. Thither we went for a rest, and to give the children the habit of talking French. At Dinan, in an old farmhouse, we ruralised amidst orchards and amongst the Breton peasantry. Very nice and quiet and healthy. There our youngest boy was born, Martin William, who was immediately inscribed on the army books as liable for service in the French Army if he reached the age of eighteen on French soil. During that part of our stay at Dinan I painted the 24th Dragoons, who were stationed there, leaving the town by the old Porte St. Malo for the front, a great crowd of people seeing them off. I had mounted dragoons and peasants for the asking as models.

My husband was knighted—K.C.B.—in this interval, at Windsor. We went to live in Ireland from Dinan, in 1888, under the Wicklow Mountains, where the children continued their healthy country life in its fulness. The picture I had painted of the departing dragoons went to the Academy in 1889, and in 1890 I exhibited *An Eviction in Ireland,* which Lord Salisbury was pleased to be facetious about in his speech at the banquet, remarking on the "breezy beauty" of the landscape, which almost made him wish he could take part in an eviction himself. How like a Cecil!

The 'eighties had seen our Government do some dreadful things in the way of evictions in Ireland. Being at

Glendalough at the end of that decade, and hearing one day that an eviction was to take place some nine miles distant from where we were staying for my husband's shooting, I got an outside car and drove off to the scene, armed with my paints. I met the police returning from their distasteful "job," armed to the teeth and very flushed. On getting there I found the ruins of the cabin smouldering, the ground quite hot under my feet, and I set up my easel there. The evicted woman came to search among the ashes of her home to try and find some of her belongings intact. She was very philosophical, and did not rise to the level of my indignation as an ardent English sympathiser. However, I studied her well, and on returning home at Delgany I set up the big picture which commemorates a typical eviction in the black 'eighties. I seldom can say I am pleased with my work when done, but I *am* complacent about this picture; it has the true Irish atmosphere, and I was glad to turn out that landscape successfully which I had made all my studies for, on the spot, at Glendalough. What storms of wind and rain, and what dazzling sunbursts I struggled in, one day the paints being blown out of my box and nearly whirled into the lake far below my mountain perch! My canvas, acting like a sail, once nearly sent me down there too. I did not see this picture at all at the Academy, but I am very certain it cannot have been very "popular" in England. Before it was finished my husband was appointed to the command at Alexandria, and as soon as I had packed off the *Eviction*, I followed, on March 24th, and saw again the fascinating East.

My journey took me *viâ* Venice, where the P. & O. boat *Hydaspes* was waiting. Can any journey to Egypt be more charming than this one, right across Italy?

Oh! you who do not think a journey a mere means of getting to your destination as quickly as possible, say, if you have taken the Milan-Verona-Padua line, is there anything in all Italy to surpass that burst on the view of the Lago di Garda after you emerge from the Lonato tunnel? On a blue day, say in spring? If you have not gone that way yet, I beg you to be on the look-out on your left when you do go. This wonderful surprise is suddenly revealed, and almost as quickly lost. Waste not a second. I put up at the "Angleterre" at Venice, on the Riva, because from there one sees the lagunes and glimpses of the open sea beyond, and the air is open and fresh.

"*March 28th.*—Took gondola for the big P. & O. S.S. which is to be my home for the next six days. I at once saw the ship was one of their smartest boats, and all looked very festive on board. Luncheon was served immediately after my arrival, and I found a bright company thereat assembled, with Sir Henry and Lady Layard at their head; some come to see friends off and others to go on. We amalgamated very pleasantly, and great was the waving of handkerchiefs as we slowly steamed past the Dogana and the Riva, our returning friends having gone on shore in gondolas whose sable sides were hidden in brilliant draperies. The sashes of the gondoliers' liveries flashed in coloured silks and gold fringes; the sea sparkled. I rejoiced. The Montalba girls gave us a salvo of pocket handkerchiefs from their balcony on the Giudecca. What a gay scene! Lady Layard, on leaving, introduced Mrs. H.M., who was to join her husband at Brindisi for a long trip in the big liner from England, and I was very happy at the prospect of her pleasant and intellectual companionship thus far."

And so we passed out in the early night on the dim Adriatic, after a sunset farewell to Venice, which remains to me as one of the tenderest visions of the past. That voyage to Alexandria is more enjoyable, given fair weather, than most voyages, because one is hardly ever out of sight of land, and such classic land, too! The Ionian Islands, "Morea's Hills," Candia. But what a pleasure it is to see on the day before the arrival the signs that the landing is near at hand. The General in Command will be waiting at sunrise on the landing stage, perhaps the light catching the gold lace on his cap, appearing above the turbans of the native crowd.

Of course every one who has been to Egypt knows the feeling of disappointment at the first sight of its shores, low-lying and fringed with those incongruous windmills which the Great Napoleon vainly planted there to teach the natives how better to make flour. In vain. And so were his wheelbarrows. The natives preferred carrying the mud in their hands. And the city, how it fails to give you the Oriental impression you are longing for, with its pseudo-Italian architecture, its hard paved streets, and dusty boulevards and squares. Government House on the Boulevard de Ramleh was comfortable, roomy and airy, but I missed the imagined garden and palm trees of the Cairo official residence.

"*April 3rd.*—We have a view of Cleopatra's Tomb (so called) to the right, jutting out into the intensely blue sea, but the other arm of the bay (the old Roman harbour) to our left, covered with native houses and minarets, is partly hidden by an abomination which hurts me to exasperation, one of those amorphous buildings of tenth-rate Italian vulgarity and dreariness which are being run up here in such quantities, and rears its gaunt expanse close behind this house. To cap this erection it has received the title of 'Bombay Castle.' Never mind, I shall soon, in my happy way, cease to notice what I don't like to see, and shall enjoy all that is left here of the original East and its fascinating barbaric beauty. Will took me for a most interesting drive, first to Ras-el-Tin, during which we threaded a conglomeration of East and West which was bewildering. There were nightmarish Italian '*palazzi*' loaded with cheap, bluntly-moulded stucco; glaring streets, cafés, dusty gardens, over-dressed Jewish and Levantine women driving about in exaggerated hats, frocks and figures; and there also appeared the dark narrow bazaars and original streets, the latticed windows, the finely-coloured robes of the natives, the weird goats, the wolfish dogs, straying about in all directions. Mounds of rubbish everywhere; some only the leavings of newly-built houses, some the remains of the bombardment's havoc, oth-

ers the dust of a once beautiful city whose loveliness in old
Roman times must have been supreme.

"Only here and there was I reminded of the charm of
Cairo—a tree by a yellow wall, a group of natives eating
sugar cane, a water-seller with his tinkling brass cups and a
rose behind his ear, and so on. We then had a really enjoyable drive along the Mahmoudieh Canal, which was balm
to my mind and eyes. All along the placid water on the
opposite bank ran Arab villages with their accompaniments
of palms, buffaloes, goats, water jars, native men and
women in scriptural robes; water wheels; square-shaped,
almost windowless mud dwellings, so appropriate under
that intense light. On our bank were the remnants of
Pashadom in the shape of gimcrack palaces closed and let
go to ruin, on account of fashion having betaken itself to
the suburb of Ramleh. These dwellings were, however, so
hidden in deep tropical gardens of great and rich beauty
that they did not offend.

"Beyond the Arab villages on the other bank appeared
Lake Mareotis, and there was a poetical feeling about all
that region. It was so strange to have on one side of a narrow band of water old Egypt and the life of the East going
on just as it has been for ages past, and on the other the
ephemeral tokens of the sham and fleeting life to-day, and
this all the way along a drive of some two miles. This is the
fashionable drive, and to see young Egypt on horseback,
and old Jewry in carriages, passing and repassing up and
down this cosmopolitan Rotten Row is decidedly trying.
My admired friends, the running syces, though, redeem the
thing to me. Their dress is one of the most perfect in shape,
colour and material ever devised. The air was rich with the
scent of strange flowers, some of which billowed over
entrance gates in magnificent purple masses."

I must be excused for having shown irritation in my
Diary at starting. I soon adapted myself to the entourage,
and I hope I "did my manners" as became my official
responsibilities. I liked the Greeks best of all—nay, I got

very fond of these handsome, sunny people.

It was a curiously cosmopolitan society, and I, who am never good at remembering the little feuds that are always simmering in this kind of mixed company, must have sometimes made mistakes. I heard a Greek woman, who had dined with us the previous evening, informing her friends in a voice fraught with meaning, "*Imaginez, hier au soir chez le Général Monsieur Gariopulo a donné le bras à Madame Buzzato!*" The recipients of this information were filled with mirth. What *had* I done in pairing off these two for the procession to dinner?

The British were entrenched at Ramleh. The little stations on the railway there gave me quite a turn at first sight. One was "Bulkley," the next "Fleming," then "Sydney O. Schutz," and finally San Stefano at railhead, and a casino with a corrugated iron roof under that scorching sun. Oh, that I should see such a thing in Egypt! Cheek by jowl with the little villas one saw weird Bedouin tents and wild Arabs and their animals, carrying on their existence as if the Briton had never come there.

The incongruities of Alexandria became to me positively enjoyable; and the desert air, as ever, was life-giving. My little Syrian horse, "Minnow," carried me many a mile alongside my husband's charger, over that pleasant desert sand. But an occasional khamseen wind gave me a taste of the disagreeable phase of Egyptian weather. I name, with the vivid recollection of the khamseen's irritating qualities, the experience of paying calls (in a nice toilette) under its suffocating puffs. And how the flies swarm; how they settle in black masses on the sweetmeats sold in the streets, and hang in tassels from the native children's eyes. Oh yes, there *is* a seamy side to all things, but it isn't my way to turn it up more than is necessary. Here may follow a bit of Diary:

"*May 22nd.*—We had a memorable picnic at Rosetta today, with thirty of the English colony. I had long wished to visit this ancient city, brick-built and half deserted, a once opulent place, but now mournful in its decay. I longed to see old Nile once more. We chartered a special train and left Moharram Bey Station at 8 a.m. I was much pleased with the seaside desert and the effects of mirage over Aboukir Bay. The ancient town of Edkou struck me very much. It was built of the small brown Rosetta brick, and was placed on a hill, giving it a different aspect from the usual Arab pale-walled villages which are usually built on level ground. It had thus a peculiar character. Shortly before reaching Rosetta the land becomes richly cultivated. There is a subtle beauty about the cultivated regions of this fascinating land of Egypt which I feel very much. It is the beauty of abundance and richness as well as of vivid colour.

"At Rosetta dense crowds of natives awaited us and some police were detailed to escort us through the town. I heard some of the women of our party wishing they could pick the blue tiles off the minarets, but for my part I prefer them under their lovely sky and sunshine, rather than ornamenting mantelpieces in a Kensington fog. A little *musharabieh* lattice is still left here in the windows and has not yet been taken to grace the British drawing-rooms of Ramleh. We strolled about the bazaars and into the old ramshackle mosques, and, altogether, exhausted the sights. Everywhere in Rosetta you see beautiful little Corinthian marble columns incorporated with the Arab buildings, and supporting the ceilings and pulpits of the mosques. They are daubed over with red plaster. Very often a rich Corinthian capital is used as a base to a pillar by being turned upside down, so that the shaft, crowned with its own capital, possesses two—one at each end—an arrangement evidently satisfactory to the barbarian Arabs who succeeded the classic builders of the old city. Almost every angle of a house has a Greek column acting as corner stone. But the brown brickwork is very dismal, and but for the vivid colours of the people's dresses the monotony of tone would be displeasing. This is Bairam, and the people during the three days' feast succeeding the dismal Ramadam Fast are in their most radiant dresses, and revelry and feasting are going on everywhere. Such a mass of moving colour as was the market-place of Rosetta to-day these eyes, that have seen so much, never looked upon before.

"At last, when we had climbed into enough mosques and poked about into houses, and through all the bazaars (the fish bazaar was trying), we went down to the landing stage and took boat for the trysting place, about a mile up the broad, wind-lashed Nile. Will and the Bishop of Clifton, sole remaining straggler from the late pilgrimage to the Holy Land, and half our party had gone on before us; and, after a quick sail along the palm-fringed bank, we arrived at the pretty landing place chosen for our picnic. We found a tent pitched and the servants busy laying the cloth under a dense sycamore, close to an old mosque whose onion-shaped dome and Arab minaret gave me great pleasure as we came in sight of them. I was impatient to make a sketch. I lost no time, and went off and established myself in a palm grove with my water colours. The usual Egyptian drawbacks, however, were there—flies, and puffs of sand blown into one's eyes and powdering one's paints. On the Mahmoudieh Canal I am exempt from the sand nuisance, and nothing can be pleasanter than my experience there, sitting in an open carriage with the hood up, and not a soul to bother me.

"Our return to Rosetta was lively. As we were then going against the wind, we had to be towed from the shore, and it was very interesting to watch the agility of our crew dodging in and out of the boats moored under the bank and deftly disengaging the tow-rope from the spars and rigging of these vessels. A tall Circassian *effendi* of police cantered on his little Arab along the bank to see that all went well with us. The other half of our party chose to sail and progress by laborious tacking from one side of the wide river to the other, and arrived long after we did. We all met at the house of the Syrian postmaster, where he and his pretty little wife received us with native politeness, and gave us coffee and sweets. Our return journey was most pleasant, and we got to Alexandria at 8 p.m. Twelve charming hours.

"*May 24th.*—The Queen's birthday. Trooping of the colour at 5 p.m. on the Moharrem Bey Ground. Most successful. Will, mounted on a powerful chestnut, did look a commanding figure as he raised his plumed helmet and led the ringing cheers for the Queen which brought the pretty ceremony to a close. The sun was near setting behind the height of Komeldik, and lit up the roses in the men's helmets and garlanded round the standard. In the evening a dull and solemn dinner to the heads of departments and their wives. A difficult function. We had the bands of the Suffolks playing outside the windows, which were wide open on the sea. I went out sketching in the morning, very early. I should have been at my post all day on such an occasion, I confess. Will said I was like Nero, fiddling while Rome was burning.

"*May 29th.*—The Mediterranean Fleet is here. Great interchange of cards, firing of salutes, etc., etc. All very ceremonious, but productive of picturesqueness and colour and effect, so I like it very much. The Khedive Tewfik, too, has arrived, with the Khediviah, for the hot season from Cairo. Will, of course, had to be present at the station this morning for the reception of our puppet, and it was not nice to see the Union Jack down in the dust as the guard of honour of the Suffolks gave the salute. Our dinner to-night was the admiral and officers of the newly-arrived British squadron.

"*June 2nd.*—To the Khediviah's first reception at the harem of the Ras-el-Tin Palace. I had two Englishwomen to present, rather an unmanageable pair, as seniority appeared to be claimed erroneously at the last moment by the junior. This reception has become a most dull affair now that Oriental ways are done away with. Dancing girls no longer amuse the guests, nor handmaidens cater to them with sweetmeats during the audience, and there is nothing left but absolute emptiness. The Vice-Reine sits, in European dress, on a divan at the end of a vast hall, and the visitors sit in a semi-circle before her on hard European chairs reflected in a polished *parquet*, speaking to each other in whispers and furtively sipping coffee. She addresses a few remarks to those nearest her, and the pauses are articulated by the click of the ever-moving fans of the assembly. The ladies-in-waiting and girl slaves move about in a mooning way in the funniest frocks, supposed to be European, but some of them absolutely frumpish. Melancholy eunuchs of the bluest black, in glossy frock coats, rise and bow as one passes along the passages to or from the presence, and it is a relief to get out through the jealously-walled garden into the outer world.

"I find it difficult to converse in a harem, being so bad at small talk. I upset the Vice-Reine's equanimity by telling her (which was quite true) that I had heard she was taking lessons in painting. '*Moi, madame?!! Oh! je n'aurais pas le courage!*' It was as bad as when I told her, in Cairo, how much I liked poking about the bazaars. '*Vous allez dans les bazaars, madame?!!*' So I relapsed into talking of illnesses, which subject I have always found touches the proper note in a harem. They say the Vice-Reine delights in these audiences, as they are amongst the great events of her days. She is a beautiful woman, a Circassian, and of lovely whiteness.

"Finished the delicate sketch of the loveliest bit of the canal, where the pink minaret and the black cypress are. I wish I could do just one more reach of that lovely waterway before I leave! There is a particular group of oleanders nodding with heavy pink blossom by the water's edge against a soft blurred background of tamarisk, where women and girls in dark blue, brilliant orange, and rose-coloured robes come down to fetch water in their amphoræ. There is another reach lined for the whole length of the picture with tall waving canebrakes, above whose tender green tops appears the delicate distance of the lagoons of Mareotis; there is— but ah! each bend of that canal reveals fresh beauties, and often as Will has driven me there, I am as eager as ever to miss no point in the lovely sequence.

"*June 14th.*—All my days now I am sketching more

continuously, as the arduous work of paying calls has relaxed greatly. This evening we drove again far beyond Ramleh on the old route followed by Napoleon to reach Aboukir, and I finished the sketch there."

And so on, till my departure a few days later. I had wisely left my oils at home at Delgany, and thus got together a much larger number of subjects, the handier medium of water-colour being suited to the official life I had to attend to.

CHAPTER SEVENTEEN

MORE OF THE EAST

MY return voyage was made on board the Messageries boat to Marseilles. This gave me the Straits of Messina as well those of Bonifacio. On passing Ajaccio I don't think a single French passenger gave a thought to Napoleon. I was intent on taking in every detail of that place, as far as I could see it through a morning mist. Corsica looked very grand, crowned with great snow-capped mountains.

I lost no time in getting home to the children, and passed the rest of the summer in the green loveliness of Ireland, returning to Egypt, in the following October, *viâ* Venice again. Every soldier's wife knows what it is to be torn in two between the husband far away abroad and the children one must leave at home. The trial is great, no doubt of it. Then there is this perplexity: whether it would be well to take one of the children with one and risk the dangers of the journey and the climate at the other end. Parents pay heavily for our far-flung Empire!

On the morning of my departure from Venice I woke to the call of the sunbeams pouring into my room, and, behold, as I went to the window, the dome of the "Salute" taking the salute, as we say in the Army, of the sunrise! And the Dogana's gilded globe responding, too. Joy! our start at least will be calm. Till midday I had Venice to myself, and I could stroll about the Piazza and little streets, and recollect myself in peaceful meditation in St. Mark's. What delicate loveliness is that of Venice! Those russet reds and creamy whites and tender yellows, and here and there bits of deep indigo blue to give emphasis to the colour scheme. And that tender opalesque sky, and the gilded statues on domes and towers, and the rich mosaics twinkling in the hazy light! These things make one feel a love for Venice which is full of gratitude for so beautiful a thing.

At 12.30 I took gondola and was rowed to my old friend the *Hydaspes* lying in the Giudecca, and was just in time to sit down to a truly Hydaspian luncheon, which was crowded. To my indescribable relief the captain told me I should have a cabin all to myself as last time. At two o'clock we cast off, and that effective passage all along the front of the city was again made which so impressed me the preceding spring; and then we turned off seawards, winding through the channel marked out by those white posts with black heads which, even in their humble way, are so harmonious in tone and are beloved by painters, carrying out as they do the whole artistic scheme. Every fishing boat we met or overtook gave one a study of harmonies. Now it was an orange sail with a red upper corner in soft sunlight against the flat blue-purple of the distant mountains and the vivid green of the Lido; now, composing with a line of rosy, snowy mountain tops that lay like massive clouds on the horizon, would rise a pale cool grey-white sail, well in the foreground, with its upper part tinted a soft mouse-grey and its lower border deep terra-cotta red. The sea, pale blue; the sky thinly veiled with clouds of a rosy dove-grey. Nowhere does one see such delicacy of colouring as here. Then the market boats looked well, full of vegetables, whose cool green came just where it should for the completion of the colour study. To think that the Local Board, or whatever those modern vulgarians are called, of Venice are advocating the complete suppression of those coloured sails, to be replaced by plain white ones all round. Hands off, *mascalzoni!* All this enchantment gradually faded away in the mists of evening and of distance, and we were soon well out to sea.

"*Sunday,*—At 9 a.m. Brindisi in bright, low sunshine," says the Diary. "To Missa Cantata; much pleasant strolling. What animation all day with the loading and unloading, the coming and going of passengers, the cries and laughter of the population thronging the quays! The *Britannia* from London was already in, and I watched the transfer of my heavy luggage from her to the *Hydaspes* with a hawk's eye. I had a genuine compliment on landing paid to my accent. Those pests, the little beggar boys, who hang on to the English and can't be shaken off, attacked me at first till I turned on them and shouted, 'Via, *birrrrichini!*' One of them pulled the others away: "Come away, don't you see she is not English!' The Italians still think *Gl' Inglesi* are all millionaires and made of *scudi.*

"*November 12th.*—What indescribable joy this afternoon to see the crew busy with the preparations for our arrival tomorrow morning!

"*November 13th.*—Of course I began to get ready at 3 a.m. and peer out of the porthole on the waste of starlit waters as I felt the ship stopping off the distant lighthouse. We lay to a long time waiting for the dawn before proceeding to enter the harbour. The sun rose behind the city just as we turned into the port. I looked towards the distant landing stage. Half a mile off, with my wonderful sight, I saw Will, though the sun was right in my eyes. I knew him not only by his height, but by the shining gold band round his cap. We were a long time coming in and swinging round alongside, and, before the gangway was well down, Will sprang on to it and, in spite of the warning shouts of the sailors, was the first to board the *Hydaspes.*"

I was back in Egypt; to be there once more was bliss. The now brimming Mahmoudieh saw me haunting it again; the predominating red of the flowering trees and creepers that I noted before had made place for enchanting variations of yellow, and all the vegetation had deepened. The heat was great at first. I was particularly struck by the enhanced beauty of the date palms, whose golden and deep purple fruit now hung in clusters under the graceful branches. But all too soon came a good deal of rain, to my indignation. Rain in Egypt! The natives say we have brought it with us. I never saw any in Cairo nor upstream.

The Governor of the city had invited us to make use of a little *dahabiyeh,* the *Rose,* for a cruise on the Lower Nile, and on November 20th we started. My husband had already welcomed on their arrival, in a worthy manner, the officers of the French fleet, with whom he was in perfect sympathy; but my Diary records the happy necessity for our departure by the scheduled time on board the *Rose* on that very November 20th. That morning the German squadron arrived and the thunder of its guns gave us an intentional send-off! They were duly honoured, of course, but the General himself was away.

It was a nine days' cruise to the mouth of the Nile and back. Quite a different reading of the Nile from the one I have recorded in my letters to my mother, and reproduced in *From Sketch Book and Diary.* Very few tourists or even serious travellers have come so far down, so that one is less afraid of being forestalled by abler writers in recording one's impressions there. It was pretty to see the big Turkish flag fluttering at our helm, and a beautifully disproportionate pennon streaming in crimson magnificence from the point of the little vessel's curved felucca spar. But our first days were damping: "*November 22nd.*—Oh, the rain! Alas, that I should see Egypt under such deluges, and see in this land the deepest, ugliest mud in the world. We had to moor off the residence of the Bey, to whom this *dahabiyeh* belongs, last night, as we wished to pay him our respects and tender him our thanks this morning. He made us stay to luncheon, and a very excellent Arab repast it was. I got on well with him as he spoke excellent French! but his mother! Oh! it was heavy, as she could only talk Turkish, and my translated remarks didn't even get a smile out of her. I must say the Mohammedan women are deadly.

"We proceeded on our voyage very late in the day, on account of this visit which common civility made necessary. The weather brightened up at sunset and nothing more weird have I ever seen than the mud villages, cemeteries, lonely tombs, goats, buffaloes and wild human beings that loomed on the banks as we glided by, brown and black against that sky full of racing clouds that seemed red-hot from the great fiery globe that had just sunk below the palm-fringed horizon. These canal banks might give many people the horrors. I certainly think them in this weather the most uncanny bits of manipulated nature I have ever seen. I was fortunate in getting down in colour such a telling thing, a goatherd in a Bedouin's burnous, which was wildly flapping in the hot wind against the red glow in the west, driving a herd of those goats I find so effective, with their long, pendant ears, and kids skipping in impish gambols in front. 'Apocalyptic' apparition, caught, as we left it astern, in that portentous gloaming! I shall make something of this. As to the inhabitants of those regions, to contemplate their life is too depressing. As darkness comes on you see them creeping into their unlighted mud hovels like their animals. On the Upper Nile, at least, the fellaheen have glorious air, the sun, the clean, dry sand, but here in that mud—!

"*November 23rd.*—No more rain. At Atfeh we left the canal at last, by a lock, and I gave a sigh of relief and contentment, for we were on the broad bosom of Old Nile. After a delay at this mud town to buy provisions we pushed out into the current and with eight immensely long 'sweeps' (the wind was against sailing) we made a good run to Rosetta, on whose mud bank we thumped by the light of a pale moon. The rhythmic sound of those splashing oars and of the chant of the oarsmen in the minor key, with barbaric 'intervals' unknown to our music, continued to echo in my ears—it all seemed wild and strange and haunting.

"*November 24th.*—Began this morning a sketch of Rosetta to finish on our return from rounding up our outward
voyage at the western mouth of the great river where we
saw it emerge into a very desolate, grey Mediterranean. I
may now say I have a very good idea of the mighty river for
upward of a thousand miles of its course—a good bit further, both below and above stream, than the authoress of *A
Thousand Miles up the Nile* knew it, whom in my early days I
longed to emulate and, if possible, surpass! An old-fashioned book, now, I suppose, but all the more interesting for
that. Furling sail, for the wind had been fair to-day, we
turned and were towed back to Fort St. Julian, where we
moored for the night.

"*November 25th.*—After a nice little sketch of the Fort
St. Julian, celebrated in Napoleonic annals, we started off,
and reached Rosetta in good time, so that I was able most
satisfactorily to finish my large water-colour of the place. I
was rather bothered where I sat at the water's edge by the
small boys and a very persistent pelican, which kept flying
from the river into the fish market and returning with
stolen fish, to souse them in the water before filling its
pouch, in time to avoid capture by the pursuing brats.

"*November 26th.*—From Rosetta we glided pleasantly to
Metubis, one of the many shining cities, as seen from afar,
that become heaps of squalid dwellings when viewed at
close quarters. But the minarets of those phantom cities
remain erect in all their beauty, and this city in particular
was transfigured by the most magnificent sunset I have ever
seen, even here."

The wild town of Syndioor was our mooring place for the
next night, and at sunrise we were off homewards. Syndioor
and the opposite city of Deyrout were veiled in a soft mist,
out of which rose their tall minarets in stately beauty, radiant in the level light. The effect on the mind of these
ruined places, once magnificent centres of commerce and
luxury, is quite extraordinary. They are now, all of them,

derelicts. And so in time we slipped back into the canal, landing under the oleanders of our starting place. The crew kissed hands, the *reis* made his obeisance, and we returned to the hard stones and rattle of the Boulevard de Ramleh, refreshed. The Germans were gone.

Balls, picnics, gymkhanas and dinners were varied by intervals of water-colour sketching in the desert. One picnic, out at Mex, to the west of Alexandria, was distinguished by a great camel ride we all had on the soft-paced, mouse-coloured mounts of the Camel Corps, the Englishwomen looking so nice in their well-cut riding habits, sitting easily on their tall steeds. I managed to secure several sketches that day of the men and camels of the corps, and have one sketch of ourselves starting for our turn in the desert. Our ponies took us back home. The sort of day I liked. As I record, the completeness of my enjoyment was caused by my having been able to put some useful work in, as usual. I had a Camel Corps picture *in petto* at this time.

"*February 13th, 1891.*—We had the Duke of Cambridge to luncheon. He arrived yesterday on board the *Surprise* from Malta, and Will, of course, received him officially, but not royally, as he is travelling incog., and he came here to tea. To-day we had a large party to meet him, and a very genial luncheon it was, not to say rollicking. The day was exquisite, and out of the open windows the sea sparkled, blue and calm. H.R.H. seemed to me rather feeble, but in the best of humours; a wonderful old man to come to Egypt for the first time at seventy-two, braving this burning sun and with such a high colour to begin with! One felt as though one was talking to George III. to hear the 'What, what, what? Who, who, who? Why, why, why?' Col. Lane, one of his suite, said he had never seen him in better spirits. I was gratified at his praise of our cook—very loud praise, literally, as he is not only rather deaf himself, but speaks to people as though they also were a 'little hard of hearing.' 'Very good cook, my dear' (to me). 'Very good cook, Butler' (across the table to Will). 'Very good cook, eh, Sykes?' (very loud to Christopher Sykes, further off). 'You are a *gourmet*, you know better about these things than I do, eh?' C.S.: 'I ought to have learnt something about it at Gloucester House, sir!' H.R.H. (to me): 'Your health, my dear.' 'Butler, your very good health!' Aside to me: 'What's the Consul's name?' I: 'Sir Charles Cookson.' 'Sir Charles, your health!' When I hand the salt to H.R.H. he stops my hand: 'I wouldn't quarrel with her for the world, Butler.' And so the feast goes on, our august guest plying me with questions about the relationship and antecedents of every one at the table; about the manners and customs of the populace of Alexandria; the state of commerce; the climate. I answer to the best of my ability with the most unsatisfactory information. He started at four for Cairo, leaving a most kindly impression on my memory. The last of the old Georgian type! 'Your mutton was good, my dear; not at all *goaty*,' were his valedictory words."

Mutton *is* goaty in Egypt unless well selected. I advise travellers to confine themselves to the good poultry, and to leave meat alone. What I would have done without our dear, good old Magro, the major domo who did my housekeeping out there, I dread to think. His name, denoting a lean habit of body, was a misnomer, for he was rotund. A good, honest Maltese, his devotion to "Sair William" was really touching. I was only as the moon is to the sun, and to serve the sun he would, I am convinced, have risked his life. I came in for his devotion to myself by reason of my reflected glory. One morning he came hurtling towards me, through the rooms, waving aloft what at first looked like a red republican flag, but it proved to be a sirloin or other portion of bovine anatomy which he had had the luck to purchase in the market (good beef being so rare). "Look, miladi, you will not often meet such beef walking in the street!" He laid it out for my admiration. This is the way he used to ask me for the daily orders: "What will miladi command for dinner?" "Cutlets?" (patting his ribs); "a loin?"

(indications of lumbago); "or a leg?" (advancing that limb); "or, for a delicate *entrée*, brains?" (laying a finger on his perspiring forehead). "Oh, for goodness' sake, Magro, not brains!" When the day's work was done he would retire to what we called the "Ah!-poor-me-room"—his boudoir—where, repeating aloud those words so dear to his nationality, he would take up his cigar. Government gave him £250 a year for all this expenditure of zeal.

While on the subject of Oriental housekeeping, I must record the following. Our predecessors of a former time had what to me would have been an experience difficult to recover from. They were giving a large Christmas dinner, and the cook, proud of the pudding he had mastered the intricacies of, insisted on bringing it in himself, all ablaze. It was only a few steps from the kitchen to the dining-room. Holding the great dish well up before him, he unfortunately set fire to his beard, and the effect of his dusky face approaching in the subdued light of the door, illuminated in that way by blue flames, must have been satanic.

"*March 14th.*—Lord Charles Beresford, who has relieved the other ship with the *Undaunted*, invited us all to luncheon on board, but Will and I could not stay to luncheon as we had guests; nevertheless, we had a very interesting morning on board. On arriving at the Marina we found Lady Charles, Lady Edmund Talbot, Colonel Kitchener,[11] whose light, rather tiger-like eyes in that sunburnt face slightly frightened me, and others waiting to go with us to the *Undaunted* in the ship's barge and a steam launch. Lord Charles received us with his usual sailor-like welcome, and we had a tremendous inspection of the ship, one of our latest experiments in naval machinery—a belted cruiser. She will probably cruise to the bottom if ever the real test comes. A torpedo was fired for us, but it gambolled away like a porpoise, ending by plunging into a mudbank. I wish they would diverge their direction like that in war, detestable inventions!

"*April 1st, 1891.*—I am now quite in the full swing of

Egyptian enjoyment. No more Egyptian rain! Excellent accounts from home, and my intention of going back is rendered unnecessary. How thankful I am, on the eve of our departure for Palestine, for the 'all well' from home!"

My entries in the Diary during that unique journey, and my letters to my mother, are published in my book, *Letters from the Holy Land*. I illustrated it with the water colours I made during our pilgrimage, and I was most delighted to find the little book had an utterly unexpected success. It was nice to find myself among the writers! To have ridden through this land from end to end is to have experienced a pleasure such as no other part of the earth can give us. Had I had no more joy in store for me, that would have been enough.

As the railway was not opened till the following year the mind was not disturbed, and could concentrate on the scenes before it with all the recollection it required. I called our progress "riding through the Bible." Many a local allusion in both Testaments, which had seemed vague or difficult to appreciate before, opened out, so to say, before one's happy vision, and gave a substance, a vitality to the Scripture narrative which produced a satisfaction delightful to experience. Perhaps the strongest longing in my childhood's mind had been to do this journey. To do it as we did, just our two selves, and in the fresh spring weather, was a happy circumstance.

As I look back to that time which we spent amidst the scenes of Our Lord's revealed life on earth, no portion of it produces such a sense of mental peace as does the night of our arrival on the shores of the Sea of Galilee. *There* were no crowds, no distractions, not a thing to jar on the mind. Before and around one, as one sat on the pebbly strand, appeared the very outlines of the hills His eyes had rested on, and far from modern life encroaching on one's sensitiveness, the cities that lined those sacred shores in His time had disappeared like one of the fleeting cloud shadows which the moon was casting all along their ruined sites. His words came back with a poignant force, "Woe unto thee, Chorazin! Woe unto thee, Bethsaida!...and thou, Capernaum, which art exalted unto heaven..." Where were they? And the high waves raced foaming and breaking on the shingle, blown by a strong though mild wind that came across from the dark cliffs of the country of the Gadarenes. One seemed to feel His approach where He had so often walked. One can hardly speak of the awe which that feeling brought to the mind. He was quite near!

Undoubtedly the effect of a journey through the Holy Land *does* permanently impress itself upon one's life. It is a tremendous experience to be brought thus face to face with the Gospel narrative. We returned to the modern world on May 1st. This time I left Alexandria in company with my husband on June 3rd, and on landing at Venice we at once went on to Verona, where he was anxious to visit the battlefield of Arcole.

CHAPTER EIGHTEEN

THE LAST OF EGYPT

HERE at Verona in her richest dress, her abundant and varied crops filling the landscape, one might say, to overflowing; not a space of soil left untilled, and, all the way along our road to San Bonifacio for Arcole, the snow-capped Alps were shimmering in the blue atmosphere on one hand, and a great teeming plain stretched away to the horizon on the other.

I noticed the fine physique of the peasantry, and their nice ways. Every peasant man we met on the road raised his hat to us as we passed. At San Bonifacio we got out of the carriage and, turning to the right, we walked to Arcole, becoming exclusively Napoleonic on reaching the famous marsh. History says that a soldier saved Napoleon from drowning early in the battle by pulling him out of the water in that marsh, "by the hair!" I pondered this *bald* statement,

and came to the conclusion that the thing must have happened in this wise. Young Bonaparte in those early days
wore his hair very long, and gathered up into a queue. Had
he been close-cropped, as his later experience in Egypt
compelled him to be, the history of the world might have
been very different. As I looked into the water from the
famous little bridge, I saw the place where the young con-
queror slipped and plunged in. The soldier must have
caught hold of the pigtail, and with the good grip it afforded him pulled his drowning general out. Between the little
bridge and the spot where he sank Napoleon raised the
obelisk which we see to-day. Thus do I like to realise interesting events in history.

Our driver on the way back became a dreadful bore, for
ever turning on the box to chatter. First he informed us that
Arcole was called after Hercules, "a very strong man" (great
thumping of biceps to illustrate his meaning), which we
knew before. Then, when within sight of the battlefield of
Custozza, where our dear Italians got such a "dusting" from
the Austrians, he informed us that he had been in the battle, and that the Italians had *blasted* the enemy. "*Li abbiamo
fulminati.*" "Oh, shut up, do! *Basta, caro!*"

Our afternoon stroll all over Verona merged into a
moonlight one which takes first rank in my Italian chronicles. The effect of a roaring Alpine torrent (for such is the
Adige at this season of melting snows) rushing and swirling
through the heart of that ancient city, between embank-
ments bordered with domed churches, with towers and
palaces, I found quite unique. Mysterious, too, it all felt in
the lights and profound shades of the moonlight. Above
rose the hills with very striking serrated outlines, crowned
with fortresses.

The rest of the summer saw me at home at Delgany. I
must say the "Green Isle" for summer, following Egypt for
winter, makes a very pleasant combination. My husband
had returned to Alexandria on August 23rd, and I and a
wee child followed in November. I had half accomplished

my next Academy picture at home, and I took it out to finish in Egypt—*Halt on a Forced March: Retreat to Corunna*. A study of an artillery team this time, giving the look of the spent horses, "lean unto war." It was very well placed at the Academy in the fresh first room, and well received, but it was too sad a subject, perhaps, so I have it still. There were no half-starved horses in all Wicklow, I am happy to say, look where I would for models. I had well-to-do ones to get tone and colour from, but I bided my time. In Egypt I had plenty of choice, and had I not been able to put the finishing touches to my team *there*, the picture would never have been so strong—an instance of my favourite definition when I am asked, "What is the secret of success?" "*Seize opportunities*."

So on December 10th, 1891, I, with the little child I had safely brought out with me, landed once more at Alexandria. The big charger and the grey Syrian pony had now a black donkey alongside for the desert rides, which were the chief pleasure of our life out there.

But the winter grew sad. On January 7th, 1892, the Khedive Tewfik died rather mysteriously, it was said, but his death was announced as the result of that plague we call the "flu," which reached even to the East. Just eight days later poor Albert Victor, Duke of Clarence, fell a victim to it, and in the same way died Cardinal Manning. Also some of our own friends at Alexandria went down. And yet never was there more brilliant weather, so softly brilliant that one could hardly realise the presence of danger. All the balls and other festivities were stopped, of course. I had ample time to finish my *Halt on a Forced March* in this long interval, so boring and depressing to Alexandrian society. Soon things returned to pleasantly normal conditions, however, and being free from the studio on sending my picture off, I went in whole-heartedly for the amenities of my official position. The Private View at the far-away Royal Academy was in my mind on the occasion of my giving away the prizes at some athletic sports, for I knew it was just then in full blast, April 29th, 1892. I knew my quiet picture could not make anything of a stir, and I chaffed myself by suggesting that the "three cheers and one cheer more" proposed by the English consul at the end of the prize-giving, which rent the sunset air in that dusty plain in my honour, should be all I ought to expect. It would be a *little* too much to receive in two quarters of the globe at the same moment, allowing for difference of time!

I call upon my Diary again: "*May 18th.*—We joined a picnic in the very palm grove through which the Turks fled from the French pursuit under Bonaparte to find death in the surf of Aboukir Bay. We were shaded by clumps of pomegranate trees in flower as well as by the waving, rustling palms, and a cool wind blew round us most pleasantly, while the white and grey donkeys that brought us rested in groups, their drivers and the villagers squatting about them in those unconsciously graceful attitudes I love to jot down in my sketch book. The moving shadows of the palm branches on the sand always capture my observation; no other tree shadows produce that effect of ever-interlacing forms. Far away in the radiant light lay the region where the terrible naval battle took place later, to our credit. Altogether our party was surrounded by frightful reminiscences, in the midst of which the picnic went its usual picnicky way. We rode back to Alexandria by the light of the stars.

"*May 23rd.*—A wonderful day, full of colour, movement and interest. Young Abbas II., the new Khedive, was received here on his arrival from Cairo, the whole population, swelled by strange wild Asiatics from distant parts, filling the streets and squares through which he was to pass. Will, of course, had to receive him at the station. The crowd alone was a pleasure to look at. The Khedive seemed a squat young man with a round pink and white painted face. They say he loves not the English. What I enjoyed above all was the drive we took soon after, all the length of the line of reception, to Ras-el-Tin. Oh, those narrow streets of the old quarter, filled with numberless varieties of Oriental costumes. Now and then the crowd was threaded by troops, some on horseback, some perched on camels, and, to give the finishing touch of variety, the native fire brigade went by, wearing the brass helmets of their London *confrères*, very surprising headgear bonneting their black and brown faces."

I, with the little child, left for home on June 7th, viâ Genoa, well provided with a good stock of studies of camels and Camel Corps troopers. These were for my 8-foot picture, destined for the next Academy. Many a camel had I stalked about the Ramleh desert to watch its mannerisms in movement. I got quite to revel in camels. Usually that interesting beast is made utterly uninteresting in pictures, whereas if you know him personally he is full of surprises and one never gets to the end of him.

The voyage to my dear old Genoa was full of beautiful sights, with one exception. I don't know what old Naples was like—I know it was frightfully dirty—but I saw it modernised into a very horrid town, a smudge of ugliness on one of the ideal beauties of the world. It gave me a shock on beholding it as we entered the harbour, and so I leave the town itself severely alone, with its new, barrack-like buildings looking gaunt and gritty in the burning June sunshine. The cloisters of the Certosa at Sant' Elmo are very beautiful, and I much enjoyed the church and splendid *Descent from the Cross* of Spagnoletto. There was just time for a dash up there before leaving at 12 noon. As we steamed out towards Ischia I got the oft-painted (and, alas! oleographed) view of Vesuvius across the whole extent of the bay from off Posilipo. Certainly nowhere on earth can a fairer scene be beheld, and greater grace of coast and mountain outline. Then the fair scene melted away into the tender haze of the June afternoon—blue and tender grey, the volcanic islands one by one disappeared and the day of my first sight of the Bay of Naples closed.

June 12th was a most memorable day, a day of deepest,

sweetest, and saddest impressions and memories for me. In the afternoon I made ready for our approach to that part of the world where the brightest years of my childhood were spent—the Gulf of Genoa. In order not to lose one moment away from the contemplation of what we were approaching, I packed up all our things before three o'clock, did all the *fin de voyage* paying and tipping, and then, my mind free for concentration, I stationed myself at the starboard bulwark, binocular in hand. At long last I saw in the haze of the lovely afternoon a shadowy outline of rocky mountain which my heart, rather than my eyes, told me was Porto Fino, for never had I seen it before from out at sea, at that angle. But I knew where to look for it, and while to the other passengers we seemed still out of sight of land I saw the shadowy form. Then little by little the whole coast grew out of the haze and I saw again, one after the other, the houses we lived in from Ruta to Albaro. With the powerful glass I had I could see Villa de' Franchi and its sundial, and see how many windows were open or shut at Villa Quartara as we passed Albaro, and see the old, well-loved pine tree and cypress avenue of the latter *palazzo*.

"The sight of Genoa in the lurid sunset glow, with its steep, conical mountains behind it, crowned with forts, half shrouded in dark grey clouds, was very impressive. 'La Superba' looked her proudest thus seen full face from the sea, seated on her rocky throne. By the by, when *will* people give up translating 'superba' by 'superb'? It is rather trying. 'Genoa the Superb'! Ugh!"

I worked away well in the pleasant seclusion of Delgany, at my 8-foot canvas whereon I carried very far forward my *Review of the Native Camel Corps at Cairo.* I had already a water-colour drawing of this subject, which I had made while the scene was fresh in my mind's eye. I had been indebted to the then General commanding at Cairo for the facilities afforded me to see, at close quarters, a charge of the native Camel Corps, which impressed me indelibly. I had driven out of Cairo to the desert, where the manœuvres

were taking place, and, getting out of the carriage opposite
the saluting base, I placed myself in front of the advancing
squadrons, so timing things that I got well clear at the right
moment. I wanted as much of a full-face view as possible.
The attitudes of the men, wielding their whips, the movements of the camels, the whole rush of the thing gave me
such a sensation of advancing force that, as soon as the
"Halt!" was sounded, and the 300 animals had flung themselves on their knees with the roar and snarl peculiar to
those creatures when required to exert themselves, I hastened back to Shepheard's and marked down the salient
points. The men were of all shades, from *fellaheen* yellow to
the bluest black of Nubia, and it was a striking moment
when they all leapt off their saddles (as the camels col-
lapsed), panting, and beginning to re-set their disordered
accoutrements. In those days the saddles were covered with
red morocco leather, with fringed strips that flew out in the
wind, adding, for the artist, a welcome aid to the representation of motion. Now, of course, that precious bit of colour is
gone, and the necessity for khaki invisibility reaches even to
the camel saddle, which is now a stiff and unattractive dun-
coloured object.

For my last and most brilliant visit to Egypt I took out
our eldest little girl, and a very enjoyable trip we had, *viâ*
Genoa. Of course, I took out the picture to finish it on its
native sands. I had the richest choice of military camels,
arms and accoutrements, and a native trooper or two, as
models, but only for studies. I was careful to have no posed
model to paint from in the studio, otherwise good-bye to
movement. These graceful Orientals become the stupidest,
stiff lay figures the moment you ask them to pose as models.
Besides, the sincere Mohammedans refuse to be painted at
all. I have never used a Kodak myself, finding snapshots of
little value, but quick sketches done unbeknown to the
sketchee and a good memory serve much better. The picture,
I grieve to say, was hung not very kindly at the Academy,
but at the Paris Salon it was received with all the

appreciation I could desire.

What pleased me particularly in this last sojourn in Egypt was our visit to Cairo, where I was so happy during my first experience, when I described my sensations as being comparable to swimming in Oriental colour, light, and picturesqueness. The only thing that jarred was the tyranny of Cairo society, which compelled one to appear at the diversions, whether one liked it or not. Nevertheless, I gained a very thorough knowledge of the wondrously beautiful mosques, having the advantage of the guidance of one who knew them all intimately—Dean Butcher. It was a true pleasure to have him as *cicerone,* and I am grateful to him for his most kindly giving up his time for little C. and me. My husband had long ago been acquainted with every nook and corner of Cairo, but Dean Butcher had made a special study of these mosques, and I think he was pleased with the way we took in the fascinating information he gave me and the child.

It's a far cry from Cairo to Aldershot! On November 1st, 1893, my husband's command of the 2nd Infantry Brigade began there. Much as I loved Egypt, it was a great delight for me to know that the parting from the children was not to be repeated. I had had Egypt to my heart's content.

After returning home from Egypt, at Delgany, on June 17th, 1893, I set up my next big picture, *The Réveil in the Bivouac of the Scots Greys on the Morning of Waterloo—Early Dawn.* I was able to make all my twilight studies at home, all out of doors; not a thing painted in the studio. I pressed many people into my service as models, and I think I got the light on their fine Irish faces very true to nature. I even caught an Irish dragoon home on leave in the village, whose splendid profile I saw at once would be very telling.

Cairo
1885

The Native
Camel Corps

Jethou
1893

The Bersaglieri

THE EGYPTIAN CAMEL-CORPS AND THE BERSAGLIERI.

ALDERSHOT MANŒUVRES. THE ENEMY IN SIGHT.

CHAPTER NINETEEN
ALDERSHOT

AND now our Irish home under the glorious Wicklow Mountains broke up, and I was to become acquainted with life in the great English camp. The huts for officers were still standing at that time, wooden bungalows of the quaintest fashion, all the more pleasing to me for being unlike ordinary houses. The old court-martial hut became my studio, four skylights having been placed in it, and I was quite happy there. I worked hard at *The Réveil*, and finished it in that unconventional workshop.

To say that Aldershot society was brilliant would be very wide of the mark. How could it be? But to us there was a very great attraction close by, at Farnborough. There lived a woman who was and ever will be a very remarkable figure in history, the Empress Eugénie. She hadn't forgotten my husband's connection with her beloved son's tragic story out in South Africa, nor her interview with him at Camden Place, and his management of the Prince's funeral at Durban. We often took tea with her on Sundays during our Aldershot period, her "At Home" day for intimate friends and relatives, at the big house on the hill. She became very fond of talking politics with *Sair William*, and always in English, and she used to sit in that confidential way foreign politicians have, expressive of the whispered divulgence of tremendous secrets and of occult plots and plans in various parts of the world. She talked incessantly with him, but was a bad listener; and if a subject came up in conversation which did not interest her, a sharp snap or two of her fan would soon bring things to a stop.

Entries from the Aldershot Diary:

"*January 9th, 1894.*—We went to the memorial service at the Empress's church in commemoration of the death of Napoleon III. After Mass we went down to the crypt, where another short service was chanted and the tombs of the Emperor and Prince Imperial were incensed. Between the two lies the one awaiting the pathetic widow who was kneeling there shrouded with black, a motionless, solitary figure, for whom one felt a very deep respect.

"*March 14th.*—Delightful dinner at Government House, where the Duke and Duchess of Connaught proved most cheery host and hostess. He took me to dinner, and we talked other than banalities. All the other generals' wives and the generals and heads of departments were there to the number of twenty-two.

"*March 25th.*—To a brilliant dinner at Government House to meet the Duke of Cambridge. Good old George was in splendid form, and asked me if I remembered the lunch we gave him at Alexandria. It was a most cheery evening. We sat down about twenty-eight, of whom only six were ladies. Grenfell, our old friend of Genoese days, and Evelyn Wood were there.

"*May 17th.*—A glorious day for the Queen's Review, which was certainly a dazzling spectacle. Dear old Queen, it is many a long year since she reviewed the Aldershot Division; nor would she have come but that her son is now in supreme command here. Old people say it was like old times, only that she has shrunk into a tinier woman than ever she was, and by the side of the towering Duchess of Coburg in that spacious carriage she looked indeed tiny, and nearly extinguished under a large grey sunshade. A good place was reserved for my little carriage close to the Royal Enclosure, and I enjoyed the congenial scene to the utmost. Was I not in my element? The review took place on Laffan's Plain, a glorious sweep of intense green turf which I often take little Martin to for our morning walk, and no Aldershot dust annoyed us. I was very proud of the general commanding the 2nd Brigade riding past the saluting base at the head of his troops on that mighty charger, 'Heart of Oak,' that fine golden bay, set off to the utmost advantage by the ceremonial saddle-cloth and housings of blue and gold. That general gives the salute with a very free sweep of the sword arm. The march past took a long time. As to the

crowd of officers behind the Queen's carriage, my eyes positively ached with the sight of all that scarlet and gold. I
must say this scarlet is pushed too far to my mind. It must
have now reached the highest pitch of dyeing powers. It
was a duller tone at Waterloo; and certainly still more artistic when Cromwell first ordered his men to wear it. But I
may be wrong, and it is certainly very splendid. The Duke
of Cambridge and Prince of Wales were on huge black
chargers, and wore field marshals' uniforms. It was pretty to
see the Duke of Connaught—who, at the head of his staff,
in front of the division drawn up in line, had sat awaiting
the Queen's arrival—canter up to his mother and salute her
as her carriage drove into the enclosure. Then he cantered
back to his place, a very graceful rider, and the review
began. I managed to do good work at *The Réveil* in
forenoon. What a contrast and rest to the eyes that picture
is after such glittering spectacles as to-day's. War *versus*
Parade! It was pathetic to see the Queen to-day with her
soldiers. She cannot pass them in review many more times.

"The Empress Eugénie has returned, and we had a long
interview with her the other day at her beautiful home at
Farnborough. She is by no means the wreck and shadow
some people are pleased to describe her as being, but has
the remains of a certain masculine power which I suppose
was very masterful in the great old days of her splendour.
She is not too tall, and has a fine, upright figure. She lives
apparently altogether in the memory of her son, and is surrounded by his portraits and relics, including drawings
showing him making his heroic stand, alone, forsaken,
against the savage enemy. I feel, as an Englishwoman, very
uneasy and remorseful while listening to that poor mother,
with her tearful eyes, as she speaks of her dead boy, who
need not have been sacrificed. There is no trace in her
words of anger or reproach or contempt, only most appealing grief. She has one window in the hall full to a height of
many feet of the tall grass which grows on the spot where
her treasured son was done to death by seventeen assegai

wounds, all received full in front. I remember his taking us over some artillery stables, I think, at Woolwich once. He had a charming face. The Empress rightly described to us the quality of the blue of his eyes—'the blue sky seen in water.'

"We often go to her beautiful church these fine summer days. Her only infirmity appears to be her rheumatism, which necessitates some one giving her his arm to ascend or descend the sanctuary steps when she goes to or comes from her *prie-Dieu* to the right of the altar. Sometimes it is M. Franceschini Pietri, sometimes it is the faithful old servant Uhlmann who performs this duty.

"*August 13th.*—We have had the Queen down again for another review in splendid (Queen's) weather. The night before the review Her Majesty gave a dinner at the Pavilion to her generals, and for the first time in her life sat down at table with them. Will gave me a most interesting account. In the night there was a great military tattoo, which I witnessed with C. from General Utterson's grounds. Very effective, if a little too spun out. Will and the others were standing about the Queen's and the Empress Eugénie's carriages all the time, in the grass soaked with the heavy night dew, and felt all rather blue and bored. In the Queen's carriage all was glum, while the Empress with her party chatted helpfully in hers to fill up the time. It was pitch dark but for the torches carried by long lines of troops in the distance.

"To-day was made memorable by the review held of our brilliant little division by the German Emperor on Laffan's Plain, in perfect weather. He wore the uniform of our Royal Dragoons, of which regiment he is honorary colonel, and rode a bay horse as finely trained as a circus horse (and rather suggestive of one, as are his others too, that are here), with the curb reins passing somewhere towards the rider's knees, which supply the place of the left hand, half the size of the right and apparently almost powerless. The poor fellow's shoulders are padded, too, and one sees a *hiatus* between the false, square shoulder and the real one, which is very sloping. But the general appearance was gallant, and the young man seemed full of gaiety and martial spirit. He took the salute, of course, and was a striking figure under the Union Jack which waved over his British helmet. Then followed a little episode which, if rather theatrical, was enlivening, and a pretty surprise. As the Royal Dragoons' turn came to pass the saluting base the Kaiser drew his sword and, darting away from his post, placed himself at the head of his British regiment, the Duke of Connaught replacing him at the flagstaff *pro tem*. The Kaiser couldn't salute himself, of course, so saluted the Duke, and, when the Dragoons were clear, back he came at a circus canter to resume his post and continue to receive the salute of the passing legions, as before. We all clapped him for this graceful compliment. It was smartly done. The detachment (seventy-five in number) had been sent over from Dublin on purpose for this little display. In the evening Will dined at Government House in a nest of Germans, who seemed afraid to sit well upon their chairs in the august presence of their Emperor, and sat on the very edge. One particularly corpulent general was very nearly slipping off. I went to the evening reception, no wives being asked to the dinner, as the dining-room is so small and the German suite so voluminous.

"I was at once presented to H.I.M., who talked to me, like a good boy, about my painting and about the army, which he said he greatly admired for its appearance. He is just now a keen Anglo-maniac (*sic*)! We shall have him dressing one of his regiments in kilts next. He is not at all as hard-looking as I expected, but not at all healthy. His face, seen near, is unwholesome in its colour and texture, and the eyes have that *boiled* look which suggests a want of clarity in the system, it seems to me. He is nice and natural in his manner and in the expression of his face, with light brown moustache brushed up on his cheeks. He wore the mess dress of the Royal Dragoons, and his right hand was twinkling with very 'loud' rings on every finger, coiled serpents with jewelled eyes.

"*August 14th.*—A glorious sham fight in the Long Valley and heights for the Kaiser. I shall always remember his appearance as, at the head of a large and brilliant staff of Germans and English, he came suddenly galloping up to the mound where I was standing with the children, riding, this time, a white horse and wearing his silver English Dragoon helmet without the plume. He seemed joyous as his eye took in the lovely landscape and he sat some minutes looking down on the scene, gesticulating as he brightly spoke to the deferential *pickelhauben* that bent down around him. He then dashed off down the hill and crested another, with, if you please, C. on her father's huge grey second charger careering after the gallant band, and escaping for an anxious (to me) half-hour from my surveillance. The child looked like a fly on that enormous animal which overtopped the crowd of staff horses. Adieu to the old gunpowder smoke. It has cleared away for ever. One sees too much nowadays, and that mystery of effect, so awful and so grand, caused by the lurid smoke, is gone. How much writers and painters owe to the old black powder of the days gone by!

"*September 23rd.*—Had a delightful evening, for we dined with the Empress Eugénie. I seemed to be basking in the 'Napoleonic Idea' as I sat at that table and saw my glass engraved with the Imperial 'N,' and was aware of the historical portraits of the Bonaparte Era that hung round the room. The Empress was full of bright conversation and chaff; and I find, as I see her oftener, that she has plenty of humour and enjoys a joke greatly. We didn't go in arm in arm, men and women, but *Sa Majesté* signed to me and another woman to go in either side of her. She called to Will to come and sit on her right. I was very happy and in my element. Oh! how the mind feels relieved and expanded in that atmosphere. We had music after dinner, and I had long talks on Egypt with the Empress, whose recollections of that bright land are particularly brilliant, she having been there during the jubilant ceremonies in connection with the opening of the Suez Canal. One year before the great calamities to her and her husband! She told me that just for a freak she walked several times in and out between the two pillars on the Piazzetta at Venice, that time, to brave Fate, who, it was said, punished those who dared to do this. 'Then *les évènements* followed,' she added. Well might she say that life is an up and down existence. She waved her hand up and down, very high and very low, as she said it, with a weary sigh. Her face is often very beautiful; those eyes drooping at the outer corners look particularly lovely as they are bent downwards, and her white hair is arranged most gracefully. She is always in black.

"Will has accepted the extension of his command here to my great pleasure; the chief charm to us in this place is the neighbourhood of the Empress. That makes Farnborough unique. Not only is she so interesting, but now and then there are visitors at her house whose very names are sonorous memories. The other day as we came into her presence she went up to Will and asked him to let Prince Murat, Ney (Prince de la Moscowa) and Masséna (duc de Rivoli), see some of the regiments in his brigade at their barracks. When the inspection was over these three illustrious Names came to lunch with us, and I sat between Murat and Masséna, with *le Brave des Braves* opposite. What's in a name? Everything, sometimes. I thought myself a very favoured creature last Sunday as I sat by Eugénie at her tea table and she sprinkled my muffin with salt out of her little muffineer. I am glad to know she likes me and she is very fond of Will. One Sunday she and I and the Marquise de Gallifet were sitting together, and the Empress was talking to the latter about *The Roll Call*, pronouncing the name in English, but Madame, who looked somewhat stony and unsympathetic, could not pronounce the name when the Empress asked her to, and made a very funny thing out of it.

The Empress tried to teach her, making fun of her attempts which became more and more comic, combined with her frigid expression. At last the Empress turned to me and asked me to show how it ought to be said in the proper way; but, as she had just given me an enormous chocolate cream, I was for the moment unable to pronounce anything with this thing in my cheek, and she went into fits of laughter as I made several attempts to say the unfortunate name. So it was never pronounced, and Madame la Marquise looked on as though she thought we were both rather childish, which made the Empress laugh the more. The least thing, if it is at all comical, sends her into one of her laughing fits which are very catching—except by Gallifets.

"Talking of camel riding (and they say she rode like a Bedouin in the desert) I sent her into another fit which brought the tears to her eyes by saying I always forgot '*quel bout de mon chameau se lève le premier*' at starting. But she sent me into one of my own particular fits the other day. I was telling her, in answer to her enquiry as to insuring pictures on sending them by sea, that I thought only their total loss would be paid for, and what the artist considered an injury of a grave nature amounting to total loss might not be so considered by the insurance company. 'And if,' she said, 'you have a portrait and a hole is made right through one of the eyes?' Here she slowly closed her left eye and looked at me stolidly with the right, to represent the injured effigy, 'would you not get compensation?' The one-eyed portrait continued to look at me out of the forlorn single eye with every vestige of expression gone, and I laughed so much that I begged her to become herself again, but she wouldn't, for a long time.

"There has been a great deal of pheasant shooting, particularly at the De Worms' at Henley Park, where a *chef* at £500 a year has made that hospitable house very attractive; but there has been one shoot at Farnboro' made memorable by Franceschini Pietri distinguishing himself with his erratic gunnery. Suddenly he was seen on a shutter, screaming,

as the servants bore him to the house. Every one thought
he was wounded, but it turned out he was sure he had hit
somebody else, which happily wasn't true. People are shy of
having him, after that, at their shoots, especially Baron de
Worms, who showed me how he accoutred himself by
padding and goggles, one day, bullet-proof against that
excitable little southerner, who was a member of the party
at Henley Park."

After one of the Empress's dinners at Farnboro' Hill, a
small dinner of intimate friends, we had fun over a lottery
which she had arranged, making everything go off in the
most sprightly French way. What easy, pleasant society it
was! One admired the courage which put on this brightness, though all knew that the dead weight on the poor
heart was there, so that others should not feel depressed.
Even with these kind semblances of cheeriness no one
could be unmindful of the abiding sorrow in that woman's
face.

"*January 9th, 1895.*—The anniversary of the Emperor
Napoleon's death come round again. There was quite a little stir during the service in the church. The catalfalque,
heaped up with flowers, was surrounded with scores of lighted tapers as it lay before the altar. A young priest, in a laced
cotta, went up to it to set a leaf or flower or something in its
place, when instantly one of his lace sleeves blazed. Almost
simultaneously the General, in full uniform, springing up
the altar steps without the smallest click of his sword, was
at the priest's side, beating out the fire. Not another soul in
that crowded place had seen anything. That was like Will!
We laid wreaths on the tombs in the crypt."

An entry in March of that year records good progress
with *The Dawn of Waterloo*, and mentions that we had the
honour of receiving the Empress Frederick and her hosts,
the Connaughts, and their suites, who came to see the picture. I found the Empress still more like her mother than
when I first saw her, when she and the Crown Prince Frederick dined at the Goschens'—a memorable dinner, when

the fine, serious-looking and bearded Frederick told my husband he would desire nothing better for his sons than that they should follow in his footsteps. The Empress was beaming—that is exactly the word—and a few minutes after coming into the drawing-room she showed that she was anxious to get on to the studio, to save the light. So out we sallied, walking two and two, a formidable procession, and we were nearly half an hour in the little court-martial hut. They all had tea with us afterwards, quite filling the tiny drawing-room. The Empress was very small, and as she talked to me, looking up into my face, I thought her the most taking little woman I ever saw. She had what I call the "Victoria charm," which all her sisters shared with her—absolutely unstudied, homely, and exceedingly friendly. At least it so appeared to me in a high degree in her that day. But what a sorrow she had had to bear!

The picture was taken to the Club House, there to be shown for three days to the division before Sending-in Day. The idea was Will's, but I got the thanks—undeserved, as I had been reluctant to brave the dust on the wet paint. Crowds went to see it, from the generals down to the traditional last drummer.

I thought the Academicians were again unkind in the placing of my picture, and a trip to Paris was all the more welcome as a diversion, for there I was able to seek consolation in the treat of a plunge into the best art in the "City of Light." One interesting day in May found us at Malmaison, the country house of Napoleon and Josephine. There is always something mournful in a house no longer tenanted which once echoed the talk, the laughter, the comings and goings, the pleasant and arresting sounds of voices that are long silent. But *this* house, of all houses! It was absolutely stripped of everything but Napoleon's billiard table, and the worm-eaten bookshelves in his little musty study the only "fixtures" left. The ceilings we found in holes; that garden, once so much admired and enjoyed, choked with dusty nettles. We went into every room—the one where poor derelict Josephine died; the guests' bedrooms; the dining-room where Napoleon took his hurried meals; the library where he studied; the billiard-room, where he himself often took part in a game surrounded by "fair women and brave men" in the glitter of gorgeous uniforms and radiant *toilettes*. One lends one's mind's ear to the daily and nightly sounds outside—the clatter of horses' hoofs as the staff ride in and out of the courtyards with momentous despatches; the sharp words of command; the announcement of urgent arrivals demanding instant hearing. We found our minds revelling in suchlike imaginings. The chapel, the coach-houses, the great iron gates were all there, but seen as in a dream.

We were back at Aldershot on May 30th. "The Queen's Ball, at Buckingham Palace, brilliant as ever. The Shahza-da, the Ameer of Afghanistan's son, was the guest of the evening, as it is our policy just now to do him particular honour, after having made his father 'sit up.' A pale, wretched-looking Oriental, bored to tears! The usual delightful medley of men of every nationality, civilised and semi-civilised, was there in full splendour, but the rush of that crowd for the supper-room, in the wake of royalty, was most unseemly. Every one got jammed, and it was most unpleasant to have steel cartridge boxes and sword hilts sticking into one's bare arms in the pressure. I think there was something wrong this time with the doors. I was much complimented that night on my *Dawn of Waterloo*, but that was an inadequate salve to my wounded feelings.

"*June 15th.*—A great review here in honour of the young Shahzada, who is being so highly honoured this season. I don't think I ever saw such a large staff as surrounded that pallid princeling as he rode on to the field. The whole thing was a long affair, and our bored visitor refreshed himself occasionally with consolatory snuff. The whole of the cav-alry finished up, as usual, with a charge 'stem on,' and as the formidable onrush neared the weedy youth he began to turn his horse round, possibly suspecting deep-laid treachery."

My husband and I were present when Cardinals Vaughan and Logue laid the foundation stone of Westminster Cathedral. The luncheon that followed was enlivened by some excellent speeches, especially Cardinal Logue's, whose rich brogue rolled out some well-turned phrases.

A week later we were at dinner at Farnborough Hill. "There was a large house-party, including Princes Victor and Louis Napoleon, the elder a taciturn, shy, dark man about thirty-three, and the younger an alert, intelligent officer of thirty-one, who is a colonel in the Russian cavalry, and is the hope and darling of the Bonapartists. I call him Napoleon VI. Victor went in with the Empress to dinner and Louis with me, but on taking our seats the two brothers exchanged places, so that I sat on Victor's right. I had an uphill task to talk with the studious, silent Victor, and found my right-hand neighbour much more pleasant company, Sir Mackenzie Wallace. I had not caught his name and his accent was so perfect and his idioms and turns of speech so irreproachable that I never questioned his being a Frenchman. Away we went in the liveliest manner with our French till suddenly we lapsed into English, why I don't know. This gave the Empress her chance. She began chuckling behind her toothpick and asked me in French if he had a good accent in speaking English. 'Yes, madame, very good!' 'Ah! *really* good?' (chuckle). 'Really good, madame.' 'Ah, that is well' (chuckle). I saw in Will's face I was being chaffed and guessed the truth. Much laughter, especially from Louis. He told Will, across the Empress, that he had seen an engraving of *"Scotland for Ever!"* in a shop window in Moscow, and had presented it to the mess of his own cavalry regiment, the Czar being now colonel of the Scots Greys, and that he little expected so soon to meet the painter of that picture. The dinner was very bright and sparkling, so unlike a purely English one. How gratefully Will and I conformed to the spirit of the thing. His Irish heart beats in harmony with it. I didn't quite recover from my *faux pas* at table, and, on our taking leave, brought

everything into line once more by wishing Prince Louis
'*Felicissima Sera!*' in a way denoting a bewilderment of mind
amidst such a confusion of tongues. I left amidst applause.

"*July 8th.*—There was a sham fight on the Fox Hills to-
day to which the two French princes went. Will mounted
Victor on steady 'Roly Poly,' and sent H. on 'Heart of Oak'
to attend on His Imperial Highness throughout the day.
Louis was mounted by the Duke. My General loves to honour a Napoleon, so, when he was riding home with Louis
after the fight, and the Guards were preparing to give the
General the usual salute, he begged the Imperial Colonel to
take the salute himself. 'But, General,' I am not even in
uniform!' answered Louis. 'One of your name, sir, is always
in uniform,' was the ready reply. So Louis took it. On his
way back to the Empress he stopped at our hut, and after a
glass of iced claret cup on this grilling day, he looked at my
sketches, and at the little oil picture I am painting for Miss
S.—*Right Wheel!*—the Scots Greys at manœuvres. I wonder
if he has it in him to make a bid for the French Throne!

"*July 12th*—The Queen came down to-day, and there was
a very fine display of the picked athletes of the army at the
new gymnasium in the afternoon, before Her Majesty, who
did not leave her carriage. She looked pleased and in great
good humour. She gave a dinner to her generals in the
evening at the Pavilion as she did last year. Will sat near
her, and she kept nodding and smiling to him at intervals as
he carried on a lively conversation with Princesses Louise
and Beatrice. Her Majesty expanded into full contentment
when nine pipers, supplied by the three Highland Regiments of the Division, entered the room at the close of
dinner in full blast. They tell me that each regiment jealously adhered to its own key for its skirls, or whatever the
right word is, and so in three different keys did the pibrochs
bray, but this detail was not particularly noticeable in the
general hurly-burly. The Queen stood it well, though in
that confined space it must have tried her nerves. Give me
the bagpipes on the mountain side or in the desert, where I

have heard them and loved them.

"*July 13th.*—At a very fine review for the Queen, who brought her usual weather with her. She looked well pleased, especially with the stirring light cavalry charge at the close, when Brabazon pulled up his line at full charging pace within about 12 yards (it seemed to me) of the royal carriage. Really, for a moment, I thought, as the dark mass of men and horses rolled towards us, that he had forgotten all about 'Halt!' It was a tremendous *tour de force*, and a bit of swagger on the part of this dashing hussar. That group of the Queen in her carriage, with the four white horses and scarlet coated servants; the Prince of Wales and the rest of the glittering Staff; Prince Victor Napoleon in civilian dress, his heavy face shaded by his tall black hat as he uneasily sat his excited horse; the other carriages resplendent in red and gold; the Empress's more sober equipage full of French *élégantes*, and the wave of dark hussars bursting in a cloud of dust almost in amongst the group, all the leaders of the charging squadrons with sabres flung up and heads thrown back—what a sight to please me! I feel a physical sensation of refreshment on such occasions. What discipline and training this performance showed! Had one horse got out of hand he might have flopped right into the Queen's lap. I saw one of the squadron leaders give a little shiver when all was over. On getting home I was doing something to the bearskins of my Scots Greys in "*Right Wheel!*", showing the way the wind blew the hair back, as I had just seen it at the review, while fresh in my mind, when a servant came to tell me Princess Louise was at the Hut. I had got into my painting dress with sleeves turned up for coolness. I ran in, changed in half a minute, and had a nice interview, the Duchess of Connaught being there also, and we had one of those 'shoppy' art talks which the Duchess of Argyll likes.

"*August 16th.*—My 'At Home' day was made memorable by the appearance of the Empress Eugénie, who brought a remedy for little Eileen's cold. It was a plaster, which she showed me how to use. I cannot say how touched we were by this act, so thoughtful and kind—that poor childless widow! She seems to have a particularly tender feeling for Eileen, indeed Mdlle. d'Allonvile has told me so."

The rest of the Aldershot Diary is filled with military activities up to the date of the expiration of my husband's time there, and his appointment to the command of the South Eastern District with Dover Castle as our home. But between the two commands came an interlude filled with a tour through some parts of Italy I had not seen before, and a visit to the Villa Cyrnos at Cap Martin, whither the Empress had invited us.

CHAPTER TWENTY

ITALY AGAIN

IN January, 1896, we left Aldershot on a raw foggy day, with the usual winter brown-paper sky, the essence of dreariness, on leave for the land I love best. At Turin our train for Genoa was filled with poor young soldiers off to Abyssinia, the Italian Government having followed our example in the policy of "expansion"; with what success was soon seen. An Italian told us that "good coffee" was to be had from there, amongst other desirable commodities. So the poor young conscripts were being sent to fetch the good coffee, etc. They were singing in a chorus of tenor voices as they went, after affectionately kissing the comrades who had come to see them off.

At sunrise we arrived at Naples, Vesuvius looking like a great amethyst, transparent in the golden haze from the sun which rose just behind it. I must say the Neapolitan population struck me as very wretched; the men were no better than the poor creatures one might see in Whitechapel any day, and dressed, like them, in shoddy clothing. The poor skeleton mules and horses were covered with picturesque brass-mounted harness instead of flesh, and I saw no red-sashed, brown-limbed *lazzaroni* such as were supposed to dance *tarantelle* on the shore. Certainly there is not much dancing and singing in their hungry-looking descendants.

January 17th was a memorable day, spent at Pompeii. One must see the place for oneself. Familiar with it though you may be through books and paintings, Pompeii takes you by surprise. The suddenness of that entrance into the City of the Dead *is* a surprise to a newcomer, such as I was. To come into the city at once by the "Street of Tombs," which carries you steeply upwards into the interior—no turnstiles at the gate, no ticket collectors, no leave-your-umbrella-at-the-door; this natural way of entering gave me a strange sensation as if I were walking into the past. The present day was non-existent. Though we were three and a half hours circulating about those theatres, baths, villas, shops, through the narrow streets, with their deep ruts and stepping stones, I was so absorbed in the fascination of realising the life of those days that I never needed to rest for a moment, and the day had grown very hot. One rather drags oneself through a museum, but we were here under the sky, and Vesuvius, the author of this destruction, was there in very truth, looking down on us as we wandered through the remnants of his victim.

As to beauty of colour there is here a great feast for the painter. What could surpass, on a day like that, the simple beauty of those positive reds and yellows and blues of walls and pillars in that light, backgrounded by the tender blue of mountains delicately crested with the white of their snows? The positive strong foreground colours emphasised by the delicacy of the background! The absolute silence of the place was impressive and very welcome.

The Diary had better "carry on" here: "*Sunday, January 19th.*—To Capri and Sorrento on our way to Amalfi. There is a string of names! I feel I can't pronounce them to myself with adequate relish. To Mass at 8, and then at 9 by steamer to Capri, touching at Sorrento on our way. Three hours' passage over a very dark blue sea, which was flecked with foam off Castellamare. Capri is all I expected, a mass of orange and lemon groves in its lower part, with wonderful crags soaring abruptly, in places, out of the clear green water. Tiberius's villa is perched on the edge of a fearful precipice that has memories connected with his cruelties which one tries to smother. Indeed, all around one, in those scenes of Nature's loveliness, the detestable doings of man against man are but too persistently obtruding themselves on the mind which is seeking only restful pleasure.

"We were driven to the Hotel Quisisana ('Here one gets well'), very high up on a steep ridge, where the village is, and were sorry to find our pleasure marred by being set down to *déjeuner* with as repulsive a company of Teutons as one could see. The perspective of those feeding faces, along the edge of the table, tried me horribly. They say the Germans are outnumbering the British as tourists in Italy now. Nowhere do their loud voices and rude manners jar upon our sensibility as painfully as in Italy. The *Frau* next to me actually sniffed at four bottles out of the cruet in succession, poking them into her nose before she satisfied herself that she had found the right sauce for her chop! What's to be done with such people?

"We had not much time to give to the lovely island, for the little steamer had to take us to Sorrento at two o'clock. We put up there at the Hotel Tramontano, and had a stroll at sunset, with views of the coast and Vesuvius that spread out beyond the reach of my well-meaning, but inadequate, pen. I can't help the impulse of recording the things of beauty I have seen. It is owing to a wish to preserve such precious things in my memory, to waste nothing of them, and to record my gratitude as well."

At Amalfi came the culmination to our long series of experiences of the Neapolitan Riviera. The names of Amalfi, Ravello, Salerno and Pæstum will be with me to the end, in a halo of enchantment.

On returning to Naples, of course, we paid our respects to Vesuvius. Our climb to the highest point allowable of the erupting cone was not at all enchanting, and left my mind in a most perturbed condition. There was much food for meditation when our visit was over, but at the time one had only leisure to receive impressions, and very disconcerting impressions at that. A keen north wind blew the fumes from the crater straight down my throat as I panted upwards through the sulphur, ankle deep, and I could only think of my discomfort and probable collapse. I disdained a litter. I perceived several fat Germans in litters.

An even deeper impression was made on my mind than that produced by the eruption proper on our coming, after much staggering over cold lava, near a great, crawling river of liquid fire oozing out of the mountain's side. Above our heads the great maw of the crater was throwing up bursts of rock fragments with rumblings and growls from the cruel monster. I wonder when that wild beast will make its next pounce? And down there, far, far below, in the plain lay little Pompeii, its poor, tiny, insignificant victim! Yes, for a thoughtful climber there was more than the sulphurous north wind to make him pause.

The little funicular railway had brought us up to the foot of the cone, crunching laboriously over the shoulder of the mountain, and I could not but think—"If the chain broke?" At one point the open truck seemed to dangle over space. We were sitting with our faces towards the sea and away from the cone, and (were we never to be rid of them?) two corpulent Teutons faced us, hideously conspicuous, as having apparently nothing but the blue air behind them. There was no horizon at all to the sea, the pale haze merging sea and sky into one. Then, when we alighted, we found ourselves in a restaurant with Messrs. Cook & Co.'s waiters running about. Certainly it was no time for meditating or moralising in that medley of the prehistoric and the *fin de siècle*.

I found Rome very much changed after the lapse of all those years since I was there with our family during the last months of the Temporal Power. I shall never forget the shock I felt when, to lead off, on our arrival, I conducted my husband to the great balustrade on the Pincian over-looking the city, promising him my favourite view. It was a truly striking one in the far-off days, and quite beautiful. Instead of the reposeful vineyards of the area facing us beyond the Tiber, fitting middle distance between us and St. Peter's, gaunt buildings bordering wide, straight, staring streets glistening with tramlines seemed to jeer at me in vulgar triumph, and I am not sure that I did not shed tears in private when we got back to our hotel. One fact, howev-er, brought a sense of mental expansion as I surveyed that view, which should have made amends for the sensitive contraction of my artist's mind. That great basilica yonder was mine now! A return to Rome had another touch of sad-ness for me. Our father had been so happy there in introducing his girls to the city he loved. He seemed now to be ever by my side as the well-remembered haunts that were left unchanged were seen again. Leo XIII. was now Pope. On one particular occasion in the Sistine Chapel, at Mass, I was struck by the extraordinary effect of his white, utterly ethereal face and fragile figure as he stood at the altar, relieved against the background of Michael Angelo's exceedingly muscular *Last Judgment.* And, now, what of this *Last Judgment?* The action of our Lord, splendidly rendered as giving the powerful realisation of the push which that heavy arm is giving in menace to the condemned souls towards the Abyss on His left (I had almost said the *shove!*), is realistic and strong. But what a gross conception! Our modern minds cannot be impressed by this fleshly rendering of such a subject, a rendering suitable to the coarser fibre of the Middle Ages. I could positively hate this fresco, were I not lured, as a painter, to admire its technical power.

Our visit to the Empress at Cap Martin followed, on our way home to Aldershot. She received us with her usual genial grace. The place, of course, ideal, and the typical blue weather. We were made very much at home. Madame le Breton told me I was to wear a *table d'hôte* frock at dinner, and Pietri told Sir William a black tie to the evening suit was the order of the day. .

"*February 13th.*—The Villa Cyrnos is in a wood of stone pines, overhanging the sea on a promontory between Mentone and Monte Carlo. It is in the French Riviera style, all very white—no Italian fresco colouring. Plentiful striped awnings to keep off the intense sunlight. Cool marble rooms, polished parquets, flowers in masses—a sense of grateful freshness with reminders of the heat outside in the dancing reflections from the sea. Indeed, this is a charming retreat. Madame d'Arcos and her sister, Mrs. Vaughan, were there, who having just arrived from England, were full of accounts of the arrival of the remains of Prince Henry of Battenberg from Ashanti, and the funeral, at which Madame d'Arcos had represented the Empress. The different episodes were minutely described by her of this, the last act of the latest tragedy in our Royal Family. She had a sympathetic listener in the poor Empress.

"*February 14th.*—A sunny day marred, to me, by a visit to Monte Carlo, where the gambling is in fullest activity. The Empress wanted us all to go for a little cruise in a yacht, but though the sea was calm enough I preferred *terra firma*, and her ladies drove me to Monto Carlo. Hateful place! The lovely mountains were radiant in the low sunshine of that afternoon and the sea sparkling with light, but a crowd of over-dressed riff-raff was circulating about the casino and pigeon-shooting place, from which came the ceaseless crack of the cowardly, unsportsmanlike guns. I record, with loathing, one fellow I saw who came on the green, protected from the gentle air by a fur-lined coat which his valet took charge of while his master maimed his allotted number of clipped victims, and carefully replaced as soon as all the birds were down. A black dog ran out to fetch each fluttering thing as it fell. I was glad to see this hero was not an English man. Inside the casino the people were massed round the gaming tables, the hard light from the circular openings above each table bringing into relief the ugly lines of their perspiring faces. The atmosphere was dusty and stifling, and the hands of these horribly absorbed people were black with clawing in their gains across the grimy green baize. I drank in the pure, cool air of the sunset loveliness outside when I got free, with a very certain persuasion that I would never pay a second visit, except under polite compulsion, to the gambling palace of Monte Carlo.

"*February 15th.*—The Empress took us quite a long walk to see the corps of the '*Alpins*' at the Mentone barracks and back by the rocky paths along the shore. She is very active, and is looking beautiful.

"*Sunday, February 16th.*—All of us to Mass at the little Mentone church. The dear Empress gave me a little holy picture during the service and said, 'I want you to keep this.' There is at times something very touching about her."

I sent a small picture this year to the "New Gallery," instead of the Academy, feeling still the effects of their unkindness in placing *The Dawn of Waterloo* where they did the preceding year.

CHAPTER TWENTY ONE

THE DOVER COMMAND

AND now Dover Castle rises into prominence above the horizon as I travel onward. My husband was offered Colchester or Dover. He left the choice to me. How could there be a doubt in my mind? The Castle was the very ideal, to me, of a residence. Here was History, picturesqueness, a wide view of the silver sea, and the line of the French coast to free the mind of insularity. So to Dover we went, children, furniture, horses, servants, dogs and all, from the Aldershot bungalow. As usual, I was spared by Sir William all the trouble of the move, and while I was comfortably harboured by my ever kind and hospitable friends, the Sweetmans, in Queen's Gate, my husband was managing all the tiresome work of the move.

It was a pleasure to give dances at the Constables' Tower, and the dinners were like feasts in the feudal times under that vaulted ceiling of the Banqueting Hall. Our boys' bedroom in the older part of this Constables' Tower had witnessed the death of King Stephen, and a winding staircase conducted the unappreciative London servants by a rope to their remote domiciles. The modernised part held the drawing-rooms, morning-room, library, and chief bedrooms, while in the garden, walled round by the ramparts, stood the tower whence Queen Mary is said to have gazed upon her lost Calais. My studio had a balcony which overhung the moat and drawbridge. What could I have better than that? No wonder I accomplished a creditable picture there, for I had many advantages. I place *"Steady, the Drums and Fifes!"* amongst those of my works with which I am the least dissatisfied. The Academy treated me well this time, and gave the picture a place of honour. These drummer-boys of the old 57th Regiment, now the Middlesex, are waiting, under fire, for the order to sound the advance, at the Battle of Albuera. That order was long delayed, and they and the regiment had to bear the supreme test of endurance, the keeping motionless under fire. A difficult subject, excellent for literature, very trying for painting. I had had the vision of those drummer-boys for many years before my mind's eye, and it is a very obvious fact that what you see strongly in that way means a successful realisation in paint. Circumstances were favourable at Dover. The Gordon Boys' Home there gave me a variety of models in its well-drilled lads, and my own boys were sufficiently grown to be of great use, though, for obvious reasons, I could not include their dear faces in so painful a scene. The yellow coatees, too, were a tremendous relief to me after that red which is hard to manage. I remember asking Detaille if he ever thought of giving our army a turn. "I would like to," he said, "but the red frightens us." The bandsmen of the Peninsular War days wore coatees of the colour of the regimental facings. After long and patient researches I found out this fact, and the facings of the 57th, being canary yellow, I had an unexpected treat. I remember how the Duke of York[12] at an Aldershot dinner had characteristically caught up this fact with great interest when I told him all about my preparations for this picture. I am glad to know this work belongs to the old 57th, the "Die Hards," who won that title at Albuera. "Die hard, men, die hard!" was their colonel's order on that tremendous day.

Many interesting events punctuated our official life at Dover:

"*August 15th, 1896.*—Great doings to-day. We had a busy time of it. Lord Salisbury was installed Lord Warden in the place of Lord Dufferin. Will had the direction, not only of the military part of the ceremonies but of the social (in conjunction with me), as far as the Constables' Tower was concerned. Everything went well. Lord and Lady Salisbury drove in a carriage and four from Walmer up to our Tower, and, while the procession was forming outside to escort them down to the town, they rested in our drawing-room for about half an hour, and Lord Dufferin also came in.

"I had to converse with these exalted personages whilst officers in full uniform and women in full toilettes came and went with clatter of sabre and rustle of silk. To fill up the rather trying half-hour and being expected to devote my attention chiefly to the new Lord Warden, I bethought myself of conducting him to a window which gave a bird's-eye view of the smoky little town below. I moralised, *à la* Ruskin, on the ugliness of the coal smoke which was smudging that view in particular, and spoiling England in general. On reconducting the weighty Salisbury to a rather fragile settee I morally and very nearly physically knocked him over by this felicitous remark: 'Well, I have the consolation of knowing that the coalfields of England are finite!' 'What?' he shouted, with a bound which nearly broke the back of that settee. I don't think he said anything more to me that day. Of course, I meant that smokeless methods would have to be discovered for working our industries, but

I left that unsaid, feeling very small. It is my misfortune
that I have not the knack of small talk, so useful to official
people, and that I am obliged to propel myself into conversation by pronouncements of that kind. Shall I ever forget
the catastrophe at the L—s' dinner at Aldershot, when I
announced, during a pause in the general conversation, to
an old gentleman who had taken me in, and whose name I
hadn't caught, that there was one word I would inscribe on
the tombstone of the Irish nation, and that word was—
Whisky. The old gentleman was John Jameson.

"But to return to to-day's doings. I had to consign to C.,[13]
as my deputy, the head of the table for such of the people as
were remaining at the Castle for luncheon as I myself had
to appear at that function at the Town Hall. The procession, military, civil and civic—especially civic—started at
12 for the 'Court of Shepway,' where much antique ceremonial took place. When they all reached the Town Hall after
that, Lord Salisbury first unveiled a full-length portrait of
the outgoing Lord Warden, at the entrance to the Banqueting Hall, and complimented him on so excellent a likeness
with a genial pat on the back. We were all in good humour
which increased as we filed in to luncheon and continued
to increase during that civic feast, enlivened by a band.
Trumpets sounded before each speech, and the sharp clapping of hands called, I think, 'Kentish Fire,' gave a local
touch which was pleasingly original. I am glad, always, to
find the county spirit still so strong in England, and
nowhere is it stronger than in Kent. It must work well in
war with the county regiments.

"I am afraid Lady Salisbury must have got rather knocked
out of time coming to the Castle, by all the saluting, trum-
peting and general prancing of the guard of honour. She
was nervous crossing our drawbridge with four 'jumpy' horses which she told me had never been with troops before!
Altogether I don't think this was a day to suit her at all. I
heard the postillion riding the near leader shout back to the
coachman on the box as they started homeward from our

door, 'Put on both brakes *hard!*' Away went the open carriage which had very low sides and no hood, and Lord
Salisbury, being very wide, rather bulged over the side.
Wearing a military cape, lent him by my General, the day
turning chilly, he had a rather top-heavy appearance, and
we only breathed freely when that ticklish drawbridge, and
the very steep drop of the hill beyond it, were passed. So
now let them rest at Walmer. Will will do all he can to
secure peace for them there."

On August 20th I went to poor Sir John Millais' funeral
in St. Paul's. The ceremony was touching to me when I
thought of the kind, enthusiastic friend of my early days
and his hearty encouragement and praise. They had placed
his palette and a sheaf of his brushes on the coffin. Lord
Wolseley, Irving, the actor, Holman Hunt and Lord Rose-
bery were the pall-bearers. The ceremony struck me as
gloomy after being accustomed to Catholic ritual, and the
undertaker element was too pronounced, but the music was
exquisite. So good-bye to a truly great and sincere artist.
What a successful life he had, rounded by so terribly painful
a death!

One of the most interesting of the Dover episodes was
our hiring of "Broome Hall" for the South-Eastern District
manœuvres in the following September. The Castle was too
far away for working them from there, so this fine old Elizabethan mansion, being in the very centre of the theatre of
"war," became our headquarters. There we entertained Lord
Wolseley and his staff as the house-party. Other warriors
and many civilians whose lovely country houses were dot-
ted about that beautiful Kentish region came in from
outside each day, and for four days what felt to me like a
roaring kind of hospitality went on which proved an aston-
ishing feat of housekeeping on my part. True, I was liberally
helped, but to this day I marvel that things went so
successfully. Everything had to be brought from the Castle—servants in an omnibus, *batterie de cuisine,* plate, linen
and all sorts of necessary things, in military waggons, for the

house had not been inhabited for a long while. All the food was sent out from Dover fresh every day, by road—no village near. The house had been palatially furnished in the old days, but its glory was much faded and so ancestral was it that it possessed a ghost. A pathetic interest attaches to "Broome" to-day, and I should not know it again in its renovated beauty. Lord Kitchener restored it to more than its pristine lustre, I am told.

The morning start each day of all these generals (Sir Evelyn Wood was one of them) from the front door for the "battle" was a pleasing sight for me, with the strong cavalry escort following. After the gallant cavalcade had got clear I would follow in the little victoria with friends, hoping in my innermost heart that I was leaving everything well in hand behind me for the hungry "Cocked Hats" on their return.

On March 30th, 1897, I had a glimpse of Gladstone. We were on the pier to receive a Royalty, and the "Grand Old Man" was also on board the Calais boat. He was the last to land and was accompanied by his wife. He came up the gangway with some difficulty, and struck me as very much aged, with his face showing signs of pain. I had not seen him since he sat beside me at a dinner at the Ripons' in 1880, when his keen eye had rather overawed me. He was now eighty-eight! The crowd cheered him well, but the old couple were past that sort of thing, and only anxious to seek their rest at "Betteshanger," a few miles distant, whither Lord Northbourne's carriage whirled them away from public view.

And now comes the Diamond Jubliee of Queen Victoria. I think my fresh impressions written down at the time should be inserted here as I find them. Too much national sorrow and suffering brought to us by the Great War, and too many changes have since blurred that bright picture to allow of posthumous enthusiasm for its chronicling to-day. Were I to tone down that picture to the appearance it has to me at the present time it would hardly be worth showing.

"June 22nd, 1897.—Jubilee Day. I never expected to be
so touched by what I have seen of these pageants and
rejoicings, and to feel so much personal affection for the
Queen as I have done through this wonderful week. Thinking of other nations, we cannot help being impressed with
the way in which the English have comported themselves
on this occasion—the unanimity of the crowds; the willing-
ness of every one concerned; all resulting in those huge
pageants passing off without a single jar. My place was in
the courtyard of the Horse Guards; Will's place was on his
big grey before St. Paul's, at Queen Anne's statue, to keep
an eye on things. I had an effective view of the procession
making the bend from Whitehall into the courtyard, and
out by the archway into the parade ground. This gave me
time to enjoy the varied types of all those nationalities
whose warriors represented them, as they filed past at close
quarters. But we had five hours of waiting. These hours
were well filled up for me, so continually interested in
watching the movements of the troops as they took up their
positions for receiving the procession and saluting the
Queen. I think in the way of perfect dress and of superfine,
thoroughbred horseflesh, Lord Lonsdale's troop of Cumber-
land Hussars was as memorable a group as any that day.
They wore the 'sling jacket,' only known to me in pictures
and old prints of the pre-Crimean days, and to see these
gallant-looking crimson pelisses in reality was quite a
delightful surprise.

"The sun burst through the clouds just as the guns
announced to us that the Queen had started from Buckingham Palace on her great round by St. Paul's at 11.15. So we
waited, waited. Presently some one called out, 'Here's Captain Ames,' and, knowing he was the leader, we nimbly ran
up to our seats. It seemed hardly credible that the journey
to St. Paul's and the ceremony there, and the journey
homewards could have occupied so comparatively brief an
interval. I think the part of the procession which most
delighted me was the cohort of Indian cavalry, and then the

gorgeous bunch of thirty-six princes, each in his national dress or uniform. These rode in triplets. You saw a blue-coated Prussian riding with a Montenegrin on one side and an Italian bonneted by the absurd general's helmet now in vogue on the other. Then came another triplet of a Persian, whose breast was a galaxy of diamonds flashing in the sun, an Austrian with fur pelisse and busby (poor man, in that heat), and the brother of the Khedive, wearing the familiar *tarboosh*, riding a little white Arab. Then followed an English admiral in the person of the Duke of York, a Japanese mannikin on his right, and a huge Russian on his left, and so on, and so on—types and dresses from all the quarters of the globe in close proximity, so that one could compare them at a glance. The dignified Indian cavalry were superb as to dress and *puggarees*, but the faces were stolid, very unlike the keen, clean-cut Arab types which so charmed me in Egypt and Palestine. There certainly were too many carriages filled with small Germans. Then came the colonial escort to the Queen's carriage. As they came on and passed before us I do not exaggerate when I say that there seemed to pass over them an ever-deepening cloud-shadow, as it were, from the white Canadians riding in front, through ever-deepening shades of brown down to the blackest of negroes, who rode last. What an epitome of our Colonial Empire! Then, finally, before the supreme moment, came Lord Wolseley, the immediate forerunner of the Royal carriage. He looked well and gallant and youthful. Then round the curve into the courtyard the eight cream-coloured horses in rich gala harness of Garter-blue and gold! So quick was the pace that I dared not dwell too long on their beauty for I was too absorbed in the Queen during that precious minute. There she was, the centre of all this! A little woman, seated by herself (I had not time to see who sat facing her) with an expressionless pink face, preoccupied in settling her bonnet, which had got a little crooked, as though nothing unusual was going on, and that was the last I saw of her as she passed under the dark archway, facing homeward.

"*June 26th.*—Off from Dover at 2 a.m. for Southampton, by way of London, to see the culminating glory of the Jubilee—the greatest naval review ever witnessed. At eight we left Waterloo in one of the 'specials' that took holders of invitation cards for the various ocean liners that had been chartered for the occasion. Our ship was the P. and O. *Paramatta*, and very pleased I was on beholding her vast proportions, for I feared qualms on any smaller vessel. There were meetings on board with friends and a great luncheon, and general good humour and complacency at being Britons. The day cleared up at 10.30, and only a slight haze thinly veiled the mighty host of the Channel Fleet as we slowly steamed towards it along the Solent. Gradually the sun shone fully out and the day settled into steady brilliance.

"Well, I have been so inflated with national pride since beholding our naval power this day that if I don't get a prick of some sort I shall go off like a balloon. Let us be exultant just for a week! We won't think of the ugly look of India just now and all the nasty warnings of the bumptious Kaiser and the rest of it. We can't while looking at Britannia ruling the waves, as we are doing to-day. Five miles of ships of war five lines deep! When all these ships fired each twenty-one guns by divisions as the Prince of Wales steamed up and down the lines, and the crews of each vessel in turn gave such cheers as only Jack Tar can give, it was not the moment to threaten us with anything. I shall never forget the aspect of this fleet of ours, black hulls and yellow funnels and 'fighting tops' stretching to east and west as far as the eye could reach and beyond, the mellow sunlight full upon them and the slowly-rolling clouds of smoke that wrapped them round with mystery as their countless guns thundered the salute! Myriads of flags fluttered in the breeze, the sea sparkled, and in and out of those motionless battleships all manner of steam and sailing craft moved incessantly, deepening by the contrast of their hurry the sense one had of the majestic power contained in those reposing monsters...Every one is saying, 'And to think that not a single ship has been recalled from abroad to make up this display!' We are all very pleased, and have the good old Nelson feeling about us." On June 28th the Queen held her Jubilee Garden Party in the Buckingham Palace grounds. There we looked our last on her.

I took four of the children, in August, to Bruges, that old city so much enjoyed by me in my early years. I was charmed to see how carefully all the old houses had been preserved, and, indeed, I noticed that a few of them, vulgarly modernised then, were now restored to their original beauty. How well the Belgians understand these things! Seventeen years after this date the eldest of the two schoolboys I had with me was to ride through that same old Bruges as A.D.C. to the general commanding "The Immortal 7th Division," which, retiring before the German hordes, was to turn and help to rend them at Ypres.

In 1898 I exhibited a smaller picture than usual—*The Morrow of Talavera*, which was very kindly placed at the Academy—and I began a large Crimean subject, *The Colours*, for the succeeding year. I had some fine models at Dover for this picture. In making the studies for it I had an interesting experience. I wanted to show the colour party of the Scots Guards advancing up the hill of the Alma in their full parade dress—the last time British troops wore it in action—Lieutenant Lloyd Lindsay carrying the Queen's colour. It was then he won the V.C. Lord Wantage (that same Lloyd Lindsay), now an old man, but full of energy, when he heard of my project, conducted me to the Guards' Chapel in London, and there and then had the old, dusty, moth-eaten Alma colours taken down from their place on the walls, and held the Queen's colour once more in his hand for me to see. I made careful studies at the chapel, and restored the fresh tints which he told me they had on that far-away day, when I came to put them into the picture. I was in South Africa when the Academy opened in the following spring.

On September 11th, 1898, we received the terrible news of the assassination of the Empress of Austria. I had seen her every Sunday and feast day at our little Ventnor church, at Mass, during her residence at Steep Hill Castle. She had the tiniest waist I ever saw—indeed, no woman could have lived with a tinier one. She was beautiful, but so frigid in her manner; she seemed made of stone, yet she rode splendidly to hounds—altogether an enigma.

October 27th, 1898, I thoroughly enjoyed. It was a day after my own heart—picturesque, historical, stirring, amusing. Sir Herbert Kitchener, *the* Sirdar *par excellence*, was received at Dover on his arrival from the captured Khartoum with all the prestige of his new-won honours shining around him. My husband had decided that the regulation military honours "to be accorded to distinguished persons" were applicable to the man who was coming, and so a guard of honour (Highlanders) with the regimental colour was drawn up at the pier head, the regimental officers in red and the staff in blue. The crowd on the upper part of the pier was immense and densely packed all along the parapet, and the Lower Pier, reserved for special people, was crowded, too. It was a calm, grey, yet bright day, and the absence of wind made things pleasant. Great gathering of Cocked Hats at the entrance gates, and we all walked to the landing stage. There was a dense smudge of black smoke on the horizon. I knew that meant Kitchener. Keeping my eye on that smudge, I took but a distracted part in the small talk and frequent introductions of distinguished persons come from afar to welcome the man of the hour, "the Avenger of Gordon." I was conducted to the head of the landing steps, together with such of the staff as were not to go on board the boat with the General. Then the smudge got hidden behind the pier end, but I could see the ever-increasing swish and swirl of the water on the starboard side of the hidden steamer, and soon she swept alongside; a few vague cheers began, no one in the crowd knowing the Sirdar by

sight. When, however, the General went on board and
shook hands, this proclaimed at once where the man was,
and cheer upon cheer thundered out. I have never, before
or since, seen such spontaneous enthusiasm in England.
After a little talk (my husband and he were long together
on the Nile) and after the delivery of letters (one from the
Queen) and telegrams, during which the hurrahs went on
in a great roar and multitudinous pocket handkerchiefs
fluttered in a long perspective, the big, solid, stolid, sunburnt Briton stepped on English soil once more. While
shaking hands with me he seemed astonished and amused
at all that was going on and, looking over my head at the
masses of people above, he lifted his hat, and thenceforth
kept it in his hand as he was escorted to the Lord Warden
Hotel. He had asked his A.D.C., on first catching sight of
the reception awaiting him, "What is all this about?"

Then there was an Address at the hotel to which he listened with an ox-like patience, and after that the enormous
company of invited guests went to lunch. In his speech my
husband paid the Sirdar the compliment of saying that the
traditional Field Marshal's baton would be found in his
trunk when the customs officers opened it at Victoria.
Kitchener spoke so low I could not hear him. Had he been
less immovable one could have plainly seen how utterly he
hated having to make a speech. His travelling dress looked
most interestingly incongruous amidst the rich uniforms
and the glossy frock-coats as he stood up to say what he had
to say. As we all bulged out of the hotel door the cheers
began again from the crowds. I took care to look at the people that day, and I was struck by their *unanimity*. All ranks
were there, and yet on every face, well bred or unwashed, I
saw the same identical expression—one of broad, laughing
delight. Such were my impressions, which I noted down, as
usual, at the moment, and I have lived to see that remarkable man work out his life, and end it with a tragedy that
will hold its place in history; my husband's prophecy, put in
those playful words at Dover, fulfilled; a threatening disaster

IN WESTERN IRELAND.
A "JARVEY" AND "BIDDY."

A DESPATCH-BEARER, BOER WAR, AND THE HORSE-GUNNERS.

to the Empire turned into victory with the aid of that extraordinary mind and physical endurance; and the burning fire
of that personality quenched, untimely, in the icy depths of
a northern sea.

CHAPTER TWENTY TWO

THE CAPE AND DEVONPORT

ON November 12th, 1898, my husband sailed for South
Africa, there to take up the military command, and to
act as High Commissioner in place of Sir Alfred Milner,
home on leave. His staff at Dover loved him. Their send-off
brought tears to his eyes. I, C. and the A.D.C. saw him off
from Southampton, to rejoin him in the process of time at
the Cape. We little knew what a dark period in his life
awaited him out there, brought about by the malice of
those in power there and at home. It is too sacred and too
painful a subject for me to record it here further than I have
done. The facts will be found in his *Autobiography*. I left
England on February 18th, 1899, with three of the children,
leaving the two eldest boys at college. It was a very painful
leave-taking at the Waterloo Station. My mother was there
and all the dear ones, whom I did not expect to see again
for two or three years—my mother perhaps ever again. Yet
in a few months we were back there! My theory that one
should try and not fret about the future, which is an
absolutely unknown quantity, proved justified. I have
chronicled our voyage out in my former little book, and
described one night at Madeira—a night of enchantment
under the moon.

I need not go over the days on the "blue water" again,
nor our strange life beyond the Equator, where, though I
was filled with admiration for the beauty of our surroundings, I never felt the happiness which Italy, Egypt or
Palestine had given me. Very absurd, no doubt, and sentimental, but my love of the old haunts made me feel

resentful of the topsy-turvy state of things I found down there. The crescent moon on what (to me) was the wrong side of the sunset, the hot north wind, the cold blast from the south, the shadows all inverted,—no, I did not enjoy this contradiction to my well-beloved traditions. There was, besides, a local melancholy in that strange beauty I cannot describe. All this may be put down to sentimentality, but a very real melancholy attaches to South Africa in my mind in connection with my husband, who suffered there for his honesty and devotion to the honour of the Empire he served. The authorities accepted his resignation of the Cape command which he tendered for fear of embarrassing the Government, and he accepted the command of the Western District in its place, which meant Devonport. So on August 22nd we all embarked for Home.

There we found the campaign of calumny, originated in South Africa against Sir William, in its acutest phase. The Press was letting loose all the poison with which it was being supplied, and I consequently went through, at first, the bitter pain of daily trying to intercept the vilest anonymous letters, many of them beer-stained missives couched in ill-spelt language from the slums. Not all the reparation offered to my husband later on—the bestowal of the Grand Cross of the Bath, his election to the dignity of Privy Councillor, his selection as the safest judge to investigate the South African war stores scandals, not to name other acts conveying the *amende honorable*—ever healed the wound.

His offence had been a frank admission of sympathy for a people tenacious of their independence and, knowing the Boers as he did, he knew what their resistance would mean in case of attack. He was appalled at the prospect of a war, not against an army but against a people, involving the farm-burnings and all the horrors which our armies would have to resort to. He would fain have seen violence avoided and diplomacy used instead, knowing, as he did, that the old intransigent Dopper element would die out in time, and the new generation of Boers, many of whom were educated

at our universities, intermarrying with the English, as they
were already doing, would have brought about that very
union of the two races within the Empire which has been
reached to-day through all that suffering. In case, however,
war should be decided on he employed the utmost vigour
allowed to official language to warn those in power of the
necessity for enormous forces in order to ensure success.
Some of his despatches were suppressed. The idea at Headquarters was an easy march to Pretoria. What I have
alluded to as the malice which prompted the campaign of
calumny had caused the report to be spread that our initial
defeats were owing to his wilful neglect in not warning the
directing powers of the gravity of their undertaking.

The chief interest I found in our new appointment was
caused by the frequent arrivals of foreign men-of-war,
whose captains were received officially and socially, and
there were admirals, too, when squadrons came. It was
interesting and amusing. Lord and Lady Charles Scott were
at the Admiralty and, later, Sir Edward Seymour, during our
appointment. The foreign sailors prevented the official
functions from becoming monotonous, and we got a certain
amount of pleasure out of this Devonport phase of our
experiences. I carried my painting "through thick and
thin," and did well, on the whole, at the Academy. I had
the "consuming zeal"—a very necessary possession. One
year it was a big tent-pegging picture (I don't know where
its purchaser is now), which was well lighted at Burlington
House. Then a Boer War subject, *Within Sound of the
Guns*—well placed; followed by an Afghan subject, *Rescue
of Wounded*, which to my great pleasure was given an excellent place in the *Salle d'Honneur*. I also accomplished other
smaller works and exhibited a great number of water
colours. It is a medium I like much. I also prepared for the
Press my *Letters from the Holy Land* there which I have
already mentioned. My publishers, Messrs. A. and C. Black,
reproduced the water-colour illustrations very faithfully.

Our French sailor guests were always bright, so were

the Italians, but the Japanese were very heavy in hand,
and conversation was uphill work. It was mainly carried
on by repeated smiles and nods on their part. When their
big ships came in on one occasion the Admiralty gave
them the first dinner, of course, and at the end the band-
master had the happy thought of giving a few bars out of
Arthur Sullivan's "Mikado" before the Emperor's health
was drunk, the National Air not being in his repertory.
Some one asked the Jap admiral if he recognised it. "Ah!
no, no, no!" came the usual smiling and nodding answer.
At the Port Admirals' I was to learn that in the navy you
mustn't stand up for our Sovereign's health, by order of
William IV. This resulted one evening in our sitting for
"The King" and standing up for "The Kaiser." There were
the German admiral and officers present. I thought that
very unfortunate.[14]

Well, Devonport in summer was very delightful, but
Devonport in winter had long periods of fog and gloom. I
had the blessing of another trip to Italy, this time with our
eldest daughter, starting on a dark wintry day in early
March, 1900. Sir William's work prevented his coming with
us. Viâ Genoa to Rome lay our happy way. Of course, it
wasn't the Rome I first knew, but the shock I received when
revisiting it four years before this present visit had already
introduced me into the new order, and I now knew what to
see, enjoy, and avoid. There were several new things to
enjoy: above all, the Forum, now all open to the sky! In the
dear old days that space was a rather dreary expanse of
waste land where some poor old paupers were to be daily
seen, leisurely labouring under the delusion that they were
excavating. They grubbed up the tufts of grass and scraped
the dust with pocket-knives, and the treasures remained
comfortably tucked away from public view. Then the much-
abused Embankment. The dignified sweep of its lines leads
the eye up, as it follows the flow of the stream, to the dignity of St. Peter's, whereas, formerly, in its place, unbeautiful
masses of mouldering houses tottered over the Tiber and

gave that long-suffering river the reflections of their drain-
pipes. Then, the two end arches of that most estimable
Ponte Sant' Angelo are now cleared of the old mud which
blocked them up malodorously and docked the lovely thing
of its symmetry. Then, finally, Rome is clean!

We had the good fortune to be present at two very striking Papal functions, striking as bringing together Catholics
from a wide-flung circle embracing some remote nationalities unknown by sight to me. The first was the Pope's
Benediction in St. Peter's on March 18th. We were standing altogether about three hours in the crowd at the Tomb,
well placed for seeing the Holy Father. He was taken round
the vast basilica in his *sedia gestatoria,* and blessed a wildly
cheering crowd. I never saw a human being so like a spirit
as Leo XIII. He looked as white as his mitre as he leant forward and stretched his arm out in benediction from side to
side, borne high above the helmets of the Noble Guard.
One heard cheers in all languages, and a curious effect was
produced by the whirling handkerchiefs, which made a
white haze above the dark crowd. I have often heard secular
monarchs cheered, and that very heartily, but for a Pope it
seems that more than ordinary loyalty prompts the cheer-
ers. The people seem to give out their whole being in their
voices and gestures.

The Diary says: "I am glad I have seen that old man's face
and his look, as though it came to us from beyond the
grave. At times the cheers went up to the highest pitch of
both men's and women's voices. A strange sound to hear in
a church."

A spring day spent at the well-known Hadrian's Villa,
under Tivoli, is not to be allowed to pass without a grateful
record. It is a most exquisite place of old ruins, cypresses,
olives and, at this time, flowering peach trees, violets and
anemones. It is an enchanting site for a country house.
Hadrian chose well. From there you see the delicately-pen-
cilled dome of St. Peter's on the rim of the horizon to the
west, and behind you, to the north, rise the steep foot-hills

of the mountains, some crowned with old cities. The ruins of the villa are all *minus* the lovely outer coating which used to hide the brickwork, and poor Hadrian would have felt very woeful had he foreseen that all the white loveliness of his villa was to come to this. But as bits of warm colour and lovely surface those brick spaces take the sun and shadow beautifully between the dark masses of the cypresses and feathery grey cloudiness of the olives. Nowhere is the "touch and go" nature of life more strikingly put before the mind than in dead Rome, where so much magnificence in stone and marble and mosaic and bronze has fallen into lumps of crumbling brick.

On March 26th we attended the Papal Benediction in the Sistine Chapel, which is a remarkable thing to see. It was a memorable morning. The floor of the chapel was packed with pilgrims, some of them rough men and women from remote regions of the north-east, whose outlandish costumes were especially remarkable for the heavy Cossack boots, reaching to the knee, worn by both sexes. One wondered how these people journeyed to Rome. What a gathering of the faithful we looked down on from our gallery! The same ecstatic cheering we had heard in St. Peter's announced the entrance of Leo XIII. There he was, the holy creature, blessing right and left with that thin alabaster hand, half covered with a white mitten. With all their hoarse barbaric cheering, I noticed how those peasants, who had so particularly attracted me, remembered to bend their heads and most devoutly make the sign of the cross as he passed. They almost monopolised my study of the motley crowd, but I was aware of the many nationalities present, and the same enthusiasm came from them all. At such times a great consolation eases the mind, saddened, as it often is, by the general atmosphere of declining faith in which one has to live one's ordinary life in the world. After the Mass came the presentation of the pilgrims at the altar steps. The Pope had kind words for all, bending down to hear and to speak to them, and often stroking the men's heads. One huge Muscovite peasant knelt long at his feet, and the Pope kept patting the rough man's cheek and speaking to him and blessing him over and over again. At the sight of this a wild *"hourah!"* broke from his fellow villagers. Where in the world was their village? In the mists of remoteness, but here in heart, unmistakably. Following the swarthy giant three sandy-haired German students, carrying their plumed caps in their hands and girt with rapiers, presented some college documents to receive the Papal benediction, and a great many men and women knelt and passed on, but the Pope seemed in no way fatigued. As he was borne out again he waved us an upward blessing with his white and most friendly countenance turned up to us.

Our Roman wanderings included a visit to the Holy Father's Vatican gardens, which are part of the little temporal kingdom a Pope still possesses, and to his tiny "country house" therein, where he goes for change of air (!) in the summer, about two stone-throws from the Vatican. I note: "There are well-trimmed vineyards there; there are pet birds and beasts in a little 'zoological gardens'; there is the arbour where he has his meals on hot days; and, finally, we were conducted to his little villa bedroom from whose window one of the finest views of Rome is seen, dominated by the Quirinal, within (let us hope) shaking hands distance." We heard the "Miserere" at St. Peter's on Good Friday—very impressive, that twilight service in the apse of the great basilica! The unaccompanied voices of boys sounded in sweetest music—one hardly knew whence it came—and the air seemed to thrill with the thin angelic sound in the waning light as one by one the candles at the altar were put out. At the last Psalm the last light was extinguished, and the vast crowd with its wan faces remained lighted only by the faint glimmer that came down from the pale sky through the high windows. Then good-bye to Rome. We left for Perugia on April 22nd. I certainly ought to be grateful for having had yet another reception by my Umbrian Hills! And such a reception that April afternoon, with the low sun gilding everything into fullest beauty! I did my best to secure that moment in miserably inadequate paint from the hotel window immediately on arrival. Better than nothing. But no more of Perugia, nor of dear old Florence on our way to academic Padua; no more of Verona. I have much yet to record on getting home, and after!

CHAPTER TWENTY THREE

A NEW REIGN

SIR WILLIAM was asked by Lord Wolseley to take up the Aldershot command in the absence of Sir Redvers Buller, who was struggling very desperately to retrieve our fortunes in the Boer War; so to Aldershot we went from Devonport, where my husband's command ran concurrently. How intensely England had hoped for the turning of the tide when Buller was given the tremendous task of directing our armies! We forget the horrors the nation went through in those days because the late War has made us pass through the same apprehensions multiplied by millions, but there the fact remains in our history that we nearly suffered a terrible catastrophe at the time of which I am writing. Buller, on leaving for the Cape, had said to my husband how fervently he wished he possessed his gift of imagination, and, indeed, that is a very precious gift to a commander. This truly awful state of things—our terrible losses, and the temporary lowering of our military prestige (thank heaven, so gloriously recovered and enhanced in the World War!)—were the answer to the repeated assertion made, when we were at the Cape, by those who ought to have known, that "the Boers won't fight." How this used to enrage my husband, whose "gift of imagination" made him see so clearly the danger ahead. Well, all this is of the long ago, and, as I have already noted, it is better to say little now; but the sense of injustice lives!

Buller had a great reception at Aldershot on his return

from South Africa. I never saw a more radiantly happy face on a woman than poor Lady Audrey's, who had been in a state of most tense anxiety during her dear Redvers' absence. As the train steamed into the station the band struck up "See the Conquering Hero comes!" The horses of his carriage were unharnessed, and the triumphal car was drawn by a team of firemen to Government House. At the entrance gate a group of school children sang "Home, sweet Home"; my husband hauled down his flag and Buller's was run up, and so that episode closed.

We had inhabited a suburban-looking villa on the road to Farnborough during the absence of Sir Redvers, not wishing to disturb the anxious watcher at Government House, and very often we saw the Empress, just as in the old days. She told us the dear Queen was very ill, worse than the world was allowed to know. My husband had always said the war would kill her, for she had taken our losses cruelly to heart, and so it happened on January 22nd, 1901. The resumed Devonport Diary says:

"A day ever to be marked in English history as a day of mourning. Our Queen is dead. At dinner S. brought us the news that she passed away at 6.30 this afternoon. We were prepared for it, but it seems like a dream. To us who have been born and have lived all our lives under her sovereignty it is difficult to realise that she is gone.

"*January 23rd, 1901.*—A dull gloomy day, punctuated by 81 minute guns, which began booming at noon. All the royal standards and flags hanging half-mast in the fog, on land and afloat.

"*January 24th.*—At noon-day all standards and flags were run up to the masthead, and a quick thunder of guns proclaimed the accession of Edward VII. At the end the band on board the guardship *Nile* struck up 'God Save the King.' The flags will all be lowered again until the day after Queen Victoria is laid to rest. Edward VII! How strange it sounds, and how events and changes are rolling down upon us every hour now. Albert Edward will be a greater man as Edward VII!

"*February 5th.*—The Queen was buried to-day beside her husband at Frogmore. It is inexpressibly touching to think of them side by side again. Model wife and mother, how many of your women subjects have strayed away, of late, from those virtues which you were true to to the last!

"*February 16th.*—There is great indignation amongst us Catholics at Edward VII. having been called upon to take the oath at the opening of Parliament which savours so much of the darkest days of 'No Popery' bigotry. I think it might have been modified by this time, and the lies about 'idolatry' and the 'worship' of the Virgin Mary eliminated. Could not the King have had strength of mind enough to refuse to insult his Catholic subjects? I know he must have deeply disliked to pronounce those words.

"*August 6th.*—Again the flags to-day are at half-mast, and so is the royal standard, and this time, on the men-of-war, it is the German flag! The Empress Frederick died yesterday." I never mentioned at the time of our visit to the Connaughts at Bagshot, when we were first at Aldershot, a touching incident concerning her. Sir William sat next to her at dinner, and, *à propos* of a really fine still-life picture painted by her, which hung over the dining-room door in the hall, he asked her whether she still kept up the painting. "No," she said, "I have cried myself blind!" What with one Empress crying as though her heart would break in speaking to him that time at Camden Place and this Empress telling him she had cried herself blind—! The illness and death of the Kaiser Frederick must have been a period of great anguish.

During this summer I was very busy with my picture of the *10th Bengal Lancers at Tent Pegging*, a subject requiring much sunshine study, which I have already mentioned.

In September, Lord Roberts—"the miniature Field Marshal," as I call him in the Diary—came down on inspection, and great were the doings in his honour. "How will this little figure stand in history? Will's well-planned defence against a night attack from the sea came off very well this dark still night, though the navy were nearly an hour late. There was too much waiting, but when, at last, the enemy torpedo boats and destroyers appeared, the whole Sound was bordered with such a zone of fire that, had it been real war, not a rivet of the invader's flotilla would have left in possession of its hold. 'Bobs' must have been gratified at tonight's display, which he reviewed from Stonehouse.

"Our Roberts dinner was of twenty-two covers, and the only women were Lady Charles Scott, myself and C. A guard of honour was at the front door, and presented arms as the Field Marshal arrived, the band playing. He certainly is diminutive. A nice face, soldierlike, and a natural manner. With him that too jocose Evelyn Wood and others. 'Bobs,' of course, took me in to dinner, and, on my left, Lord Charles Scott took in C. Will took in Lady Charles. The others—Lord Mount Edgcumbe, H.S.H. Prince Louis of Battenberg (in command of the *Implacable*), Admiral Jackson, and so forth—subsided into their places according to seniority. Every man in blue or red except one rifleman. Soft music during dinner and two bars of the National Anthem before the still unfamiliar 'The King, God bless him!' at dessert. Will still feels a little—I don't know how to express it— of the mental hesitation before changing 'the Queen' which he felt so strongly at first. He was very truly attached to her. I was back in the drawing-room in good time to receive the crowd, who came in a continuous flow, all with an expectant smile, to pay homage to the Lion. I don't think I forgot anybody's name (coached by the A.D.C.) in all those introductions, but that item of my duties is a thing I dread. I never saw people in such good humour at any social function before. We certainly *do* love to honour our soldiers. But, all the time, things are not going too well with us in the war!

"*September 14th*. Again the flags half-mast! Now it is the 'Stars and Stripes.' Poor President McKinley succumbed today to his horrible wound. The surgeons wouldn't let him die for a long while, though he asked them to. They did their best.

"*March 7th, 1902.*—And now for the royal visit, the principal occasion for which is the launching of the great battleship the *Queen*, by Queen Alexandra. Will was responsible for all matters ashore, as the admiral was for those afloat. Lady Charles and I had to be on the platform at North Road to receive Their Majesties, the only other women there being Lady Morley and the Plymouth Major's daughter, bearing a bouquet for presentation. The royal train had an engine decorated in front of its funnel with an enormous gilt crown, and I was pleased, as it majestically glided into the station, to see that it is possible even in railway prose to have a little dash of poetry. The band struck up, the guard of honour presented arms with a clang. First, out sprang lacqueys carrying bags and wraps who scurried to the royal carriages waiting outside, and out sprang various admirals and diplomats in hot haste, all with rather anxious faces veneered with smiles. And then, leisurely, the ever lovely and self-possessed Queen and her kindly and kingly escort, wearing, over his full-dress admiral's uniform, a caped overcoat. Salutes, bows, curtseys, smiles, handshakes. Will presents the great silver Key of the Citadel, which Charles II. had made for locking the Great Gate against the refractory people. Edward VII. touches it and the General Commanding returns it to the R.A. officer, who has charge of it. We all kiss the King's hand as seeing him for the first time to speak to since his accession. The Queen withdraws her hand quickly before any officer can salute it in like manner, which looks a little ungracious. Whilst the General and Admiral are introducing their respective staffs to the King, the Queen has a little chat with me and asks after my painting and so forth. She is very fond of that water colour I did for her album at Dover of a trooper of her 'own' 19th Hussars at tent-pegging. Lady Charles and I did not join in the procession through the Three Towns to the dockyard, but hastened home to avoid the crowd.

"In the evening we dined with Their Majesties on board

the royal yacht over part of which floating palace C. and I
had been conducted in the morning. Whatever the yacht's
sailing value may be she certainly cuts out the Kaiser's
Hohenzollern in her internal splendour. When it comes to
washstand tops of onyx and alabaster; and carpets of
unfathomable depth of pile, and hangings in bedrooms of
every shade of delicate colour, 'toning,' as the milliners say,
with each particular set of furniture; and the most elaborately beautiful arrangements for lighting and warming
electrically, and so on, and so on—one rather wonders why
so much luxury was piled on luxury in this new yacht which
the King, I am told, does not like on the high seas. Her
lines are not as graceful as those of the old *Victoria and
Albert*, and it is said she 'rolls awful'!

"Well, to dinner! As we drove up to the yacht, which is
moored right opposite the Port Admiral's house and is the
habitation of the King and Queen during their sojourn
here, we saw her outlined against the pitch black sky by
coloured electric lamps, which was pretty. Equerries, secre-
taries and Miss Knollys received us at the top of the
gangway, and the ladies of the Queen soon filed into the
ante-chamber (or cabin) where they and we, the guests,
awaited Their Majesties. Full uniform was ordered for the
men, and we ladies were requested to come in 'high, thin
dresses,' as, it appears, is the etiquette on board royal
yachts. There were the Admiral and Lady Charles, the
Duke and Duchess of Buccleugh, Lord and Lady St. Germans, Lord Walter Kerr, Lord Mount Edgcumbe ('the
Hearl,' as he is known to Plymothians), the Bishop of
Exeter, Lady Lytton and others up to about thirty-six in
number. The King, still dressed as an admiral, and the
Queen in a charming black and white semi-transparent
frock, with many ropes of pearls, soon came in, and, the
curtseying over, we filed into the great dining saloon brilliantly lighted and splendid. The King led in his daughter,
Princess Victoria. Buccleugh led in the Queen, and so on.
How unlike the painfully solemn, whispered dinners of dear

old Queen Victoria was this banquet. We shouted of neces-sity, as the band played all the time. The King and Queen seem to me to have acquired an *expanded* dignity since they have come to the Throne. Will and I could not do justice to the dinner as it was Friday, but that didn't matter. After the sweets the head servant (what Goliaths in red liveries they all are!) handed the King a *snuff box!* I was so fascinat-ed by the sight of the descendant of the Georges engaged in the very Georgian act of taking a pinch that my eyes were riveted on him. I love history and am always trying to revive the past in imagination. It is true that 'a cat may look at a King,' but then I am *not* a cat (at least I hope not). I only trust His Majesty didn't mind, but he certainly saw me!

"After dinner we women went down with the Queen to her boudoir, where an Egyptian-looking servant wearing a *tarboosh* handed us coffee of surpassing aroma, and Her Majesty showed us her beloved little Japanese dog and some of the pretty things about the room. She then asked us to see her bedroom (which I had already seen that morning) and the little dog's basket where he sleeps near her bed. She is still extremely beautiful. Her figure is youthful and shape-ly, and all her movements are queenly. The King had quite a long talk with Will about this dreadful Boer War which is causing us all so much anxiety, after we went up again. He then came over to me, and after a few commonplaces he came nearer and in a confidential tone began about Will. I think he is fond of him. What he said was kind, and I knew he wanted me to repeat his sympathetic words to my hus-band afterwards. He spoke of him as a 'splendid soldier.' I know he had in mind the painful trial Will had gone through. It was late when Their Majesties bade us good-night.

"*March 8th.*—The great day of the launch of H.M.S. *Queen*. I wonder if the hearts of the sailors beat anxiously to-day at all! A quieter, more unemotional-looking set of men than those naval bigwigs could nowhere be seen in the

world. But, first of all, there was the medal-giving at the
R.N. Barracks, where Ladies Poore and Charles Scott, Mrs.
Jackson and myself had to receive the King and Queen by
the side of our respective husbands on a raised daïs in the
centre of the huge parade ground. It was very cold, and the
Queen told me she envied me my fur-lined coat. Will said I
missed an opportunity of making a pendant to Sir Walter
Raleigh! The function was very long, for the King had to
give a medal to each one of the three hundred bluejackets
and marines who passed before him in single file. At the
launching place we all assembled on a great platform, and
there in front of us stood the huge hull of the battleship,
the ram projecting over the little table on which the Queen
was to cut the ropes. That red-painted ram was garlanded
with flowers, and the bottle hung from the garland, com-
pletely hidden under a covering of roses. It contained red
Australian wine, a very sensible change from the French
champagne of former times. Down below an immense
crowd of workmen waited, some of them right under the
ship, and all round, in the different stands, were dense
masses of people. We were soon joned by three German
naval grandees and two Japanese *leprechauns*, one an admiral, a toadlike-looking creature in a uniform entirely copied
from ours. Our new allies are not handsome. Then came
the Bishop of Exeter, in robes and cap and with a peaked
beard, a living Holbein in the dress of Cranmer. How could
I, a painter, not delight in that figure? I told a friend that
bishop had no business to be alive, but ought to be a painting by Holbein, on panel. What does she do but whisk off
straight to him and Mrs. Bishop and tell them! Our privi-
leged group kept swelling with additions of officers in full
glory and smart women in lovely frocks, and bouquets were
brought in, and everything was to me perfectly charming.
Monarchy calls much beauty into existence. Long may it
endure!

"At last there was a stir; the monarchs came up the
inclined approach and the band struck up. They took their

places facing the ship's bows, and Cranmer on panel by Holbein blessed the ship in as nearly a Catholic way as was possible, with the sign of the cross left out. A subordinate held his crozier before him. A hymn had previously been sung and a psalm, followed by the Lord's Prayer. Then came the 'christening' (strange word), a picturesque Pagan ceremony. The Queen brightened up after the last 'Amen' and, nearing the table, reached over to the flower-decked bottle; then, stepping back, swung it from her against the monstrous ram, saying, 'God bless this ship and all that sail in her.' I heard a little crack, and only a few red drops trickled down. This wouldn't do, for she immediately seized the bottle again and, stepping well back this time and holding the bottle as high over her head as the ropes would allow, flung it with such violence that it smashed all to pieces and the red wine gushed over her hands and sleeves and poured out its last drops on the table. A great cheer rang out at this, and the King laughingly seemed to say to her, 'You did it this time with a vengeance!' She flushed up, looking as though she enjoyed the fun. Then came the great moment of the cutting by the Queen of the little ropes that held the monster bound as by silken threads. Six good taps with the mallet, severing the six strands across a 'turtle back' in the centre of the table, and away flew the two ropes down amongst the cheering crowd of workmen and, automatically, down came the last two supports on either side of the yet impassive hull. Still impassive—not a hair's breadth of movement! A painful pause. Some men below were pumping the hydraulic apparatus for all they were worth. I kept my eye on the nose of the ram, gauging it by some object behind. Firm as a rock! At last a tiny movement, no more than the starting of a snail across a cabbage leaf. 'She's off!' A hurricane of cheers, and with the most admirable and dignified acceleration of speed the great ship, seeming to come into life, glided down the slips and, ploughing through the parting and surging waters, floated off far into the Hamoaze to the strains of 'Rule Britannia.' Queen

Alexandra, in her elation, made motions with her arms as though she was shoving the ship off herself. Scarcely had the battleship *Queen* passed into the water than the blocks displaced by her passage were rolled back, still hot as it were from the friction, into the position they had occupied before she moved, and the King, stepping forward, turned a little electric handle at the table, and lo! the keel plate of the *Edward VII.* slowly moved forward and stopped in its position on the blocks as the germ of the new battleship. The King, in a loud voice, proclaimed that the keel plate of the *Edward VII.* was 'well and truly laid,' and a great cheer arose and 'God Save the King,' and all was over. A new battleship was born.[15] We met Their Majesties at the Port Admiral's at tea, and Will dined with them, together with some of his staff.

"*March 10th.*—Saw Their Majesties off. I wonder if they were getting tired of seeing always the same set of faces and smiles? I am going to present C. at Court on the 14th, and my function twin, Lady Charles, is going there, too, so I shall feel it will be a case of 'Here we are again,' when I meet the royal eye that night. In the evening the news of Methuen's defeat and capture by Delarey. To think this horror was going on the day we received the King and Queen at North Road Station!

"*March 14th.*—The King's Court was much better arranged than formerly, as we had only to make two curtseys—nothing more—instead of having to run the gauntlet of a long row of princes and princesses who were abreast of Queen Victoria (or her representative), and who used to inspect one from head to foot. These were now grouped behind the monarchs, and formed a rich, subdued background to the two regal figures on their thrones. (What a blessing to the aforesaid princes and princesses to be spared the necessity of passing all those nervous women in review, and by daylight, too!) Altogether the music and the generally more festive character of the function struck one as a great and happy improvement on the old dispensation. The

King and Queen didn't exactly say, 'How do you do again?' as I appeared, but looked it as I met their smiling eyes. This is the first Court of the King's reign.

"*March 27th.*—Cecil Rhodes died yesterday. I am glad I saw him at the Cape. One morning just at sunrise I and the children were driving to Mass during the mission and, as we passed over the railway line, we saw people riding down from 'Grootschuur.' The foremost horseman was Cecil Rhodes, looking very big and with a wide red face. He gave me a searching look or stare as if trying to make out who I was in the shade of the carriage hood. So I saw his face well.

"*April 3rd.*—Will and I are invited by the King and Queen to see them crowned at Westminster. I am to wear 'court dress with plumes but without train.' But what if the nightmare war is still dragging on in June? The time is getting short! We hear the King is getting anxious. Lord Wolseley's trip to the Cape (for his health!) is supposed to have really to do with bringing about peace. But "ware politics' for me. They are not in my line. What a wet blanket would be spread as a pall over all the purple canopies in Westminster Abbey if war was still brooding over us all! Imagine news of a new Methuen disaster on the morning of June 26th!"

On Varnishing Day that spring at the Royal Academy I found that my tent-pegging picture could not look to greater advantage, but it was in the last room, where the public looks with "lack-lustre eyes," being tired.

On June 21st I left to attend the Coronation of Edward VII., spending two days at Dick's monastery at Downside on the way, high up in the Mendip Hills. I note: "I had a bright little room at the guest house just outside the precincts. That night the full moon, that emblem of serenity, rose opposite my window, and I felt as though lifted up above that world into which I was about to plunge for my participation in the pomp of the Coronation in a few hours. It is inexpressibly touching to me to see my son where he is. A hard probation, for the Benedictine test is long and severe, as indeed the test is, necessarily, throughout the Religious Orders.

"*June 24th*—Memorable day! I was passing along Buckingham Palace Road at 12.30 when I saw a poster: 'Coronation Postponed'! Groups of people were buying up the papers. Of course, no one believed the news at first, and people were rather amusedly perplexed. No one had heard that the King was ill. On getting to Piccadilly I saw the official posters and the explanation. An operation just performed! and only yesterday Knollys telling the world there was 'not a word of truth in the alarming rumours of the King's health.' I and Mrs C. went to a dismal afternoon concert at 2.30 to which we were pledged, and which the promoters were in two minds about postponing, and we left in the middle to stroll about the crowded streets and watch the effect of the disastrous news. There was something very dramatic in the scene in front of the palace—the huge crowd waiting and watching, the royal standard drooping on the roof (not half-mast yet?), and the sense of brooding sorrow over the great building, which held the perhaps, dying King. What a change in two or three hours!

"*June 26th.*—This was to have been the Coronation Day. General dismantling. Those dead laurel wreaths still lying in the gutters are said to be the same that were used at the funeral of King Humbert. What a weird thought! The crowds are thinning, but still, at night, they gaze at the little clumps of illuminations which some people exhibit, as the King is going on well. '*Vivat Rex*' flares in great brilliancy here and there. The words have a deeper meaning than usual. Long may he live!

"*June 27th.*—This was to have been the day of the royal procession. Where is that rose-colour-lined coach I so looked forward to? Lying idle in its cover. Every one is moralising. Even the clubmen, Will tells me, are furbishing up little religious platitudes and texts; many are curiously superstitious, which is strange."

On our return home I was very busy in the studio. There was much galloping and trotting of horses up and down in the Government House grounds for my studies of movement for my next Academy picture (dealing with Boer War yeomanry) and others.

"*August 9th.*—King Edward VII. was crowned to-day. At about 12.40 the guns firing in the Sound and batteries announced that, at last, the Coronation was consummated. We were asked to the ceremony, but could not go up this time."

A little tour in France, with my husband and our two girls, made in September, 1902, gave us sunny days in Anjou on the Loire. The majestic rivers of France are her chief attraction for the painter, and to us English Turner's charm is inseparably blended with their slowly flowing waters. We were visitors at a *château* at Savonnières, near Angers, for most of the time, and our hosts took care that we should miss none of the lovely things around their domain. The German *Ocean Greyhounds* of the Hamburg-Amerika line used to call at Plymouth in those days, huge, three-funnel monsters which, I think, we have since appropriated, and one of these, the *August Marie*, bore us off to Cherbourg in all the pride of her gorgeous saloons, flower-decked tables, band, and extraordinary bombastic oleographs from allegorical pictures by the Kaiser William II. As we boarded her the band played "God Save the King," the captain receiving Sir William with finished regulation attention, and hardly had the great twin engines swung the ship into the Sound to receive her passengers, than with another swing forward, which made the masts wriggle to their very tops, she was off. It was the "Marseillaise" as we reached France. That band played us nearly the whole way over. A really pretty idea, this, of playing the national air of each country where the ship touched.

It was vintage time at Savonnières, which was a French "Castagnolo," a most delightful translation into French of that Italian patriarchal home. There were stone terraces

garlanded with vines bearing—not the big black grapes of
Tuscany, but small yellow ones of surpassing sugariness. We
were in a typical and beautiful bit of France, peaceful, plen-
teous, and full of dignity. They lead the simple life here
such as I love, which is not to be found in the big English
country houses, as far as I know. I was truly pleased at the
sight of the peasantry at Mass on the Sunday. The women
in particular had that dignity which is so marked in their
class, and the white lace coifs they wore had many varieties
of shape, all most beautiful, and were very *soignées* and
neatly worn. Not an untidy woman or girl amongst these
daughters of the soil.

I was anxious to see "Angers la Noire," where we stayed
on our way from Savonnières to Amboise. But the black
slate houses which gave it that name are being turned into
white stone ones, and so its grim characteristic is passing
away. Give me character, good or bad; characterless things
are odious. I don't suppose a more perfect old Angevin
town exists than Amboise. It fulfilled all I required and
expected of it. How Turner understood these towns on the
broad, majestic Loire! He occasionally exaggerated, but his
exaggerations were always in the right direction, emphasis-
ing thus the dominant beauties of each place and their local
sentiment. Which recalls the deep charm of the rivers of
France more subtly to the mind, Turner's series or an album
of photographs? Turner's mind saw more truly than the
camera. The castle of Amboise is superb and its creamy
white stone a glory. Then came Blois, with a quite different
reading of a castle, where plenty of colour and gilding and
Gothic richness gave the character—not so restful to eye
and mind as Amboise. Through both the *châteaux* we were
marshalled along by a guide. I would sooner learn less of a
place, by myself, than be told all by a tiresome man in a
cicerone's livery. Plenty of horrors were supplied us at both
places, vitiating my otherwise simple pleasure as a painter
in the sight of so much beauty.

We returned to Plymouth Sound on a lovely day, and

there our blue launch, with that bright brass funnel I had so long agitated for, was awaiting us, and we landed at the steps of Mount Wise as though we had merely been for a trip to Penlee Point.

I found my picture of the yeomanry cantering through a "spruit" in the Boer War, *Within Sound of the Guns*, admirably placed this time at Burlington House, in the spring of 1903. I had greatly improved in tone by this time. Millais' remark once upon a time, "She draws better than any of us, but I wish her *tone* was better," had sunk deep.

On July 14th, 1903, the Princess Henry of Battenberg (as the title was then), with a suite of six, paid us a visit of two days at Government House, and we had, of course, a big reception, which was inevitable. Our guest hated the ordeal of all those presentations, being very retiring, and I sympathised. I heard her murmur to her lady, Miss Bulteel, "I shall die," as the first arrival was announced. And there she had to stand till I and the A.D.C. had finished terrifying her with about 250 people in succession. What a tax royalty has to pay! There was the laying of a foundation stone, a trip in the launch up the Tamar, and something to be done each day, but with as many rests as we could squeeze in for our very *simpatica* princess. The drive through the streets of Plymouth showed me what the crowd looks like from royalty's point of view as I sat by her side in the carriage. I remarked to her what bad teeth the people had. "They are nothing to those in the north," the poor dear said. How often royalty has to run that gauntlet of an unlovely and cheering crowd!

I was now to go through the great ordeal of witnessing our dear Dick's[16] taking his vows. This was on September 4th, 1903, at Belmont Minster, Hereford.

On July 10th, 1904, a German squadron of eighteen men-of-war came thundering into the Sound, and on the 12th we assembled a Garden Party of about three hundred guests to give the three admirals and their officers a very proper welcome. Eighteen beautiful ships, but all untried. I lunched on board the flagship, the *Kaiser Wilhem II.*, on the previous day, and anything to equal the dandified "get up" of that war vessel could not be found afloat. Wherever there was an excuse for a gold Imperial crown, there it was, relieved by the spotless whiteness of its surroundings. The fair-haired bluejackets were extremely clean and comely, but struck me as being drilled too much like soldiers, and wanting the natural manner of our men. The impression on my mind at the time was that immense care and pains had been taken to show off these brand-new ships and to rival ours, but that they were not a bit like their models. The General dined in state on board that evening. Oh! the veneer of politeness shown to us these days; the bowings, the clicking of heels, the well-drilled salutes; and all the time we were joking amongst ourselves about the certainty we had that they were taking soundings of our great harbour. As usual, they were allowed to do just as they liked there. It is a tremendous thought to me that I have lived to hear of the surrender of Germany's entire navy. How often in those days we allowed ourselves to imagine a modern *possible* Trafalgar, but such a cataclysm as this was outside the bounds of any one's imagination.

I devoted a great deal of my time to getting up a "one-man-show," my first of many, composed of water colours, and in accomplishing the Afghan picture I have already mentioned as being so much honoured by the Hanging Committee at the Academy in the spring of 1904. My husband's command of the Western District terminated on January 31st, 1905, and with it his career in the army, as he had reached the retiring age. The Liberal Party was very keen on having him as an M.P., representing East Leeds. I am glad the idea did not materialise. I know what would have happened. He would have set out full of honest and worthy enthusiasm to serve the *Patria*. Then, little by little, he would have found what political life really is, and thrown the thing up in disgust. An old story. *Non Patria sed Party!* So utterly outside my own life had politics been that I had an amused sensation when I saw the Parliamentary world opening before me, like a gulf!

"*January 31st, 1905.*—Will is to stand for East Leeds. It is all very sudden. Liberals so eager that he has almost been (courteously) hustled into the great enterprise. Herbert Gladstone, Campbell-Bannerman and other leaders have written almost irresistible letters to him, pleading. When he goes to the election at Leeds he is to be 'put to no expense whatever,' and they are confident of a 'handsome majority.' We shall see! Besides all this he is given a most momentous commission at the War Office to investigate certain ugly-looking matters connected with the Boer War stores scandal that require clearing up. I am glad they have done him the 'poetical justice' of selecting him for this.

"*February 13th.*—We went to a very brilliant and (to me) novel gathering at the Campbell-Bannermans'. All the leaders of the Liberal Party there, an interesting if not very noble study. All so cordial to Will. Tremendous crush, but nice when we got down to the more airy tea room. The snatches of conversation I got in the general hubbub all sounded somewhat 'shoppy.' Winston Churchill, a ruddy young man, with a roguish twinkle in his eye, Herbert Gladstone and his lovely wife, our bluff, rosy host and other 'leaders' were very interesting, and we met many friends, all on the 'congratulate.' All these M.P.'s seem to relish their life. I suppose it *has* a great fascination, this working to get your side in, as at a football match."

The general election in course of time swept over England and brought in the Liberal Party with an overwhelming majority. My husband did not stand for East Leeds. He had to abandon the idea, as a Catholic, on account of the religious difficulties connected with the Education Act.

Our life in the glorious west of Ireland, which followed our retirement from Devonport, has been so fully described by this pen of mine in *From Sketchbook and Diary*, that I give but a slight sketch of it here. Those were days when one could give one's whole heart, so to speak, to Erin, before the dreadful cloud had fallen on her which, as I write, has lent her her present forbidding gloom. That will pass, please God!

To come straight through from London and its noise and superfluous fuss and turmoil into the absolute peace and purity of County Mayo in perfect summer weather was such a relief to mind and body that one felt it as an emancipation. Health, good sleep, enjoyment of pure air and noble scenery; kindly, unsophisticated peasantry—all these things were there, and the flocks and herds and the sea birds. In the midst of all that appealing poetry, so peculiar to Ireland, I had a funny object lesson of a prosaic kind at romantic Mulranny, on Clewe Bay. In the little station I saw a big heap in sackcloth lying on the platform—"Hog-product from Chicago"—and the country able to "cure" the matchless Irish pig! I went on to get some darning wool in the hamlet—"Made in England"—and all those sheep around us! Outside the shop door a horse had the usual big nosebag— "Made in Austria"! All these things, with a little energy, should have come out of the place itself, surely? I thought to encourage native industry, when found, by ordering woollen hose at the convent school. No two stockings of the same pair were of equal length. The bay was rich in fish, and one day came a little fleet of fishing boats—from France! There was Ireland to-day in a nutshell. What of tomorrow? Is this really Ireland's heavy sleep before the dawn?

I have seen some of the most impressive beauties of our world, but never have I been more impressed than by the solemn grandeur of the mountain across Clewe Bay they call Croagh Patrick, as we saw it on the evening of our arrival at Mulranny. The last flush of the after-glow lingered on its dark slopes and the red planet Mars flamed above its cone, all this solemn beauty reflected in the sleeping waters. At Mulranny I spent nearly all my days making studies of sheep and landscape for the next picture I sent to the Academy—A Cistercian Shepherd. This gave me a period of the most exquisitely reposeful work. The building up of this picture was in itself an idyll. But the public didn't want idylls from me at all. "Give us soldiers and horses, but pastoral idylls—no!" People had a slightly reproachful tone in their comments after seeing my poor pastoral on the Academy walls. Some one said, "How are the mighty fallen!"

We made our home in the heart of Tipperary, under the Galtee Mountains. It seemed time for us to seek a dignified repose, "the world forgetting, by the world forgot," but we did not succeed in our intention. In 1906 my husband went on a great round of observation through Cape Colony and the (former) Boer Republics on a literary mission. I and E. went off to Italy, meanwhile; Rome as our goal. There I had the great pleasure of the companionship of my sister, and it may be imagined with what feelings we re-trod the old haunts in and about that city together.

"*April 9th, 1906.*—We had a charming stroll through the Villa d'Este gardens, where the oldest, hoariest cypresses are to be seen, and fountains and water conduits of graceful and fantastic shape, wherever one turns, all gushing with impetuous waters. The architects of these gardens revelled in their fanciful designs and sported with the responsive flood. Cascades spout in all directions from the rocks on which Tivoli is built. We had *déjeuner* under a pergola at the inn right over one of these waterfalls, where, far below us, birds flew to and fro in the mist of the spray. Nature and art have joined in play at Tivoli. I always have had a healthy dislike of burrowing in tombs and catacombs. The sepulchral, bat-scented air of such places in Egypt—the land, of all others, of limpid air and sunshine and dryness—is not in any way attractive to me, and I greatly dislike diving into the Roman catacombs out of the sunny Appian Way. On former occasions I went through them all, so this time I kept above ground. I learnt all that the catacombs teach in my early years, and am not likely to lose that tremendous impression.

"*April 10th.*—A true Campagna day, as Italianised as I could make it. We had a frugal *colazione* under the pergola

of an Appian Way-side inn, watched by half a dozen hungry
cats, that unattractive, wild, malignant kind of cat peculiar
to Italy. The girl who waited on us drew our white wine in a
decanter from what looked like a well in the garden. It had,
apparently, not 'been cool'd a long age in *that* deep-delved
earth,' but it did very well. I was perfectly happy. This old-
fashioned *al fresco* entertainment had the local colour
which I look for when I travel and which is getting rarer
year by year. Our Colosseum moonlight was more weird
than ever. At eleven we had our moon. It was a large, battered, woeful, waning old moon, that looked in at us
through the broken arch. An opportune owl, which had
been screeching like a cat in the shade, flitted across its
sloping disc just at the supreme moment."

To receive Holy Communion at the hands of the Holy
Father is a privilege for which we should be very thankful.
It was mine and E.'s on Easter morning that year, at his private Mass in the Sistine Chapel. There I saw Pius X. for the
first time. Goodness and compassion shine from that sad
and gentle face. It is the general custom to kiss the 'Fisherman's ring' on the Pope's hand before receiving, but Pius X.
very markedly prevents this. One can understand! Our
audience with the Holy Father took place on the eve of our
departure. There was a never-absent look with him of what
I may call the submissive sense of a too-heavy burden of
responsibility. No photographs convey the right impression
of this Pope. He was very pale, very spiritual, very kind and
a little weary; most gentle and touching in his manner. The
World War at its outset broke that tender heart. I sent him
my *Letters from the Holy Land*, for which I received very
urbane thanks from one of the cardinals. I don't think the
Holy Father knows a single word of English, and I wonder
what he made of it.

As to our tour homeward, taking Florence and Venice on
the way, I think we will take that as read. I revel in the
Diary in all the dear old Italian details, marred only by the
change I noticed in Venice as regards her broken silence.

The hurry of modern life has invaded even the "silent city," and there is too much electric glare in the lighting now, at night, for the old enjoyment of her moonlights. It annoyed me to see the moon looking quite shabby above the incandescent globes on the Riva.

From Venice to the Dublin Castle season is a big jump. We had an average of twenty-one balls in six weeks in each of the two seasons 1907-1908. Little did I think that it would be quite an unmixed pleasure to me to do *chaperon* for some five hours at a stretch; but so it turned out. It all depends what sort of daughter you have on the scene! The Aberdeens were then in power.

Lady Aberdeen was untiring in her endeavours to trace and combat the dire disease which seemed to fasten on the Irish in an especial manner. She went about lecturing to the people with a tuberculosis "caravan." She brought it to Cashel, and my husband made the opening speech at her exhibition there. But her addresses came to nothing. The lungs exhibited in the "caravan" in spirits of wine appealed in vain. She actually asked the people that day to go back to their discarded oatmeal "stirabout"! They prefer their stewed tea and their artificially whitened, so-called bread, with the resultant loss of their teeth. My experiences at the different Dublin horse shows were sociable and pleasant. There you see the finest horses and the most beautiful women in the world, and Dublin gives you that hospitality which is the most admirable quality in the Irish nature.

Sir William spent the remaining days of his life in trying, by addresses to the people in different parts of the country, to quicken their sense of the necessity for industry, sobriety, and a more serious view of existence. They did not seem to like it, and he was apparently only beating the air. I remember one particularly strong appeal he made in Meath at a huge open-air meeting. I thought to myself that such warnings, given in his vivid and friendly Irish style, touched with humour to leaven the severity, would have impressed his hearers. The applause disappointed me. Well, he did his best to the very last for the country and the people he loved. He had vainly longed all his life for Home Rule within the Empire. Was this, then, all that was wanting?

I recall in this connection an episode which was eloquent of the hearty appreciation of his worth, quite irrespective of politics. At a banquet given in Dublin to welcome Lord and Lady Granard, after their marriage, he was called upon to respond for "the Guests." For fully one minute the cheers were so persistent when he rose that he had to wait before his opening words could be heard. The company were nearly all Unionists.

After all the misunderstandings connected with Sir William's association with the Boer War and its antecedents had been righted at last, these words of a distinguished general at Headquarters were spoken: "Butler stands a head and shoulders above us all."

The year 1910 is one which in our family remains for ever sacred. My dear mother died on March 13th.

On June 7th a very brave soldier, who feared none but God, was called to his reward. Here my Diary stops for nearly a year.[17]

CHAPTER TWENTY FOUR

MOSTLY A ROMAN DIARY

PALM SUNDAY, 1911, found me in Rome, on the eve of my son's ordination as priest. One of those extraordinary occurrences which have happened in my life took place that day. Four of us joined at the appointed place and hour: I and Eileen from Ireland (Dick, already in Rome) and Patrick, just landed, in the nick of time, from India! We three met at the foot of the Aventine and went up to Sant' Anselmo, where we knew we should see *the other one* during the Palm Sunday Mass, though not to speak to till after the long service was ended. He intoned the Gospel as deacon, and when his deep voice reached us in the gallery we looked at each other with a smile. None of us had seen him for a more or less long time.

"Holy Saturday. The great day. Dick assumed the chasuble, and is officially known now as Father Urban, though 'Dick' he will ever remain with us. The weather was Romanly brilliant, but I was anxious, knowing that these young deacons were to be on their knees in the great Lateran Church, fasting, from 7 a.m. We three waited a long time in the piazza of the Lateran for the pealing of the bells which should announce the beginning of the Easter time, and which was to be the signal for our entry into the great basilica at 9.15. We had places in two balconies, right over the altar. Below us stood about forty deacons, with our particular one in their midst, each holding his folded chasuble across his arms ready for the vesting. The sight of these young fellows, in their white and gold deacons' vestments, was very touching. Each one was called up by name in turn, and ascended the altar steps, where sat the consecrating bishop, who looked more like a spirit than a mere human creature. When Urbano Butler (pronounced *Boutler*, of course, by the Italian voice) was called, how we craned forward! To me the whole thing was poignant. What those boys give up! ('Well,' answers a voice, 'they give up the world, and a good thing too!')

"We went, when the ceremony was completed, into a side chapel to receive the newly-made young priests' first blessing. These young fellows ran out of the sacristy towards the crowd of expectant parents and friends, their newly-acquired chasubles flying behind them as they ran, with outstretched hands, for the kisses of that kneeling crowd that awaited them. What a sight! Can any one paint it and do it justice? Old and young, gentlefolk and peasants, smiling through tears, kissing the young hands that blessed them. Dick came to his mother first, then to his soldier brother, then to his sister, and I saw him lifting an aged prelate to his feet after blessing him. Strangers knelt to him and the others, and I saw, in its perfection, what is meant by 'laughing for joy' on those young and holy faces. There was one exception. A poor young Irish boy, somehow, had no relative to bless—no one—he seemed left out in his corner, and he was crying. Perhaps his mother was 'beyond the beyond' in far Connemara? I heard of this afterwards. Had I seen him, I would certainly have asked his blessing too. So it is—always some shadow, even here.

"As soon as we could get hold of Dick, in his plain habit, we hurried him to a little *trattoria* across the piazza, where his dear friend and chum, John Collins,[18] treated him to a good cup of chocolate to break his long fast."

It was quite a necessary anti-climax for me when we and our friends all met again at the hotel and sat down, to the number of fifteen, to a bright luncheon I gave in honour of the day. A very celebrated English cardinal honoured me with his presence there.

"*Easter Sunday.*—Patrick, Eileen and I received Holy Communion in the crypt of Sant' Anselmo from Dick's hands at his first Mass. These few words contain the culmination of all.

"*April 17th.*—In the afternoon we were all off, piloted by Dick, to the celebrated Benedictine monastery of Monte Cassino, a long way down towards Naples, to spend a few days, Patrick as guest within the precincts, and E. and I lodging at the guest-house, which forms part of the monastic farm, poised on the edge of a great precipice. The sheer rock plunges down to the base of the mountain whereon stands the wonderful monastery. It is something to see a great domed church on the top of such a mountain, and a building of such vast proportions, containing one of the greatest libraries in the world. A mule path was all the monks intended for communication between the two worlds, but now a great carriage road takes us up by an easy zigzag.

"*April 18th.*—Every hour of our visit to Monte Cassino must be lived. I made a sketch of the monastery and the abyss into which one peers from that great height, with

angry red clouds gathering over the tops of the snowy
mountains. But my sketches are too didactic; and, indeed,
who but Turner could convey to the beholder the awful
spirit of that scene? The tempest sent us in and we had the
experience of a good thunderstorm amidst those severe
mountains that have the appearance of a petrified chaos.
Last night E. woke up to find the room full of a surprising
blue light, which at first she took to be the dawn because,
through the open windows, she heard the whole land
thrilling with the song of birds. But such a *blue* light for
dawn? She got up to see. The light was that of the full
moon and the birds were nightingales.

"I was enchanted to see the beautiful dress of the peasant
women here. Their white *tovaglie* are looped back in a more
graceful line than the Roman. The queerest little thin black
hogs, like poor relations of the tall, pink Valentia variety
which I have already signalised, browse on the steep ascent
to this great stronghold, and everything still looks wild, in
spite of the carriage road. I should have preferred coming
up here on a mule. Our suppers at the guest-house were
Spartan. Rather dismal, having to pump conversation with
the Italian guests at this festive (!) board. Our intellectual
food, however, was rich. The abbot and his monks did the
honours of far-famed Monte Cassino for us with the kindest
attention, showing very markedly their satisfaction in pos-
sessing Brother Urban, whose father's name they held in
great esteem."

On April 22nd we had the long-expected audience with
Pio Decimo. It was only semi-private and there were
crowds, including eleven English naval officers, to be presented. I had my little speech ready, but when we came into
the Pope's presence we found him standing instead of rest-
fully seated, and he looked so fatigued and so aged since I
last saw him that I knew I must keep him listening as short
a time as possible. First I presented "*Mio figlio primogenito,
ufficiale;*" then "*mio figlio Benedittino,*" and then "*mia figlia.*"
He spoke a little while to Dick in Latin, and then we knelt

and received his blessing and departed, to see him no more.

It is a great thing to have seen Leo XIII. and Pius X., as I have had the opportunity of seeing them. Both have left a deep impression on modern life, especially the former, who was a great statesman. To see the fragile scabbard of the flesh one wondered how the keen sword of the spirit could be held at all within it. It was his diplomatic tact that smoothed away many of the difficulties that obtruded themselves between the Vatican and the Quirinal, and that tact kept the Papacy on good terms with France and her Republic, to which he called on all French Catholics to give their support. It was he who forced "the man of blood and iron" to relax the ferocious laws against the Church in Germany, and to allow the evicted bishops to return to their Sees. Diplomatic relations with Germany were renewed, and the Church's laws regarding marriage and education had to be re-admitted by the Government. Even the dark "Orthodox" intolerance of Russia bent sufficiently to his influence to allow of the establishment of Catholic episcopal Sees in that country, and the cessation of the imprisonment of priests. The episcopate in Scotland, too, was restored. We owe to him that spread of Catholicism in the United States which has long been such a surprise to the onlooker. Then there are his great encyclicals on the Social Question, setting forth the Christian teaching on the relations between capital and labour; establishing the social movement on Christian lines. How clearly he saw the threat of a great European war at no very distant date from his time unless armaments were reduced. That refined mind inclined him to the advancement of the cause of the Arts and of learning. Students thank him for opening the Vatican archives to them, which he did with the words, "The Church has nothing to fear from the publication of the Truth." His is the Vatican observatory—one of the most famous in the world. It makes one smile to remember his remarks on the then young Kaiser William II., who seems to have struck the Holy Father as somewhat bumptious on the occasion of his historic visit. "That young man," as he called him, evidently impressed the Pope as one having much to learn.

What a contrast Pius X. presents to his predecessor! The son of a postman at Rieti, a little town in Venetia. I remember when a deputation of young men came to pay him their respects at the Vatican, arriving on their bicycles, that he told them how much he would have liked a bike himself when, as a bare-legged boy, he had to trudge every day seven miles to school and back. Needless to say, he had no diplomatic or political training, but he led the truly simple life, very saintly and apostolic. He devoted his energies chiefly to the purely pastoral side of his office. We are grateful to him for his reform of Church music (and it needed it in Italy!). He was very emphatic in urging frequent communion and early communion for children. His condemnation of "modernism" is fresh in all our minds, and we are glad he removed the prohibition on Catholics from standing for the Italian parliament, thereby allowing them to obtain influential positions in public life. He took a firm stand with regard to the advancing encroachment of the French Government on the liberties of the Church in his day. His policy is being amply justified under our very eyes.

We joined the big garden party, after the Papal audience, at the British Embassy. A great crush in that lovely remnant of the once glorious, far-spreading gardens I can remember, nearly all turned to-day into deadly streets on which a gridiron of tram lines has been screwed down. Prince Arthur of Connaught brought in the Queen-Mother, Margherita, to the lawn where the dancing took place. The Rennel-Rodd children as little fairies were pretty and danced charmingly, but I felt for the professional dancer who, poor thing, was not in her first youth, and unkindly dealt with by the searching daylight. To have to caper airily on that grass was no joke. It was heavy going for her and made me melancholy, in conjunction with my memories of the old Ludovisi gardens and the vanished pines.

On October 26th my youngest daughter, Eileen, was

married to Lord Gormanston, at the Brompton Oratory, the church so loved by our mother, and where I was received. Our dear Dick married them. I had the reception in Lowndes Square in the beautiful house lent by a friend.

Ireland has many historic ancestral dwellings, and one of these became my daughter's new home in Meath. Shakespeare's "cloud-capp'd towers" seemed not so much the "baseless fabric" of the poet's vision when I saw, one day, the low-lying trail of a bright Irish mist brush the high tops of the towers of Gormanston. A thing of visions, too, is realised there in a cloister carved so solidly out of the dense foliage of the yew that never monastic cloister of stone gave a more restful "contiguity of shade."

I spent the winter of 1911-12 in London, and worked hard at water colours, of which I was able to exhibit a goodly number at a "one-man show" in the spring. The King lent my good old *Roll Call*, and the whole thing was a success. I showed many landscapes there as well as military subjects; many Italian and Egyptian drawings made during my travels, and scenes in Ireland. These exhibitions in a well-lighted gallery are pleasant, and the private view day a social rendezvous for one's friends.

Through my sister, with whom I revisited Rome early in 1913, I had the pleasure of knowing many Americans there. How refreshing they are, and responsive (I don't mean the mere tourist!), whereas my dear compatriots are very heavy in hand sometimes. American women are particularly well read and cultivated and full of life. They don't travel in Europe for nothing. I have had some dull experiences in the English world when embarking, at our solemn British dinners, on cosmopolitan subjects for conversation. What was I to say to a man who, having lately returned from Florence, gave it as his opinion that it was only "a second-rate Cheltenham"? I tried that unlucky Florentine subject on another. He: "Florence? Oh, yes, I liked that—that—*minaret thing* by the side of the—the—er—" I: "The Duomo?" He: "Oh, yes, the Duomo." I (in gloomy despair):

"Do you mean Giotto's Tower?" Collapse of our conversation.

Very probably I bade my last farewell to St. Peter's that year. I had more than once bidden a provisional "good-bye" at sundown on leaving Rome to that dome which I always loved to see against the western glory from the familiar terrace on Monte Pincio, only to return, on a further visit, and see it again with the old, fresh feeling of thankfulness. My initial enthusiasm, crudely chronicled as it is in my early Diary on first coming in sight of St. Peter's, was a young artist's emotion, but to the maturer mind what a miracle that Sermon in Stone reveals! The tomb of one Simon, no better, before his call, than any ordinary fisherman one may see to-day on our coasts—and now? "TU ES PETRUS..."

CHAPTER TWENTY FIVE

THE GREAT WAR

I WAS very busy with oil brush and water-colour brush during the summer of 1913, and the succeeding winter, in Ireland, accomplishing a large oil, *The Cuirassier's Last Réveil, Morning of Waterloo*, and a number of drawings, all of that inexhaustible battle, for my next "one-man show" held on its centenary, 1915. I left no stone unturned to get true studies of dawn twilight for that *reveil*, and I got them. At the pretty house of my friends, the Egerton Castles, on a steep Surrey hill, I had my chance. The house faced the east. It was midsummer; an alarm clock roused me each morning at 2.30. I had modelled a little grey horse and a man, and set them up on my balcony, facing in the right direction, and there I waited, with palette spread, for the dawn. Time was short; the first ray of sunrise would spoil all, so I could only dab down the tones, anyhow; but they were all-important dabs, and made the big picture run without a hitch. Nothing delays a picture more than the searching for the true relations of tone without sufficient data. But this is a truism.

The Waterloo water colours were most interesting to work out. I had any amount of books for reference, records of old uniforms to get from contemporary paintings; and I utilised the many studies of horses I had made for years, chiefly on the chance of their coming in useful some day. The result was the best "show" I had yet had at the Leicester Galleries. But ere that exhibition opened, the World War burst upon us! First my soldier son went off, and then the Benedictine donned khaki, as chaplain to the forces. He went, one may say, from the cloister to the cannon. I had to pass through the ordeal which became the lot of so many mothers of sons throughout the Empire.

"*Lyndhurst, New Forest, September 22nd, 1914.*—I must keep up the old Diary during this most eventful time, when the biggest war the world has ever been stricken with is raging. To think that I have lived to see it! It was always said a war would be too terrible now to run the risk of, and that nations would fear too much to hazard such a peril. Lo! here we are pouring soldiers into the great jaws of death in hundreds of thousands, and sending poor human flesh and blood to face the new 'scientific' warfare—the same flesh and blood and nervous system of the days of bows and arrows. Patrick is off as A.D.C. to General Capper, commanding the 7th Division. Martin, who was the first to be ordered to the front, attached to the 2nd Royal Irish, has been transferred to the wireless military station at Valentia. That regiment has been utterly shattered in the Mons retreat, so I have reason to be thankful for the change. I am here, at Patrick's suggestion, that I may see an army under war conditions and have priceless opportunities of studying 'the real thing.' The 7th Division[19] is now nearly complete, and by October 3rd should be on the sea. I arrived at Southampton to-day, and my good old son in his new Staff uniform was at the station ready to motor me up to Lyndhurst where the Staff are, and all the division, under canvas. I was very proud of the red tabs on Patrick's collar, meaning so much. I saw at once, on arriving, the difference between this and my Aldershot impressions. This is *war*, and there is no doubt the bearing of the men is different. They were always smart, always cheery, *but not like this*. There is a quiet seriousness quite new to me. They are going to look death straight in the face.

"*September 23rd.*—I had a most striking lesson in the appearance of men after a very long march, *plus* that look which is quite absent on peace manoeuvres, however hot and trying the conditions. What surprises and telling 'bits' one sees which could never be imagined with such a convincing power. A team of eight mammoth shire horses drawing a great gun is a sight never to be forgotten; shapely, superb cart horses with coats as satiny as any thoroughbred's, in polished artillery harness, with the mild eyes of their breed—I must do that amongst many most *real* subjects. But I see the German shells ploughing through these teams of willing beasts. They will suffer terribly.

"*September 25th.*—Getting hotter every day and not a cloud. I brought this weather with me. Patrick waits on me whenever he is off duty for an hour or so, and it is a charming experience to have him riding by the side of the carriage to direct the driver and explain to me every necessary detail. The place swarms with troops for ever in movement, and the roll of guns and drums, and the notes of the cheery pipes and fifes go on all day. The Gordons have arrived.

"*September 26th.*—Signs of pressure. They may now be off any hour. The ammunition has all arrived, and there wants but one battery of artillery to complete the division. General Capper won't wait much longer and will be off without it if it delays and make up a battery *en route* somehow. It is sad to see so many mere boys arriving at the hotel fresh from Sandhurst. They are given companies to command, captains being killed, wounded or missing in such numbers. As to Patrick's regiment, the old Royal Irish seem to have been so shattered that they are all *hors de combat* for the present.

"*September 27th.*—What a precious Sunday this has been! First, Patrick accompanied me to Mass, said by Father Bernard Vaughan, in a secluded part of the camp, where the heather had not been ploughed up by men, horses and guns, as elsewhere, and where the altar was erected in a wooded glen. The Grenadier and Scots Guards were all on their knees as we arrived, and the bright green and gold vestments of the priest were relieved very vividly in the sunshine against the darker green background of the forest beyond. Quite a little crowd of stalwart guardsmen received Holy Communion, and two of them were sheltering with their careful hands the candles from the soft warm breeze, one at each end of the altar. We sit out in the leafy garden of the hotel and have tea there, we parents and relatives, with our boys by us at all spare moments. To-day, being Sunday, there have been extra crowds of relatives and friends who have motored over from afar. There is pathos here, very real pathos. How many of these husbands and sons and brothers I see sitting close to their dear ones, for the last time, perhaps? Who knows? The voices are low and quiet—very quiet. Patrick and I were photographed together by M.E. These little snapshots will be precious. We were nearly all day together to-day as there was a rest. All this quiet time here our brave soldiers are being shattered on the banks of the Aisne. Just now must be a tremendously important period of the fighting. We may get great news to-morrow. Many names I know beginning to appear in the casualty lists.

"*September 28th, 1914.*—Had a good motor run with the R.'s right through the field of 'battle' in the midst of the great forest—a rolling height covered with heather and bracken. Our soldiers certainly have learnt, at last, how to take cover. One can easily realise how it is that the proportion of officers killed is so high. Kneeling or standing up to give directions they are very conspicuous, whereas of the men one catches only a glimpse of their presence now and then through a tell-tale knapsack or the round top of a cap in the bracken; yet the ground is packed with men—quite uncanny. The Gordons were a beautiful sight as they sprang up to reach a fresh position. I noticed how the breeze, as they ran, blew the khaki aprons aside and the revealed tartan kilts gave a welcome bit of colour and touched up the drab most effectively. One 'gay Gordon' sergeant told us, 'We are a grand diveesion, all old warriors, and when we get out 'twill make a deeference.'"

The most impressive episode to me of that well-remembered day was when Patrick took me up to the high ground at sunset and we looked down on the camp. The mellow, very red sun was setting and the white moon was already well up over the camp, which looked mysterious, lightly veiled by the thin grey wood-smoke of the fires. Thousands of troops were massed or moving, shadowy, far away; others in the middle distance received the blood-red glow on the men's faces with an extraordinary effect. They showed as ruddy, vaporous lines of colour over the scarcely perceptible tones of the dusky uniforms. Horses stood up dark on the sky-line. The bugles sounded the "Retreat"; these doomed legions, shadow-like, moved to and fro. It was the prologue to a great tragedy.

"*September 30th.*—There was a field day of the whole of one brigade. The regiments in it are 'The Queen's,' the Welsh Fusiliers, Staffords, and Warwicks, with the monstrous 4.7 guns drawn by my well-loved mighty mammoths. The guns are made impossible to the artist of modern war by being daubed in blue and red blotches which make them absolutely formless; and, of course, no glint of light on the hidden metal is seen. Still, there is much that is very striking, though the colour, the sparkle, the gallant plumage, the glinting of gold and silver, have given way to universal grimness. After all, why dress up grim war in all that splendour? My idea of war subjects has always been anti-sparkle.

"As I sat in the motor in the centre of the far-flung 'battle,' in a hollow road, lo! the Headquarter Staff came along,

THE SHIRE HORSES: WHEELERS OF A 4.7,
A HUSSAR SCOUT OF 1917.

The Northumberland Hussars

R.F.A.

A Sandhurst Captain

A "Gay Gordon" bugler

A hot Sergeant of the Warwicks

With the Seventh Division Lyndhurst 1914

NOTES ON THE EVE OF THE GREAT WAR.

a gallant group, *à la* Meissonier, Patrick, on his skittish brown mare 'Dawn,' riding behind the General, who rode a big black (*very* effective), with the chief of the Staff nearly alongside. The escort consisted of a strong detachment of the fine Northumberland Hussars, mounted on their own hunters. They are to be the bodyguard of the General at the Front. Several drivers of the artillery are men who were wounded at Mons and elsewhere, and, being well again, are returning with this division to the Front. All the horses here are superb. Poor beasts, poor beasts! One daily, hourly, reminds oneself that the very dittoes of these men and animals are suffering, fighting, dying over there in France. Kitchener tells our General that the 7th Division will 'probably arrive after the first phase is over,' which looks as though he fully expects the favourable and early end of the present one.

"*October 2nd.*—The whole division was out to-day. I was motored into the very thick of the operations on the high lands, and watched the men entrenching themselves, a thing I had never yet seen. Most picturesque and telling. And the murderous guns were being embedded in the yellow earth and covered with heather against aeroplanes, especially, and their wheels masked with horse blankets. There they lay, black, hump-backed objects, with just their mouths protruding, and as each gun section finished their work with the pick and shovel, they lay flat down to hide themselves. How war is waged now! Great news allowed to be published to-day in the papers. The Indian Army has arrived, and is now at the *Front!* It landed long ago at Marseilles, but how well the secret has been kept! How mighty are the events daily occurring. Late in the afternoon I saw the Northumberland Hussars, on a high ridge *practising the sword exercise!* With the idea that the sword was obsolete (engendered by the Boer War experience), no yeomanry has, of late, been armed with sabres, but, seeing what use our Scots Greys, Lancers, Dragoon Guards and Hussars have lately been making of the steel, General Capper has insisted on these, his own yeomen, being thus armed. I felt stirred with the pathos of this sight—men learning how to use a new arm on the eve of battle. They were mounted and drawn up on a long, two-deep line on that brown heath, with a heavy bank of dark clouds like mine in *"Scotland for Ever!"* behind their heads—a fine subject.

"Who will look at my 'Waterloos' now? I have but one more of that series to do. Then I shall stop and turn all my attention and energy to this stupendous war. I shall call up my Indian sowars again, but *not* at play this time.

"*October 3rd.*—Sketched Patrick's three beautiful chargers' heads in water colour. Still the word 'Go!' is suspended over our heads.

"*October 4th.*—The word 'Go!' has just sounded. In ten minutes Patrick had to run and get his handbag, great coat and sword and be off with his General to London. They pass through here to-morrow on their way to embark.

"*October 5th, 1914.*—I was down at seven, and as they did not finally leave till 8.15 I had a golden half-hour's respite. Then came the parting…"

I left Lyndhurst at once. It will ever remain with me in a halo of physical and spiritual sunshine seen through a mist of sadness.

On November 2nd, 1914, my son Patrick was severely wounded during the terrible, prolonged first Battle of Ypres, and was sent home to be nursed back to health and fighting power at Guy's Hospital, where I saw him. He told me that as he lay on the field his General and Staff passed by, and all the General said was, "Hullo, Butler! is that you? Good-bye!"[20] General Capper was as brave a soldier as ever lived, but, I think, too fond for a General of being, as he said he wished to be, *in the vanguard.* Thus he met his death (riding on horseback, I understand) at Loos. Patrick's brother A.D.C., Captain Isaac, whom I daily used to see at Lyndhurst, was killed early in the War. The poor fellow, to calm my apprehensions regarding my own son, had tried to assure me that, as A.D.C., he would be as safe as in Piccadilly.

Towards the end of 1914 London had become intensely interesting in its tragic aspect, and so very unlike itself. Soldiers of all ranks formed the majority of the male population. In fact, wherever I looked now there was some new sight of absorbing interest, telling me we were at war, and such a war! Bands were playing at recruiting stations; flags of all the Allies fluttered in the breeze in gaudy bunches; "pom-pom" guns began to appear, pointing skywards from their platforms in the parks, awaiting "Taubes" or "Zeppelins." I went daily to watch the recruits drilling in the parks—such strangely varied types of men they were, and most of them appearing the veriest civilians, from top to toe. Yet these very shop-boys had come forward to offer their all for England, and the good fellows bowed to the terrible, shouting drill-sergeants as never they had bowed to any man before. What enraged me was the giggling of the shop-girls who looked on—a far harder order for the boys even than the yells of the sergeants. One of the squads in the Green Park was supremely interesting to me one day, in (I am bound to say) a semi-comic way. These recruits were members and associates of the Royal Academy. They were mostly somewhat podgy, others somewhat bald. When resting, having piled arms, they played leap-frog, which was very funny, and showed how light-heartedly my brothers of the brush were going to meet the Boche. Of the maimed and blind one met at every turn I can scarcely write. I find that when I am most deeply moved my pen lags too far behind my brush.

On getting home to Ireland I set to work upon a series of khaki water colours of the War for my next "one-man show," which opened with most satisfactory éclat in May, 1917. One of the principal subjects was done under the impulse of a great indignation, for Nurse Cavell had been executed. I called the drawing The Avengers. Also I exhibited at the Academy, at the same time, The Charge of the Dorset Yeomanry at Agagia, Egypt. This was a large oil painting, commissioned by Colonel Goodden and presented by him to his county of Dorset. That charge of the British yeomen the year before had sealed the fate of the combined Turks and Senussi, who had contemplated an attack on Egypt. One of the most difficult things in painting a war subject is the having to introduce, as often happens, portraits of particular characters in the drama. Their own mothers would not know the men in the heat, dust, and excitement of a charge, or with the haggard pallor on them of a night watch. In the Dorset charge all the officers were portraits, and I brought as many in as possible without too much disobeying the "distance" regulation. The Enemy (of the Senussi tribe) wore flowing *burnouses,* which helped the movement, but at their machine guns I, rather reluctantly, had to place the necessary Turkish officers. I had studies for those figures and for the desert, which I had made long ago in the East. It is well to keep one's sketches; they often come in very useful.

The previous year, 1916, had been a hard one. Our struggles in the War, the Sinn Fein rebellion in Dublin, and one dreadful day in that year when the first report of the Battle of Jutland was published—these were great trials. I certainly would not like to go through another phase like that. But I was hard at work in the studio at home in Tipperary, and this kept my mind in a healthy condition, as always, through trouble. Let all who have congenial work to do bless their stars!

On July 31st my second son, the chaplain, had a narrow escape. It was at the great Battle of Flanders, where we seem to have made a good *beginning* at last. Father Knapp and Dick were tending the wounded and dying under a rain of shells, when the old priest told Dick to go and get a few minutes' rest. On returning to his sorrowful work Dick met the fine old Carmelite as he was borne on a stretcher, dying of a shell that had exploded just where my son had been standing a few minutes before.

I see in the Diary: "*December 11th, 1917.*—To-day our army is to make its formal entry into Jerusalem. I can

scarcely write for excitement. How vividly I see it all,
knowing every yard of that holy ground! Dick writes from
before Cambrai that, if he had to go through another such
day as that of the 30th November last, he would go mad
with grief. He lost all his dearest friends in the Grenadier
Guards, and he says England little knows how near she was
to a great disaster when the enemy surprised us on that terrible Friday."

Men who have gone through the horrors of war say little
about them, but I have learnt many strange things from rare
remarks here and there. To show how human life becomes
of no account as the fighting grows, here is an instance. A
soldier was executed at dawn one day for "cowardice." An
officer who had acted at the court-martial met a private of
the same regiment as the dead man's that day, who
remarked to his officer that all he could say about his dead
"pal" was that he had seen him perform an act of bravery
three times which would have deserved the V.C. "My good
man," said the officer, "why didn't you come forward at the
trial and say this?" "Well, I didn't think of it, sir." After all,
to die one way or another had become quite immaterial.

One of the most important of my water colours at the
second khaki exhibition, held in London in May, 1919, was
of the memorable charge of the Warwick and Worcester
Yeomanry at Huj, near Jerusalem, which charge outshone
the old Balaclava one we love to remember, and which dif-
fered from the Crimean exploit in that we not only
captured all the enemy guns, but *held* them. I had had all
details—ground plans, description of the weather on that
memorable day, position of the sun, etc., etc.—supplied me
by an eye-witness who had a singularly quick eye and pre-
cise preception.[21] I called it *Jerusalem delivered*, for that
charge opened the gates of the Holy City to us. *The
Canadian Bombers on Vimy Ridge* was another of the more
conspicuous subjects, and this one went to Canada.

But I must look back a little: "*Monday, November 11th,
1918.*—Armistice Day! I have been fortunate in seeing

London on this day of days. I arrived at Victoria into a London of laughter, flags, joy-rides on every conceivable and inconceivable vehicle. I had hints on the way to London by eruptions of Union Jacks growing thicker and thicker along the railway, but I could not let myself believe that it was the end of all our long-drawn-out trial that I would find on arrival. But so it was. I went alone for a good stroll through Oxford Street, Bond Street, and Piccadilly. People meeting, though strangers, were smiling at each other. I smiled to strange faces that were smiling at me. What a novel sensation! The street were thronged with the *true* happiness in the people's eyes, and there was no "mafficking" no horse-play, but such *fun*. The matter was too great for rowdyism and drunkenness. The crowd was allowed to do just as it pleased for once, yet I saw no accidents. The police just looked on, and would have beamed also, I am sure, if they had not been on duty. They had, apparently, thrown the reins on the public's neck. I saw some sad faces, but, of course, such as these kept mostly away."

In deepest gratitude I felt I could be amongst the smilers that day, for both my own sons, who faced death to the very end in so many of the theatres of war to which our armies were sent, had survived.

The boat that took me back to Ireland eventually had no protecting airship serpentining above us. We could breathe freely now!

FOOTNOTES

1. A reference to Ehrenbreitstein, the castle which inspired Digby's Broadstone of Honour (*see* B. Holland's *Memoir of Kenelm Digby*, Fisher Press, Sevenoaks, 1992).
2. The cattle plague was raging in England.
3. William I., afterwards German Emperor.
4. The severe Lady Superintendent.
5. Whose son, Mr. Alfred Pollard, C.B., became the head of the British Museum Printed Book Department.
6. Manning.
7. Poor young Inman, who was killed at the fight of Laing's Nek, S. Africa.
8. *From Sketch-Book and Diary*, A. & C. Black.
9. I have just been told by an Irishman that the Valentia breed are trained for "racing!"
10. *The Campaign of the Cataracts*.
11. The late Lord Kitchener.
12. Now King George V.
13. Our eldest daughter Elizabeth, now Mrs. Kingscote.
14. Some one has explained to me, with what authority I cannot tell, that "The Sailor King" gave this order to his officers with Royal tact, being well aware that they could no more stand, at that period of the dinner, than he could himself. So we sit.

15. To die during the World War.—E.B., 1921.
16. Our second son.
17. My daughter, Lady Gormanston, who completed and edited her father's autobiography, has recorded in the After-word the circumstances of his passing.
18. Since dead.
19. Only a few survivors of the original division which I saw are left. (1916.)
20. In his little book, *A Galloper at Ypres* (Fisher Unwin), my son gives a clear account of his own experience of that battle.
21. Colonel the Hon. Richard Preston, whose book, *The Desert Mounted Corps*, is a masterpiece.

Since I closed these Memoirs my sister, Alice Meynell, has passed away.

I feel that it is not out of place to record here the fact of her desire that I should reduce the mention of her name throughout the book. In the original text it had figured much oftener alongside of my own. Her wish to keep her personality always retired prevailed upon me to delete many an allusion to her which would have graced the text, greatly to its advantage.

ELIZABETH BUTLER. 31December 1922

INDEX

INDEX

Florence, Italy, hotel at Lung' Arno, 45, Santa Maria del Carmine, 45, Santo Spirito, 45, Duomo, 45, Giotto's tower, 45, Palazzo Vecchio, 46, 48, 118, Uffizi, 46, Strozzi Palace, 46, Ricardi, 46, Ponte Vecchio, 47, S.S. Annunziata, 47, Via Santa Reparata, 47, Egyptian Museum, 50, San Salvi, 50, Brera, 51, Santa Maria delle Grazie, 51; Via Ghibellina, Michael Angelo's apartment in the, 51-2, Santa Trinità, 52, dello Scalzo, 52, Ponte alle Grazie, 119, Santa Croce, 119, San Miniato, 119

Foley cousins, models for *Listed for the Connaught Rangers*, 135

Fort St. Julian, Egypt, sketch of, 172

Fowler, Mr., engineer who collects modern pictures, 109-10

Francesco, celebrated Roman model used by E.B., 72

Frederick, Emperor, 188-90

—, Empress, *see* Victoria, Empress Frederick

Frith, R.A., William, his *Derby Day*, the epitome of a picture popular with public, 90; 122

Fulham Road, London, E.B.'s studio at No 76, 80

Fullerton, Lady Georgiana, E.B. has dinner at home of, 94

GABRIEL, Virginia, composer who cries when she sees *Balaclava*, 121

Gallifet, Marquise de, 191-2

Galloway, Mr., 89, 105

Galway, Col., E.B. lunches with, 97

Gambart, Mr., picture dealer, 95

Garibaldi, Giuseppe, 5

Gave, River, France, 140

General Omnibus Company, send E.B. grey percherons to paint, 89

Genoa, Italy, 42, 45, 120

George V., King, 207

Germania, E.B.'s Rhine cruise on the, 15-24

Gérôme, Jean-Léon, 102

Gladstone, W.E., overawes E.B. at dinner at the Marquis of Ripon's, 210, in old age, 210

Glencar, Ireland, 134-5, 154

Glendalough, Ireland, 157-8

Goldsmiths' Hall, London, ball at, 88

Gooden, Col., 259-60

Gordon, General, W.B. joins the Gordon Relief Expedition, and publishes account in his *The Campaign of the Catarracts*, 152

Gormanston Castle, Ireland, 251

Gormanston, Viscountess, *see* Miss Eileen Butler

Granard, Lord and Lady, 245

Grant, Sir Hope, 92-3

Graphic, 79, 100, 119

Gutenfels, Germany, 20

HADEN, Sir Francis Seymour, 88

ALSO FROM FISHER PRESS

G K CHESTERTON

A SHORT HISTORY OF ENGLAND

Illustrated by Mary Tyler

Chesterton's classic *A Short History of England* was written during the
Great War. While his brother and their young friends were in the
trenches of France, he felt a need to define how the country for which
they were fighting came about. Chesterton proudly claims that he is writing as an ordinary member of the public for others like himself. It is not a
history for the specialist, but a consideration of the past so as better to
understand the present. His starting point is his reflection on the English
landscape and buildings, and his insight into how these physical features
came to be what they are. The neglected side of English history, he
argues in the introductory chapter, does not consist of the little things
which the learned obscurely conceal, but rather of the large things, such
as common land and the ruins of the monasteries, which the learned frequently ignore. Though an "amateur" history his short work is shaped
with consummate skill; it is continuously entertaining, full of
Chestertonian wit and paradox, and often prophetic. The Observer has
said of him that "he is at once the most concise and fullest historian."

Chesterton shows in detail how the rights of ordinary people were
gradually taken from them by the destruction of the guilds of craftsmen,
the enclosure movement, and the rise of trading monopolies. The disso-
lution of the monasteries is seen in large part as a means whereby a small
elite enriched themselves. To Chesterton, the 19th century reforms
widening the franchise were primarily a means whereby the continuing
elite staved off revolution. They were far from a genuine attempt to
restore to the English people their traditional freedoms: those of association, ownership of land, and of the equipment needed to earn their
livelihood. This new edition of Chesterton's history is timely now that
the ordinary individual's freedom is in danger of being further eroded as
more and more decisions on how he lives his life are taken by powerful
forces residing elsewhere.

Fisher Press
£6.99   ISBN 1 874037 09 4

If you have difficulty in obtaining Fisher Press books from you local
bookshop you can order these direct from Post Office Box 41,
Sevenoaks, Kent TN15 6YN, England. Telephone/Fax 0732-761830.